E-Business
and IS Solutions

E-Business and IS Solutions:

An Architectural Approach to Business Problems and Opportunities

William J. Buffam

 **ADDISON-WESLEY**

An imprint of Addison Wesley Longman, Inc.

Boston • San Francisco • New York • Toronto • Montreal
London • Munich • Paris • Madrid • Capetown
Sydney • Tokyo • Singapore • Mexico City

Many of the designations used by manufacturers and sellers to distinguish their products are claimed as trademarks. Where those designations appear in this book and we were aware of a trademark claim, the designations have been printed in initial capital letters or all capitals.

The authors and publisher have taken care in the preparation of this book, but make no expressed or implied warranty of any kind and assume no responsibility for errors or omissions. No liability is assumed for incidental or consequential damages in connection with or arising out of the use of the information or programs contained herein.

The publisher offers discounts on this book when ordered in quantity for special sales. For more information please contact:

Pearson Education Corporate Sales Division
One Lake Street
Upper Saddle River, NJ 07458
(800) 382-3419

corpsales@pearsontechgroup.com

Visit AW on the Web at *www.awl.com/cseng/*

Library of Congress Cataloging-in Publication Data

Buffam, William J., 1948-
      E-business solutions: an architectural approach to business problems and
   opportunities / Buffam, William J.
         p.   cm.
      Includes bibliographical references and index.
      ISBN 0-201-70847-7 (pbk.)
      1. Electronic commerce—Management.   2. Industrial management—Data
   processing.   3. Management information systems.   I. Title.
   HF5548.32.B83   2000   00-060903
   658.8_4_dc21   CIP

ISBN 0-201-70847-7
Text printed on recycled paper.
1 2 3 4 5 6 7 8 9—MA—04 03 02 01 00
First printing, September 2000

Contents

EPILOGUE: TAKE-HOME THOUGHTS   233

Preface

Objectives

This book is about building information systems (IS) solutions. It emphasizes *e-business* solutions. It's not detailed enough—or thick enough—to be a hands-on how-to guide. Rather, it gives you the essential principles and practices that lead to success.

The principles presented, while mostly not new, have been inconsistently applied in real-world IS developments. And perhaps not coincidentally, real-world IS developments have suffered embarrassingly high failure rates, in excess of 50 percent by most assessments. With the arrival of the e-business era, and its forcing of the pace of business innovation, we now have less discretion than ever before to be ineffective or inefficient in our deployment of empowering information systems. In today's world, we *have* to apply information technology (IT) to our businesses, we have to do it quickly, and we have to do it right.

"Doing things right" has traditionally been addressed by applying "architecture" to information systems building. Perhaps the most overworked word in the IT buzzword glossary, the word "architecture" is invoked in support of a wide range of causes, with the only common thread being that anything touched by "architecture" is implicitly regarded as Good, while any endeavor pursued without it is automatically regarded as Bad.

Rather than discard such an admired—albeit imprecise—buzzword, I have embraced it, as you can see from the title of this book. Indeed, to discard the term would have implied, with supreme irony, a violation of the architectural principle of reuse. Rather, this book refines the more helpful senses of "architecture" into a set of finer-grain principles, which form the core of "the architectural way."

Therefore, the supporting objectives of this book are to

- define what constitutes "architecture" in the context of information systems.
- provide a high-level introduction to, and understanding of, the architectural approach to building IT solutions.
- explain the benefits of the architectural approach.

E-business presents some particular challenges of its own. This book explores these challenges and discusses how building e-business solutions differs from traditional IS solution building.

Nonobjectives

This book is explicitly *not* a detailed how-to guide, a claim supported by its modest size. Although the architectural solution-building process is presented as a series of interrelated stages, much skill is required in the execution of any of the stages, and substantial detail needs to be added in order to guide and support a live solution-building effort. This high-level overview of the solution-building process provides an overall appreciation of the activities involved and how they fit together, serves as a foundation for further study, and provides a framework for development of detailed methodologies.

Intended audience

This book is intended for the following audience.

- Business managers involved in the e-business and IS solution-building process, or whose business areas are involved in changes resulting from the introduction of IT initiatives. For this audience, the book will
  - help them interact more knowledgeably and effectively with IS professionals.
  - provide decision makers with the information necessary to evaluate the scope of effort and resources required to conduct an architectural solution-building process.
- IS professionals with limited experience, who are undergoing education and mentoring in the solution-building process. For this audience, the book will
  - provide a foundation and a reference framework on which to base further study.
  - provide references to additional resources for further study and research.
- Experienced IS professionals, for which the book will
  - serve as a reference set of high-level principles and guidelines— which are already familiar to some degree—to help in building IS solutions, independent of the details of the particular methodology they apply.
  - provide a foundation that will be helpful as a framework for constructing or adapting detailed methodologies.

A note on terminology

Terminology is a problematic area. Some terms are used in different contexts and have different connotations in each. Particularly troublesome is the choice of words to distinguish "what it does" from "how it works." When describing businesses, the term *process* has come to mean "what it does." "How it works" is the stuff of *activities,* which are performed by *business functions.* This terminology clashes with that used in describing information systems, where the *functional definition* describes "what it does," and the *implementation* describes "how it works." For consistency with most of the books I cite in the Bibliography and References, I have tried to use the same terms in the same ways. The glossary that follows summarizes these points of usage.

enterprise   An *enterprise* in the abstract refers to a commercial corporation, government agency, educational establishment, or any other unit that regards itself as self-contained with respect to its business interactions with the world at large. In the specific context of IS solution building, we may focus on a part of the enterprise rather than on its entirety. We therefore have to draw artificial boundaries to delineate our areas of focus. In describing the solution-building process, we may for convenience refer to the focus area as the *enterprise.*

IS   *IS* stands literally for "information systems." It may denote information systems in general, in a broad sense, but ordinarily *IS* carries connotations of application-level functionality.

IT   *IT* stands literally for "information technology." *IT* may describe the full spectrum of information technology, but it usually carries connotations of lower-level supporting infrastructure rather than application-level functionality.

process   I use the term *process* in the sense that has emerged in the business process reengineering literature. A business process is "what the enterprise does," in terms of the behavior visible to a customer or other external actor.

activity   An *activity* is something the enterprise does in performing a process. The sum of an enterprise's activities amounts to "how the enterprise works." An activity can be thought of as a *process step*—which is a term used by some authors. I have tried to avoid using this term in favor of *activity.*

function   The *function* of an information system is "what it does," in terms of its behavior visible to a user. A *business function* is an organizational unit—such as financial analysis, engineering, or manufacturing—that performs a related set of tasks within a business. I have tried to avoid using the term *function* in this latter sense.

Outline

Part I: Setting the Scene for Architectural Solution Building

In Part I, we look at what "architecture" is all about and how object-oriented techniques support architectural discipline. We look at the traits that distinguish e-business from information systems of the past, and we consider the effect of varying project scope on the solution-building process.

Chapter 1 – Characteristics of E-Business   E-business differs from the information systems of the past by virtue of its interenterprise nature and because of the pressing need to "do it now and do it fast." In Chapter 1, we place e-business in its evolutionary context and look at some of the environmental drivers behind it.

Chapter 2 – The Essence of "Architecture"   Chapter 2 traces the historical evolution of information systems, and proposes a set of requirements for an IS solution-building discipline in today's world. We analyze the various senses of the term "architecture" in the context of IS solution building, and we derive a set of architectural principles. We then relate our original requirements for a solution-building discipline back to our derived architectural principles and verify that the requirements are satisfied.

Chapter 3 – Object-Oriented Methods and Architectural Solution Building   The purpose of Chapter 3 is to explain how object-oriented modeling supports the architectural solution-building process and how an object-oriented approach implicitly embraces so many tenets of "the essence of architecture."

Chapter 4 – Project Scope Considerations   In Chapter 4, we discuss considerations of project scope, particularly the extraordinary logistical and management difficulties of tackling projects of very wide organizational scope. We look at some approaches to narrowing the focus of the IS solution so as to raise confidence in its political and logistical feasibility.

Part II: The Seven-Stage Solution-Building Process

Part II describes a seven-stage process for building an IS solution, beginning with business modeling and ending with a complete review of a deployed solution. This is a high-level and conceptual treatment, above the level of detail needed to serve as a how-to guide. Each stage identifies roles of participants needed to staff the project team. The individual chapters of Part II correspond to the stages of the solution-building process.

Chapter 5 – Introduction   Chapter 5 reintroduces the seven stages of the solution-building processes, shows how they interrelate, and discusses the kinds of people we'll need to carry them out. We'll also develop a set of global architectural principles that apply across all stages of solution building.

Chapter 6 – Business Modeling   Chapter 6 discusses the first stage of the architectural solution-building process—the business modeling stage—which requires a careful analysis of enterprise business drivers. Building the use-case and ideal-object models is an ideal way to perform this analysis but may not be feasible or desirable for projects of more limited scope or ambition. The analysis results in the discovery and prioritization of the business needs of the enterprise. From the prioritized list of business needs, several are selected, consistent with the intended scope of the project, to drive the remainder of the architectural solution-building process.

Chapter 7 – IS Modeling   In the IS modeling stage of the solution-building process, the results of the business modeling stage are analyzed to identify needed enabling information technologies that are key to the implementation of business solutions. In modeling terms, this stage is performed by building the use-case and ideal-object models of the required IS system.

Two complementary approaches are appropriate here: the business-driven approach and the technology-driven approach. Being complementary, the two approaches can be applied in parallel. The business-driven approach focuses on an idealized view of the business, paying attention to technology only to the extent necessary to gain confidence that technology is available to solve the targeted business needs. Conversely, the technology-driven approach focuses on the discovery of new and emerging technology and on finding innovative ways to use it in creating business advantage.

Chapter 8 – Current IS Analysis   The current IS analysis stage involves discovery and assessment of the enterprise's current IS resources in order to identify and understand their components. The current IS analysis helps evaluate IS gaps as well as identify existing resources that will fit into, or influence changes in, the IS architecture being defined. Information about existing resources, in conjunction with the IS architecture (from the next stage), aids in implementation planning.

Chapter 9 – IS Architecture Planning   The process of mapping the required functionality of the IS system onto an organized and implementable IS structure takes place in the IS architecture planning stage. This structure, defined by the IS architecture model, provides the solution application architecture as well as the technical (middleware, platform, and network) architectures that enable it. It also defines principles, standards, and guidelines that the enterprise will use to guide implementation and deployment of the architecture.

Chapter 10 – Implementation Planning In the implementation planning stage, planners establish a strategy for making the transition from the current IS environment to the one resulting from the IS architecture planning stage. This transition strategy documents key implementation tasks and priorities and identifies the assets and products that need to be developed or acquired. It defines a roadmap and a timetable for the activities to be conducted during the deployment stage.

Chapter 11 – Deployment The deployment stage consists of a multiphase process in which projects are implemented and deployed according to the priorities identified in the implementation planning stage. The IS architecture and the implementation plan guide decisions about current assets to be used, new assets to be developed or acquired, and development resources and tools to be employed during the actual deployment of individual projects. Benchmarking and proof-of-concept prototyping may be used to confirm the viability of the IS architecture, including its performance, capacity, scalability, and availability. Decisions are made relative to the role that off-the-shelf and internally developed componentry will play in the deployment.

Chapter 12 – Review The review stage provides the ongoing opportunity to assess whether the IS architecture is meeting the targeted business needs. Because deployment is likely to consist of several different phases, it may be necessary to revise the results of earlier stages of the architectural solution-building process if new information or changing conditions demand it. For example, newly acquired or newly developed systems should be added to the baseline identified in the current IS analysis stage. Planners may also need to reexamine priorities for the next project or projects to be deployed.

Part III: Let's Get Practical

Part III covers several topics that apply across the chapters of Part II, and are concerned with practical considerations of how you would move toward application of the solution-building process in reality. This book is not a how-to guide, and Part III—in spite of its title—does not convert it into one. Rather, Part III discusses a number of issues that need to be considered for practical application of the book's principles. These issues are as follows.

- enlisting outside help: the role of consultants (Chapter 13)
- methodologies: patterns for solution building (Chapter 14)
- practical considerations in conducting solution building (Chapter 15)
- issues concerning reuse (Chapter 16)

Epilogue: Take-Home Thoughts

The epilogue is a terse distillation of the principles that are the most important to retain as a lasting impression of the ideas presented in this book.

Acknowledgments

Thanks to my eQube colleagues: Sophia Hunter, Steve Wadeson, Neil Wasserman, Heather Day, Werner Schoenfeldinger, Nicola Wreford-Howard, Erich Platzer, and Mike McHugh, who may recognize some of their ideas and insights woven into the text (but sorry, folks—the "horseshoes" picture had to go). I'm especially indebted to Neil Wasserman, who recruited me into this august team in the first place.

In 1974, Gerald Weinberg generously replied, on handwritten airmail paper, to a budding author asking for advice—advice for which I am eternally grateful. *That* book never reached fruition, but those long-lasting words of encouragement supplied fuel that helped propel this latest effort.

I credit Dave Tuffs of ICL with awakening me to the concepts of architectural elegance. A hundred years ago, Dave explained to me the principle of information hiding, even before David Parnas had given it that name and explained it to the world. I sincerely hope that Dave, who is most likely unaware of his educational legacy, will hate this book a little less than he hated my syntax parser.

Another Dave, Dave Houseman of Unisys, recognized book potential in precursor documents, in spite of my protestations to the contrary. Dot Malson shepherded the book through the mechanics of publication with publisher Peter Gordon. Kathy Glidden, who managed the nuts and bolts of getting the manuscript into print, kept my spirits up, and bent over backwards to indulge my every whim.

Tom Soller, also of Unisys, has been, and continues to be, a great encouragement and fount of wisdom. Tom has a knack for imposing architectural order in unlikely places and in seemingly chaotic situations.

I am thrilled that Eleanor Buffam, my daughter, was able to respond so quickly and so creatively to my suggestions for cartoons. Wherever Eleanor's artistic genes came from, it surely wasn't from my side of the family!

Finally, I am most indebted to my wonderful wife, Joan Brewer, for putting up so long with a distracted and cranky husband.

West Chester, Pennsylvania   WJB
June 2000   *William.Buffam@unisys.com*

PART I

SETTING THE SCENE FOR ARCHITECTURAL SOLUTION BUILDING

This book is about applying architectural discipline in building information systems solutions in general, with particular emphasis on e-business. In this first part, we'll cover some groundwork and discuss some important concepts that underlie Part II. We'll see

- what the particular characteristics of e-business are as distinct from traditional information systems.
- what the word "architecture" means, and what's involved in applying architectural discipline.
- how object-oriented techniques support the cause of architecture.
- how the scope of a solution-building effort affects the methods we employ.

1

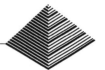

Characteristics of E-Business

First of all, we're going to see what's meant by "e-business" and how it compares with information technology as we knew it in the days before everything around us grew a leading "e-" or a trailing "dot com."

1.1   What do we mean by "e-business"?

Ask a dozen IS professionals what they understand by "e-business," and you'll probably get at least 13 different answers. To some people, "e-business" means using the Web to do business—period. To others, it covers every imaginable application of information technology to business. To help characterize e-business in the total context of IS solutions, we can think about the role of IS within an enterprise in a five-era view, as shown in Figure 1-1. This approach divides IS functionality according to the changing purposes that IS resources have evolved to serve.

The diagram shown in Figure 1-1 will reappear in Chapter 7, where we'll discuss it in a little more detail. For the moment, what I want to show is that IS solutions have been evolving to higher life forms over time, and that e-business is currently the highest life form. What distinguishes e-business from the earlier eras is that it represents IS solutions that *extend beyond the enterprise.* Interenterprise communications, and business-to-consumer communications, are the chief characteristics that distinguish e-business solutions from those of earlier eras.

This picture is a little oversimplified, because we have indeed been running interenterprise IS communications since the early 1980s, in the form of electronic data interchange (EDI) transactions. In fact, what we appreciate as *real* e-business depends on other characteristics as well:

- the use of the ubiquitous connectivity, business-to-business and business-to-consumer, provided by the Internet
- the critical mass of consumers now having access to the Internet
- the universally approachable user interface provided by the World Wide Web browser paradigm
- the availability of robust security technology

The coming together of all these forces has brought enormous potential for radical reinvention of enterprises' internal and external processes. The rapid maturation of the Internet has transformed the face of electronic communications, and the arrival and astonishing growth of the World Wide Web has made electronic communications much more usable, more standardized, and more available than ever before. With startling suddenness, the Internet has brought a general purpose and powerful information transport capability within the reach of every enterprise and consumer in the developed world.

Universal Internet availability has brought with it the opportunity for fundamental transformation of every business process. Now that every enterprise has built-in capability for computer-to-computer communication with every other enterprise, the potential for overhauling and streamlining every conceivable facet of business interaction is mind-boggling. Even more mind-boggling is the potential to create classes of business interaction never before imagined.

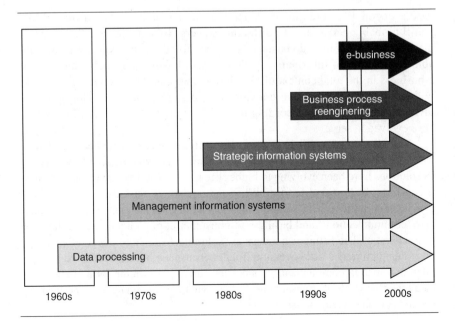

Figure 1-1 Five-era view of information systems.

EDI was the earliest form of interenterprise computer-to-computer inter-action. In the data processing era, businesses automated their business processes internally. The result was that, for example, purchase orders were printed and sent by ordinary physical mail to suppliers. Suppliers rekeyed the data from the purchase orders into their own systems, which printed out invoices. The suppliers mailed printed invoices to purchasers, who rekeyed the invoices into their own systems.

You can imagine the constant cycle of print, mail, rekey, process, print, mail, rekey, ad infinitum. What EDI did was to capture printed documents in a canonical electronic form (so as to eliminate syntactic and semantic differ-ences between businesses) and transmit them electronically to the busi-ness partner. The business partner's EDI software extracted the content of the message and simulated the rekeying exercise.

EDI was developed before the Internet was widely available for commer-cial use, and EDI transmissions were run on leased-line-based value-added networks (VANs) run by specialist EDI providers.

E-business is all about the practical realization of these mind-boggling opportunities—opportunities, in terms of business-to-business interaction over the Internet, in supply-chain planning, analysis, and automation; catalogue management; order management (entry, confirmation, tracking, fulfillment, invoicing, and payment); warehousing and inventory management; shipping and freight; pricing; promotions; taxes; duties; reporting; customer relation management; customer service; customized product and service development; marketing . . . the list is endless. And these possibilities are available to all types of enterprise, whether governmental, educational, nonprofit, or commercial.

One of the effects of e-business has been to enable a phenomenon that has been dubbed "disintermediation," wherein business functions provided by in-termediaries have become redundant, because the Internet and World Wide Web now allow end users to perform functions directly. Examples of disinterme-diation are

- elimination of entire legions of customer service representatives, whose sole function was to provide an interface between a customer and a database or process (such as a product-ordering system)
- elimination of middlemen of low added value, such as retailers of commod-ity products
- replacement of expensive physical brick-and-mortar storefronts by elec-tronic equivalents

Not without irony, a more recent effect of the proliferation of e-business has been the phenomenon of *reintermediation*. While disintermediation of one-to-one and one-to-many relationships is a natural consequence of Internet technology, perhaps less obvious is the need for new intermediation of many-to-many relationships. The Internet opens up the means and the scale through which many-to-many relationships can exist and flourish. Without intermediaries, these kinds of relationships cannot be efficient given the scale, complexity, and amorphousness of the Internet—business partners cannot economically find each other, negotiate terms, or transact business. Responding to this need, intermediaries—appearing in various guises such as trading groups, e-market makers, channel enablers, commerce networks, and online exchanges—have come into being.

E-business is good news for some, bad news for others. It's good news for those who welcome new opportunities to get a jump on traditional competitors. It's bad news for those who prefer the *status quo*. The stark reality is that e-business is not optional. It's not something your business can think about maybe taking a crack at someday. Companies that build the better e-business solutions will outperform their competitors. Companies that build the very best e-business solutions will transform themselves into *zero-latency enterprises*.[1] Companies that choose not to embrace e-business, or do so ineffectively, will underperform or be driven out of business.

E-business is mandatory.

1.2 What are the effects of e-business on architectural IS solution building?

As we progress through the book, we'll discover more of the characteristics of e-business technology and uncover more detail on how e-business considerations impose their own requirements on the solution-building process. For our purposes in this chapter, the most important realization is that e-business solutions need to be implemented *quickly*. Every day's delay represents competitive disadvantage and hard dollar losses—or lack of gain, depending on your perspective.

E-business technology is all about interoperation and integration—among your own existing solutions, and with the IS environments of your business partners. Such integration and interoperation on enterprise and interenterprise scales represent significant challenges, and a disciplined architectural approach to solution building is what you need to address these challenges.

---

[1]The term was coined by R. Schulte of the Gartner Group in the title of his August 1998 report "Introducing the 'Zero-Latency Enterprise'."

2

The Essence
of "Architecture"

In this chapter, we'll derive a set of architectural principles and develop some techniques for integrating these principles into the solution-building process. Experience shows that adhering to sound architectural principles makes the difference between ending up with an effective solution or a mediocre one. In the limit, how well you stick to the architectural way determines whether you get to the end at all or give up in despair somewhere along the way.

2.1   The evolution of information systems

In this section, we're going to trace the evolutionary path of information systems. We'll see what important influences affected the course of this evolution and the responses we made in trying to keep control and intellectual manageability of the IS environments we created.

We'll review

- how common practices of the past led to isolated computer systems.
- the reasons for the emergence of standards in the computer industry.
- the growing need for architectural discipline in building information systems.

2.1.1   The legacy of isolated systems

Computer technologies and the ways in which enterprises use them have been changing rapidly since the first computer left the laboratory. Early mainframes were expensive, difficult to program, and limited in power. By necessity, access to those systems was maintained and controlled by a highly centralized organization of specially trained experts.

Most computer systems in those days shared some common characteristics.

- Computing power was expensive, and its use was typically limited to large, processing-intensive business applications such as payroll and inventory control. Most people in an enterprise did not have direct access to computer-based information.

- Systems from different vendors could not easily communicate with one another, often leading enterprises to depend on a single line of products available from a particular manufacturer. Applications developed on one system could rarely be used on another system. Acquisition of computer equipment was usually centrally controlled.

- Low-level programming languages made applications slow to develop and hard to maintain. Both of these factors limited the ability of data processing departments to keep up with changing business requirements.

- Applications tended to be designed and developed from scratch. They displayed little uniformity in structure or implementation, making it difficult for users to transfer skills from one application to another.

As computers grew more powerful and less expensive, they served a wider range of business needs, and many more people wanted access to them. Emerging networking technologies extended computing power to more users. Former data processing departments, now evolving into information systems departments, struggled to integrate increasingly complex systems of computer resources.

The same economic forces driving the widespread application of computer technologies made it possible for more organizations to acquire and support systems dedicated to their own operations. Individual systems were typically selected to solve a specific set of business problems as expeditiously as possible. These systems served narrowly defined organizational needs but often did not take into account the needs of the enterprise as a whole.

These trends reached revolutionary proportions in the 1990s with the development of progressively more powerful desktop computers and departmental servers that could run a wide variety of commercially available software. This period also coincided with an economic climate of business mergers and acquisitions that increased the likelihood that enterprises would encounter computer systems from different vendors. The absence of universal industry standards usually meant that these multivendor systems could not easily interoperate, resulting in environments that have been referred to as isolated islands of information.

2.1.2   The emergence of standards

The declining cost of computing power and growing decentralization left many enterprises with a loose collection of computing systems that were expensive to maintain and that interoperated poorly, if at all. At the same time, there was a growing need to integrate the information available in these isolated systems. Computer users demanded access to important applications and information regardless of where they resided.

As interoperability became a more and more compelling requirement, various standards emerged to enable interoperation among heterogeneous systems. Used broadly, the term "standards" refers both to *de jure* and *de facto* standards.

- *De jure* standards are those developed and issued by officially recognized bodies, such as the International Standards Organization (ISO).
- *De facto* standards are specifications based on products that enjoy widespread acceptance in the industry but are not recognized by one of the official standards-setting bodies. Examples of de facto standards include Microsoft COM (Component Object Model) and the Sun Java technology.

The term "standards" is also used to describe agreements reached by various industry consortia. While such "standards" carry neither the formal legitimacy of de jure standards nor (necessarily) the market clout of *de facto* standards, they nevertheless represent a commitment to interoperability, at least among derivative products of participating companies. Examples of such consortia are the IETF (Internet Engineering Task Force), with such standards as the TCP/IP protocol suite; The Open Group, with such standards as the DCE (Distributed Computing Environment) and the CDSA (Common Data Security Architecture), and the RSA-led consortium that produced the PKCS (public key cryptography standards) series.

All varieties of standards benefit users when vendors develop products that work together. In addition to promoting interoperability, some standards are designed to make software more portable across platforms or to provide a common look and feel for different applications. Standards also benefit vendors by helping them focus their development resources on products for which there is an established market.

A look back at history tells us that the evolution of standards occurs quite naturally as technologies mature. Of course, to the participants in the standards-making process, it doesn't feel "natural" at all—much hard work, negotiation, and conflict resolution are involved. But in the grand scheme of things, the evolution of standards follows a fairly predictable pattern. Each advance of the technology frontier reaches a point at which the competitive advantage of unique product features is outweighed by an inability to interoperate with competitors' products. At this point, the standards-creation process exerts irresistible force on the technology. Usually, competing standards emerge, which coexist for a time in the wild, usually engaging in a fight to the death in the marketplace. For example, we have seen this scenario played out in network protocols, where the TCP/IP protocol suite emerged as the sole viable survivor after many years of coexistence with IBM's SNA, Xerox's XNS (and derivatives such as Novell's IPX), and ISO's OSI. In the LAN environment, we saw Ethernet emerge victorious from a final round against Token Ring, after earlier rounds had eliminated the broadband contenders such as IEEE 802.4 and WangNet.

In the context of standards evolution, it's worth pointing out the complicating influence of an increasingly popular ploy, which involves the driving of a particular technology through the "standards" process to gain market advantage. In the long run, the market decides, but in the short run, the business of selecting appropriate technology is obfuscated and complicated by these laundering tactics. As an IS decision maker, you need to be aware of the politics of standards and not give undue weight to the appearance of legitimacy implied by a vendor's laying claim to "standard" status. In the selection of competing standards, vendor support and viability are usually of more practical relevance than formal claims on standard status.

It's important to realize that, at any given point on the evolution timescale, there are going to be information technology services that are not standardized. Not only is such nonstandardization an inevitable feature of the standardization life cycle, it is a feature absolutely required by IT vendors if they are successfully to differentiate their products in the marketplace.

This situation appears to present a conflict. On the one hand, users of IT systems want "open" systems, which will interoperate with competitive products. On the other hand, IT vendors want to provide unique value through products with unique features, which by their nature do not lend themselves to interoperation. And ultimately, enterprise IT users themselves want to differentiate themselves from their competition through the unique value of the IT applications that run their businesses.

In fact, when we look a little deeper, we realize that there is actually little conflict. Quoting from Cook [1996]:

> *"Open systems are products in which low-value differentiation has been voluntarily eliminated by consensus."*
> *There are several important implications in this definition. They include the following:*
>
> * *Only low-value differentiation has been eliminated. This lets vendors continue to invest in high-value product features with the prospect of reasonable return on investment.*
> * *When the value of portability or interoperability (commonality) exceeds the value of differentiation (uniqueness), then the feature should be deemed as having low value and is a candidate for standardization.*

A corollary is that at any given point in time, IT products are going to be composed of unique, proprietary features at the high-value end of the spectrum, ranging to standard features at the commodity level. In between, features whose value is eroding through incipient or ongoing commoditization are going to feel pressure from the standards-making process. Inevitably, in this middle part of the value spectrum, the industry is always filled with competing and evolving standards. Vendors and users alike must decide which standards show the most promise and then select products that ease the transition between current and future systems.

While maturing standards and advances in related technologies already help users interconnect a widening variety of diverse computer systems, many problems remain unsolved.

- Computer systems serving different organizations still might not interoperate with one another, either because they do not implement the same sets of standards (or, ironically, implement the same standards but choose different, incompatible, options; or make different interpretations of the standard) or because no central authority is responsible for managing the connections among them.
- Systems continue to be created to serve narrowly defined requirements. Seldom are all the information needs of an enterprise analyzed and used as a basis for determining global system requirements.
- Even where systems are compatible, the flow of data can be impeded by organizational boundaries. Users may not have access to the data they need, or different organizations may maintain redundant and possibly inconsistent data at added cost to the enterprise as a whole.
- Users confronted with a multitude of different systems still face the challenge of working with a variety of user interfaces and command structures.

Before we leave this discussion of standards, we need to revisit the extract from Cook [1996], which said

When the value of portability or interoperability (commonality) exceeds the value of differentiation (uniqueness), then the feature should be deemed as having low value and is a candidate for standardization.

If we look at e-business technology in this light, we realize that Cook's statement isn't quite right. Many off-the-shelf e-business solutions are available and cannot be regarded as supporting only "low-value" processes. E-business changes the equation, because the *absence* of e-business capability differentiates your enterprise in a negative way. E-business capability is now table stakes, just like the telephone—without it, you can't function. This indispensability, together with the requirement for universal interoperability, creates a technology and market environment in which packaged solutions thrive. E-business has become a *business imperative* that *depends* on standardization in order to function. Therefore, Cook's statement would be more accurate if revised to read as follows:

When the value of portability or interoperability (commonality) exceeds the value of differentiation (uniqueness), then the feature should be deemed a candidate for standardization.

In other words, it is not necessary that the feature be regarded as low value to benefit from standardization.

2.1.3 The need for IS architectures

Standards alone are not enough. As more than one wag has remarked, "the great thing about standards is that there are so many to choose from," and we discussed in the preceding section why multiple competing standards are an inevitable fact of life.

An IS architecture for a specific enterprise provides a structure for selecting standards and for making decisions about the technologies and products needed to implement and maintain fully integrated information systems in response to business needs. Primary goals of comprehensive architecture planning are

- to let business missions, strategies, and processes guide the use of information technology.
- to allow for the rapid adoption of new technology for competitive advantage.

In the next section we'll look more closely at just what it is that we need from an architectural process.

2.2 "Architecture" and the original architects

We're getting closer to finding out what "architecture" is in the context of information systems, but we're still not quite ready. There's still some background we must cover first.

Let's begin by tracing the origin of the word "architecture" and how we came to be using it in the context of information technology. *Architecture* is derived from *architect,* which comes from the Greek for "builder." It's more than a little ironic that we now refer to the most abstract, front-end thinker as the "architect" and the implementer of the architect's vision as the "builder." When people were first inventing names for these roles, the "builder" himself was the "architect." According to the *American Heritage Dictionary,* an architect is "one who designs and supervises the construction of buildings or other large structures." By extension, then, a software architect is "one who designs and supervises the construction of software applications or other large software environments." So how is an "architect" different from a "designer"?

When we look at additional connotations that the word "architecture" has taken on through usage, we see an interesting pattern emerging (again quoting from the *American Heritage Dictionary*):

1. The art and science of designing and erecting buildings

2. Buildings and other large structures: *the low, brick-and-adobe architecture of the Southwest*

3. A style and method of design and construction: *Byzantine architecture*

4. Orderly arrangement of parts; structure: *the architecture of the federal bureaucracy; the broad architecture of a massive novel; computer architecture*

The pattern emerging here mirrors what was happening in the ancient craft of architecture. Architects realized that they could do their jobs more effectively and efficiently by not starting from scratch every time. For example, instead of constructing doors from individual pieces of wood, they decided on a small number of standard door sizes. So now they can build standard size door openings and buy ready-made doors from door-making specialists. The door makers can build an inventory of doors, knowing that they can be used by any builder in a variety of different buildings. Similarly, by the time plumbing went mainstream, the approach of providing standardized components that could be quickly assembled together was well established. What's equally important in the standards business is that an infinite range of *differences* are possible within the standard. Door makers can make wooden doors, glass doors, and steel doors. They can make brown doors and green doors. They can install round doorknobs or doorknobs in the shape of a serpent or monkey claw. As long as the standard size is adhered to, any one of their doors will work in a standard door frame.

It is this theme of *standardized common components* that can be used interchangeably that led to the adoption of the term "architecture" in contexts other than the business of erecting physical buildings. In the software world, however, we're dealing with much more complexity than in the world of physical buildings. We haven't made much progress in standardization of software components. We like to talk about architecture, but because of the rudimentary state of our software component industry, talk about "software architecture" usually refers to the general process of "software design" with limited and incomplete general awareness of, agreement on, or recognition of what are the parameters, constraints, guidelines, or criteria for that design.

Another theme discernible in the evolution of the usage of the word "architecture" is the connotation of a higher level of abstraction than is implied by the term "design." This theme is distinct from the common-component theme, although equally valid in its own claim to "architectural" status. The essence of this theme is that an architect is concerned with specifying an overall form, or conceptual design, that fulfills the required functions. For example, the conceptual design of a building intended to serve as a dwelling for a family of four will look very different from that of a building intended to serve as a fast-food outlet. The architect specifies the number and functions of the rooms, their sizes, and their relationships to each other and the outside world. This conceptual view allows the prospective users (the building occupants) to validate the architecture prior to investing further effort in refining the design.

2.3 Why do we need architecture in information systems?

We're going to put the cart before the horse for a moment and discuss why we need architecture, in the context of building an information system, before we complete our deliberations on exactly what architecture is in terms of activities and deliverables.

We already have an intuitive feel for what a building architect does and why the architect's job is so essential in the construction of buildings. We're going to use that insight and intuition to extrapolate to the IT world and propose a list of requirements to be fulfilled by our "architecture" in the context of IT.

At this point, our essential view of the function of a building architect is as follows.

1. The architect creates in his mind a concept of the overall form of the building to fit the intended purpose.

2. The architect creates a tangible set of blueprints that express his concept with sufficient clarity and rigor that
   - the building owners can verify that the design satisfies their needs.
   - the architect—before committing to construction—can verify, through inspection, simulation, and calculation, that the building will stand up to its anticipated load, withstand environmental conditions and requirements, and meet regulatory standards.
   - craftsmen can construct a building fulfilling that concept.

Using our experience and knowledge of the characteristics of information systems, we can extrapolate to two groups of requirements for an IS architecture. We will label the first group *fundamental requirements,* because fulfilling these requirements is essential to the building of a system that fits its intended business purpose.

In our examination of the requirements for our design discipline, we are in a sense putting aside discussion of "architecture" for the time being. Rather, we're listing the qualities we want in our design discipline. When we're done, we'll go on to look at what we think "architecture" is all about, derive a set of architectural principles, and see how well those principles satisfy our design-discipline requirements.

2.3.1 Fundamental requirements

First, we need architecture **to ensure that the IT environment is *aligned* with the business's imperatives** (its mission, objectives, and processes).

An architect's blueprints of a house allow the prospective homeowners to inspect and understand the proposed layout and design of the house and to make sure it is *aligned* with their needs and lifestyle. In addition, the blueprints provide the basis for the architect to ensure that the building meets environmental and regulatory requirements.

Analogously, an IT architecture provides the basis for IT professionals and business managers to ensure that the proposed IT system is properly aligned with the mission, objectives, and processes of their business.

An alignment of IT and business includes the following goals:

- enhance the capabilities of existing information systems
- take advantage of new strategic opportunities
- increase operational efficiency and user productivity
- support decision making by finding new opportunities to identify, gather, and distribute the information necessary to make timely and strategic decisions
- build information systems that satisfy the nonfunctional requirements of viable operations, such as the ability to handle the workload, handle an expanding workload, provide adequate security and manageability, and so on

Second, we need architecture **to help us build an IT environment that can be easily changed and extended, so as to retain its alignment with changing business imperatives.**

A business's mission, objectives, and processes are constantly undergoing change—often rapid, discontinuous, and wrenching change—in response to problems, challenges, and opportunities. Change stimuli come from all directions: from competitors, from customers, from business partners, from government, and from introduction of new technology. Business success, and indeed survival, depends on the ability to execute rapid realignment of IT systems in response to changing business imperatives.

Third, we need architecture **to help us control the costs of acquiring, developing, and maintaining IT resources.**

Information technology may be viewed as a cost, or it may be viewed as an investment. Both views are valid, and which one applies in any given situation depends on the application area and the observer's viewpoint. Either way, technology resources need to show a positive return on investment.

In the Internet age, there's a third way of looking at information technology—as underpinnings, akin to a nervous sytem, that are completely integral with the fabric of the business. In this case, we're still trying to get the most benefit for the least cost, but we recognize that the investment is not optional.

Fourth, we need architecture **to communicate appropriate views of the solution to, and among, the various stakeholders.**

This is a bland-sounding statement that superficially doesn't say much. However, its implications are profound. What it says is that the architecture must communicate the essential information to each stakeholder so as to ensure that the solution gets built, on time, within budget, while fulfilling the intended requirements. Stakeholders in the construction of a house are, for example, the owners (who need to verify that the design meets their livability needs), the construction manager (who needs to plan and manage the construction so as to deliver the building on schedule and within budget), the construction workers (who need to know the shapes, dimensions, and relative positions of the rooms, the required materials, and other such factors), and so on. The term "blueprints" is customarily used as shorthand for these kinds of plans, but clearly more is required than just building-design blueprints.

Similarly, stakeholders in an e-business solution, and their spheres of interest, include the examples listed in Table 2-1. (The "Supporting information in architecture" column lists the deliverables from the solution-building stages described in Part II of this book.)

At this point, we've covered what we may regard as the fundamental requirements for our e-business architecture. Interestingly, three of the requirements (alignment with purpose; communication with stakeholders; helping control cost of acquisition, development, and maintenance) are directly analogous to the functions of architecture in the bricks-and-mortar world. The remaining requirement (ability to change in response to changing environment) we added based on our recognition that IT systems are based on software, which is forced to change—because it can—in response to changes in its environment (a capability not common in physical buildings).

2.3.2   Enabling requirements

To realize our fundamental requirements, experience tells us that we need to specify a second-order set of requirements. We can think of these second-order requirements as essential enablers that materially assist in supplying an environment conducive to the fulfillment of the fundamental requirements.

First, we need architecture **to help keep intellectual manageability of our IT environment and the e-business processes it supports.**

We recognize by now that information systems are very complex. We need to do everything we can to simplify everything about them, so as to make them intellectually manageable. The control of complexity, and through it the ability to keep our systems understandable, is the biggest single challenge in the building of information systems. One of the most important functions of an architecture is to support a "divide-and-conquer" approach.

Human brains are not very good at dealing with a large number of unorganized concepts. Most of us can deal with only seven concepts at a time and can discriminate a range of values into only seven distinct ones. It's no accident that we think of seven colors of the rainbow, even though the visible-light spectrum is a continuous one. We label musical notes by using only seven letters, and construct scales of seven notes, even though there are 12 distinct notes to choose from. When it comes to sin, we pick seven of them as the most deadly. Perhaps

TABLE 2-1   Architecture and its value to the various stakeholders

Stakeholder	Primary areas of interest	Supporting information in architecture
Business managers whose business strategy depends on the solution	Validation that business processes are in alignment with business missions and goals Validation that the IT system is in alignment with business processes	Business strategy Business model
Software designers, integrators, and implementers	What functionality must I build? What functionality must be integrated into the solution? What's the supporting technology (platform, middleware, etc.)?	IS model IS strategy . Current IS inventory Current IS assessment Architectural principles Implementation principles
Project managers	What is the work breakdown structure? What resources are required? What elapsed times are implied? How do we roll out this solution through the organization?	Business process impact Organizational impact Transition strategy
End users	What's the user interface? How does this system help me get my job done? How do we make the transition from our current way of working?	Business process impact Organizational impact Transition strategy
System administrators	What new platforms and technology need to be integrated?	IS strategy Architectural principles Implementation principles Transition strategy
Counterparts in e-business partner enterprises	(The same considerations as those listed above apply for each role in partner enterprises.)	

we'd have less trouble obeying the Commandments if we had only seven of them to worry about instead of ten.

To keep our world intellectually manageable, we use a mental device that psychologists call "chunking," in which we chunk elementary concepts together to form a composite concept, which our brains can handle as a single concept. Thus, we have an intuitive notion of what constitutes a city—we can think of a city as a single concept, without unnecessarily demanding that our brains think in terms of its components (streets, buildings, parks, transportation systems, and so on).

By the same token, we chunk the elements of our IT environment into intellectually manageable pieces and, for most purposes, forget about the constituent parts. For example, we know that there's a TCP/IP network running underneath all of our computing resources and connecting them together, but while we're dealing with the rest of the system, we don't need to consider it in any more detail.

Second, we need architecture **to provide a framework for making and communicating technology choices.**

We need to make effective and appropriate technology choices. And we need to do it *efficiently,* given the need for rapid response. Making appropriate choices is easier in the context of overarching principles, and takes less effort. Furthermore, an overarching framework provides a common view that fosters consistency of technology choices made by different design teams contributing in different areas of the overall IT environment.

Third, we need architecture **to give us freedom of choice of IT components— through component interoperability and through component portability.**

Architectural principles help us build heterogeneous environments with all the characteristics formerly reserved for the proprietary world. In the proprietary world, which characterizes the emergence of all new technologies, you have to buy all your components from one vendor if you want to have any hope of their cooperating with each other. As technologies mature, customers demand component interoperability, so that their needs can be met by any number of vendors, not just one. Moreover, vendors themselves derive greater benefit from component interoperability than from an exclusionary, proprietary approach. Would you buy a Bloggs brand CD player that would play only CDs manufactured by Bloggs, or required you to throw away your amplifier and replace it with one made by Bloggs? No, neither would I. The same rejection slip would go out to a Bloggs e-mail system that ran on a proprietary communications stack or used a home-made encryption algorithm for secure mail.

Portability, while usually a lesser consideration than interoperability, may also be a factor. Does the software component you're evaluating run on Linux as well as on Windows NT? What about Mac?

Fourth, we need architecture **to maximize our efficiency in building and evolving the IT environment through reuse of earlier work.**

We hear a lot about the virtues of reuse these days. Object-based development environments promise reuse of already developed components. With the assistance of a repository, we can find objects that provide the functionality we need, or at least a good approximation of it, and reuse the object, adapting it to our precise needs as required.

For various reasons we won't go into here, the object reuse promise has so far gone largely unfulfilled in practice. However, the notion of reuse in the context of architecture is nevertheless valid and relevant. In fact, the notion of reuse goes to the very core of what architecture is about. Here's a direct quotation from Best [1995]: "In all uses of the word 'architecture,' the common theme is understanding of common component configurations."

The notion of *common component configurations* recurs at all levels of an IS environment. At the highest level, we will choose a common configuration as our overall system structure—our high-level functional decomposition (such as two-tier client–server, three-tier, etc.). We will choose middleware to link our application components together. A middleware environment, such as Microsoft COM, OMG CORBA, or OLTP, is an example of a common configuration that links application components together. At the lowest level, we will choose a common configuration, such as TCP/IP, for the network that links our physical systems together.

The applications themselves, which perform the business-domain specific logic that implements the business processes—and this is where that notion of *alignment* is most starkly manifested—are most efficiently designed by copying an existing pattern, rather than designing one from scratch. How to do this is a substantial topic that we'll return to later.

2.4 "Architecture" in information systems—what is it?

Now we're going to change tracks and look at how the term "architecture" is colloquially used in the context of IS.

- What activities constitute the architecture activity?
- What are the concrete deliverables of the architecture activity?

In the IT industry at large, and specifically in the referenced literature, the word "architecture" is used in several distinct senses.

1. Common-component sense—to denote a design mode based on the leveraging of reusable standard components, subassemblies, frameworks, patterns, and idioms.

2. Design sense—(a) the activity of designing a solution to meet a client's needs; (b) the design activity with the conscious imposition of principles and guidelines governing the structure of the design; (c) the formulation of standards and principles to be observed in implementing the design; (d) the design activity dealing with the higher levels of abstraction.

3. Blueprinting sense—to describe the result of applying a design recording and organization discipline, in which the design is presented and rigorously documented ("blueprinted") in various views, representing different levels of abstraction as well as the complementary viewpoints of the various stakeholders.

4. Framework sense—to denote a particular abstract framework specifically intended to be instantiated for use in building systems.

All of these senses are valid. In principle, they are independent. However, what we find is that they interact and reinforce each other as we put them into practice.

"Architecture" is best thought of as a set of principles acting on, and intimately integrated with, the total process of creating IT solutions, rather than as a discrete activity in its own right. The following sections discuss each of these different senses of the word "architecture" and abstract from each sense a set of principles that we can incorporate into the "architectural way" of solution building.

2.4.1   The common-component sense of "architecture"

The *common-component sense* of the term *architecture* is evident in the work of Best [1995], Gamma et al. [1994], and Buschmann et al. [1996]. To understand its significance, let's compare a traditional IS design with one guided by architectural principles. When we analyze the dynamics of traditional IS design, we find that it goes something like this [Best 1995]:

- understand the business domain
- abstract models for this domain
- craft application components to realize the models, perhaps attempting to excavate reusable components from previously developed systems

In contrast, there is a very distinct difference when we consciously apply an architectural approach. It goes more like this:

- understand the business domain
- match the business domain to catalogued or standardized architectural models
- adapt the components associated with these models to meet domain requirements

An architecturally driven design activity, in essence, involves identifying common components and leveraging them in the IS design, or design evolution, at hand. How do we do that?

Common components are found on several different levels. Clearly, there are going to be more common components the further away we get from the domain-specific business aspects. For example, common networking infrastructures are by now very familiar. In many situations, we'd expect to run TCP/IP over 10BaseT or 100BaseT to our servers and desktops, and expect our corporate networking utility to provide the local and wide-area connectivity the same way we expect the phone company to supply phone lines and the power company to supply power. In effect, this form of networking is so familiar and so standard that we regard it as a commodity and rarely think about it.

As we get closer to the application domain, the common components demand more of our attention. What middleware should we use? On what middleware does the existing application set depend? Is that middleware appropriate for new development, or should we introduce a new middleware environment alongside our existing one? In practice, middleware environments are commercially available, often embedded in operating systems, and well documented and well understood. Selecting a middleware environment, while not a trivial exercise, is not unduly limited by any difficulty of discovering what environments are available.

Within the application domain itself, there are patterns we can apply to reduce our development workload and increase our ease of understanding. Perhaps we can apply a model-view-controller pattern [Buschmann et al. 1996] to an application; perhaps we can fit an entire application suite into a workflow framework [Best 1995]. It is the application level that presents the greatest challenge to the architectural design paradigm. It is hard to "mine" design patterns from earlier work, and once such patterns have been mined, it is hard to catalogue and reuse them. Reuse is hard because the pattern-reuse technique is an emerging and little-known discipline with precious few tools to support it. Although the pattern-reuse technique is being successfully used by some in the industry [Best 1995, Schmidt 1999], there is much untapped potential here that could be realized with greater awareness, better tools, and available repositories of reusable patterns.

We have recently witnessed an extreme example of the use of standard components across large, disparate types of enterprises. Encouraged in part by the Y2K problem, many enterprises have adopted enterprise resource planning (ERP) packages, such as those supplied by SAP, Baan, PeopleSoft, and others. When we look at this development in light of the ecology of standards (discussed earlier), it's entirely consistent and predictable. ERP packages represent standard components that apply to the commodity aspects of an enterprise's business—those aspects that do not give the company its defining attributes constituting its competitive advantage. Adoption of ERP packages effectively means that the company adjusts its low-differentiation processes to conform to the purchased software. This is 180 degrees different from the traditional view that IT systems should be molded to support business practices. The important point here is that it is only the low-differentiation processes that are subject to this kind of standardization. As we saw earlier, low-differentiation processes may be low-value internal processes or business imperatives. Any process representing competitive advantage will need to be customized or built from scratch, and properly integrated with the standard back-office software.

2.4.2 The design sense of "architecture"

You will often encounter the word "architecture" being used as an unqualified synonym for design. In this sense, architecture is the art and science of designing and creating a structure that supports client needs. Used purely in this way, "architecture" is not very helpful. The definition addresses only one of our requirements for architecture (to ensure that the IT environment is aligned with the business's imperatives). Obviously we're going to design the system before we start writing source code. What's important is the discipline we bring to the design process, the principles and guidelines that impose order so as to shape and constrain the design in ways that will ensure its ultimate success.

Elegant design: lessons from the world of bricks and mortar

The first architectural design mode we'll look at is from the world of architecture in the physical world. This mode is beautifully described by Christopher Alexander [1979]. Alexander takes many pages to describe his concepts, and I can hardly expect to summarize his points satisfactorily here. Rather, I will attempt simultaneously to condense his points and translate them from the bricks-and-mortar world to the IS world.

Alexander speaks of the "quality without a name," which gives buildings and places their vibrancy and life force. The "quality without a name" is present when there is perfect harmony between the physical place and the events that are intended to take place there. To achieve excellent designs, as opposed to those that are merely adequate, the architect's challenge is to create and capture this "quality without a name" in his or her building designs.

By analogy, the IS architect's job is to design systems that are in perfect harmony with their intended purpose. Perhaps the word that captures this quality most aptly is "elegance." Elegance in IS solutions is elusive to define. It's a bit like pornography, in that we can't say with any precision what it *is,* but we can give examples, and we'll certainly know it when we see it.

Elegance is simplicity. Elegance is a clear, intuitive mapping between a function and its implementation. What makes elegance so desirable is the intellectual

Pathways to the Quality Without a Name

One of the better examples of realizing the "quality without a name" in the world of buildings is that of the architect faced with designing the walkways around a college campus. He realized that if he simply grassed over the whole area, then the wear patterns in the turf would reveal the traffic flows and show where to route the walkways. Thus was born a standard technique, to be reused over and over.

manageability it brings. Our IS solutions are so troublesome to build and maintain, in large part, because they are so complex. Elegance is the antithesis of complexity. Strive for elegance always.

Elegance applies at every level of the IS solution. Where an application supports a business process, the human interface of that application needs to be in perfect harmony with the performance of that process. You want the screens and menus to flow in a sequence that perfectly matches the usual flows of the business process. You want data fields to be filled in automatically, wherever the software can make an intelligent guess. You want the auto-filled field to be highlighted, so that if the user needs to override it, all that he needs to do is to type. At all costs, you want the user to feel that the application is helping and supporting him, not fighting with him. You want the user to feel that the "do-as-I-mean" option is turned on.

Elegance at the source code level means that you write obvious code, to well-established idioms, that everyone understands. The implementation supports the interface (the function, or "what it does") in an obvious way. Elegant code for factorial(n) says that factorial(1) = 1, otherwise factorial(n) = n * factorial(n-1). Ugly code that computes the same thing uses an iterative loop.

How, in practice, can we imbue our solutions with elegance, given its elusive nature? Alas, there is no systematic way to guarantee the creation of elegance—it is a quality borne of the creative, fertile mind. The blunt advice is to have only first-rate people developing your IS solutions. Of course, that's impossible, because you'd have to pay them so much that your projects would never be cost effective. Wherever possible, we try to achieve elegance by applying patterns that have acquired their own elegance through repeated reuse and continuous honing through experience. As Alexander [1979] points out, however, every design is an application of multiple patterns, themselves applied in a pattern of patterns. As a software engineer would say, the whole thing is recursive. We cannot mechanize the process—there is no escaping that you need competent, imaginative people to create designs. It is here that we may indeed need to create our own new patterns, where no suitable patterns currently exist. It is this activity—the building of a solution through the application of patterns of patterns—that comes closest to the sense given to "architecture" of design at a high level of abstraction.

Design by empirically validated principles

Let's now look at some "best practices" types of techniques that IS pioneers have developed over the years and that have been shown to be very effective in practice. Real-world application of these techniques, together with the control set of developments of projects that failed to apply the techniques, has yielded a body of empirical data to show us which practices are common to successful developments.

The extracts that follow are from Booch [1994], who notes that practical experience shows that successful systems display certain essential qualities, whereas failed systems do not.

Good software architectures are constructed in well-defined layers of abstraction, each layer representing a coherent abstraction, provided through a well-defined and controlled interface, and built upon equally well-defined and controlled facilities at lower levels of abstraction.

This principle was first described by Dijkstra in a seminal paper published in 1968 [Dijkstra 1968], and has become very familiar as an organizing principle in software systems. The "layers pattern" can lay plausible claim to the title of First Software Pattern Ever to be documented. It is indeed described as a pattern by Buschmann et al. [1996].

Good software architectures display a clear separation of concerns between the interface and implementation of each layer, making it possible to change the implementation of a layer without violating the assumptions made by its clients.

This principle was first clearly articulated by Parnas [1972], who was drawing more generalized principles from Dijkstra's paper [Dijkstra 1968]. It is the fundamental philosophy behind object orientation. An object displays its function— that is, what it does in terms of the effects a client sees—as its published interface. An object's implementation is private, being the concern of the object itself, and not of its clients. Through the formalization of this philosophy, object orientation embodies the principle of *information hiding* articulated by Parnas. The information-hiding principle holds that significant design decisions are hidden in a single module, making the design decision a property of the module's *implementation,* not its *interface.* The design decision can thus be changed without ripple effects on other modules. Of course, certain design decisions—such as those that affect how modules intercommunicate—are not inherently amenable to being hidden.

A good software architecture is simple: common behavior is achieved through common abstractions and common mechanisms.

This principle, which is a reinforcement of our definition of architecture in the *common-component sense,* is far more powerful than it first appears. Brooks [1995] observed this effect more than 25 years ago, when he noted that *conceptual integrity* (an elegant term he coined to describe this principle) was the biggest single predictor of a successful software design. A system with conceptual integrity always uses the same patterns, mechanisms, and techniques to do similar things. We don't, for example, make our users put up with an ugly terminal interface inside a DOS window for one critical function while giving them a slick, fully integrated Windows interface for everything else. Even deep within the

Anglo-American miscommunication.

source code, common idioms should be employed. For example, decide what the error-handling idiom is, and make sure it's adhered to. These common patterns and idioms have enormous positive effects on the comprehensibility of every aspect of the system.

A little analogy from everyday life might explain this vital point even better. It's often said that England and America are two great countries divided by a common language. Although the two languages may consist nominally of the same vocabulary and grammar, the idioms are different. Suppose you're waiting to go into a job interview. Another candidate emerges from her ordeal, and you make conversation. "How did it go?" would work in either language. "How did you get on?" would be perfectly standard English, but would likely draw the response "Get on what?" from an American. "Recount for me the essence of what took place during your interview" is perfectly correct from a grammatical and semantic point of view, but would leave your fellow candidate wondering what planet you were from. To make sure you're going to be understood without undue strain on your listener's brain, you have to use the right idiom.

When building information systems, conceptual integrity means that you don't, metaphorically speaking, say "How did you get on?" in some cases, "How did you make out?" in others, and "How did it go?" in still others. You pick the phrase that's going to work best in most situations and use it always.

Principles for design and implementation

Up to this point, we've been talking about principles, applying to the design activity itself, which are inherent in the architectural process. Of equal importance are standards and principles that will further govern the conduct of the design—yet aren't really inherent in any sense of "architecture"—and principles that govern the *implementation* of that design. Using the bricks-and-mortar analogy again, implementation standards and principles are analogous to building codes. We will be expanding on this topic in later chapters, as we make progressive refinements and resolution of detail in our set of principles. We will be defining principles at the IS strategy level and at the IS architectural planning level.

Implementation principles cover any topic necessary to provide the proper guidance in decision making, including guidance for technology selection and for requirements governing nonfunctional attributes of the system to be built, such as scalability, performance, and manageability.

Implementation principles can be thought of as constraints and guidelines to enforce or promote *conceptual integrity* through the later stages of solution building. Their function is to provide a decision-making framework to ensure that common behavior is achieved through common mechanisms and common abstractions.

A particular example of a principle that governs solution building—and yet isn't inherent in "architecture"—is the use of iterative design and development. We'll be seeing more of this principle in later chapters.

2.4.3   The blueprinting sense of "architecture"

The *blueprinting sense* of the word *architecture* was the focus of a widely cited 1987 paper by Zachman [1987]. Work by Spewak [1992] and Boar [1998] built on these ideas. In the Zachman approach, any methodology used to produce the design tends to lie outside the scope of the blueprinting activity. The function of the blueprinting activity is to produce blueprints that are comprehensive, rigorous, unambiguous, and comprehensible to the entire community of interest. Multiple views are produced at appropriate levels of abstraction to fulfill the needs of different stakeholders viewing the system from different angles.

There is little available evidence to suggest that approaches rigorously based on the blueprinting theme of the Zachman framework[1] ever attained a significant degree of practical application in the commercial world, although it found a niche in some government agencies. The use of this framework implies an extraordinarily high degree of commitment and discipline throughout the entire analysis,

---

[1]Note that the term "framework" is used here in a fundamentally different sense than in the *framework* sense of "architecture." Whereas the framework sense of "architecture" denotes an abstract framework to be instantiated to produce a particular solution, the Zachman framework is a device for recording the state of, and organizing the artifacts of, a design.

design, and implementation teams. Furthermore, the details of the framework itself need to be completed and customized before it is ready to be used in actual practice. The flexible form of the framework presents an effective deterrent to the development of software tools to automate and facilitate its use. The consequent unavailability of supportive tooling was one of the impediments to the widespread adoption of the Zachman framework and its derivatives.

This is not to say that the Zachman framework had no influence on software production methodology. Rather, its influence was indirect, as the ideas behind it were adopted to varying degrees by practicing IS professionals and absorbed into their own less formal approaches.

In current practice, the blueprinting function of the architecture activity is effectively integrated into the modeling activity. We model the business, and we model the information systems that support its business processes. The tools, or methods, that we use in these modeling activities perform, or incorporate, the blueprinting function. We will examine these modeling activities further in later chapters.

2.4.4   The framework sense of "architecture"

The use of the word *architecture* to denote a finished design of some kind is a contrast from all our other uses, which have the sense of a set of activities. You will see "architecture" used as a synonym for "design" in this finished-design sense, just as we see it used synonymously in the activity sense. And it's not very helpful for our purposes in either sense.

Where "architecture" in the finished-design sense is helpful is where we can abstract some more generalized, or completely domain-independent, behavior that can serve as a framework for other solutions. A framework is a pattern of interaction. To use it, we plug things into the framework that conform to its interfaces. (A PC is an example of a framework, with its ISA and PCI buses.) Notice that "architecture" in this sense is used in the bricks-and-mortar world (for example, "Byzantine architecture") as well as in the IS world.

For our purposes, "architecture" used in this sense is supportive of the common-component sense—by applying architectural principles in our solution building, we will tend to produce designs that reuse proven frameworks.

This may be a good time to reinforce a theme that I've tried to keep revisiting throughout this book. The theme is that doing things the architectural way—reusing components, patterns, and frameworks—is a substantial intellectual challenge. Applying architectural principles takes lots of imagination and creativity, and pure left-brain deductive reasoning won't do it. Best [1995] gives an excellent example of framework reuse, which simultaneously demonstrates the intellectual difficulty of actually doing it. He points out that both delinquent-account collection and repair dispatch, two apparently quite unconnected business functions, can be built on a common framework—workflow. One of the problems of reuse arises from the intellectual difficulty of realizing that techniques from a completely different business process may be applicable to the task at hand. But the greater difficulty is that it is not normal for designers to try to abstract out domain-independent considerations from domain-dependent behavior. The designer of the delinquent-account collection software, even if she has managed to make the mental leap to realize that the repair-dispatch framework can be reused, is likely to have to spend too much time cleansing the framework of its domain dependencies to make the effort worthwhile.

2.5   Summary of the "architectural way"

So far, we've seen a set of requirements that we want this mysterious thing called "architecture" to fulfill, a set of meanings that are commonly attached to the word "architecture," and some discussion on what general principles we can derive from the various meanings of "architecture." What we have to do to reach closure is to summarize the approach that we have synthesized and called "the architectural way," and validate that the approach does indeed meet the requirements we laid out for the design discipline.

We'll summarize the "architectural way" as follows.

- **Solution fitted to client needs.** The most fundamental characteristic of architecture is that we design a solution to fit our client's needs.
- **Empirically validated principles.** We conduct our design according to the vital principles that have been found to be common to successful systems, and absent from failed efforts:
  - a clear separation of concerns between interface and implementation
  - construction based on a hierarchy of well-defined layers of abstraction

  (Readers who are paying particularly close attention will have noticed the omission of *common behavior achieved through common abstractions and common mechanisms,* which appeared in the earlier section on empirically validated principles. The reason for this principle's omission is that this current list elevates its status—see *conceptual integrity,* below.)
- **Design and implementation principles and guidelines.** The architectural design process specifies overarching principles and guidelines that will govern the design process and the implementation of the design.
- **Components, patterns, and frameworks.** As far as possible, we assemble our systems from available prebuilt components, in commonly understood and well recognized patterns, structured around familiar frameworks. Adherence to *de jure* and *de facto* standards is the purest form of this principle.
- **Conceptual integrity, and elegance in all things.** We strive always for the elegant solution, for the simple and obvious. We reject the complex and obscure. Adhering to the *implementation principles and guidelines,* we use

common mechanisms and common abstractions to achieve common behavior. Intellectual manageability is paramount.

- **Formal description and recording.** We use a formal description and recording discipline that represents the requirements for the IS system and its functional and environmental characteristics at various levels of abstraction. All stakeholders in the system can relate to one or more representations of the system specification to verify that their needs are being met and that they understand how to advance the realization of the system to the next level of refinement.

Table 2-2 recalls our requirements for the design discipline and relates how the various aspects of the "architectural way" help satisfy those requirements.

Table 2-2   How the "architectural way" satisfies design-discipline requirements

Requirement	How "architecture" addresses the requirement
Ensure that the IT environment is *aligned* with the business's imperatives (its mission, objectives, and processes)	Solution fitted to client needs
	Formal description and recording
	Empirically validated principles
Help build an IT environment that can be easily changed and extended, so as to *retain* its alignment with changing business imperatives.	Formal description and recording
	Components, patterns, and frameworks
	Empirically validated principles
	Conceptual integrity, and elegance in all things
Help control the costs of acquiring, developing, and maintaining IT resources.	Conceptual integrity, and elegance in all things
	Components, patterns, and frameworks
	Empirically validated principles
Communicate appropriate views of the solution to, and among, the various stakeholders.	Formal description and recording
	Empirically validated principles
	Design and implementation principles and guidelines
Help keep intellectual manageability of the IT environment and the e-business processes it supports.	Formal description and recording
	Conceptual integrity, and elegance in all things
	Components, patterns, and frameworks
	Empirically validated principles

(continued)

Table 2-2   How the "architectural way" satisfies design-discipline requirements (*continued*)

Requirement	How "architecture" addresses the requirement
Provide a framework for making and communicating technology choices.	Formal description and recording
	Design and implementation principles and guidelines
Provide freedom of choice of IT components.	Components, patterns, and frameworks
	Empirically validated principles
Maximize efficiency in building and evolving the IT environment through reuse of earlier work.	Components, patterns, and frameworks
	Empirically validated principles

3

Object-Oriented Methods and Architectural Solution Building

Part II of this book bases much of its description of the solution-building process on the use of the object-oriented approach. This treatment does *not,* however, mean that following the architectural way demands that you *must* use formal OO techniques and tools—although OO is indeed the preferred approach. We will see later how some of the benefits of object orientation can be gained even in the absence of a formal OO environment.

The reason for basing a description of the solution-building process on the OO paradigm is that object orientation captures many of the facets of the "architectural way" in one package. Just as we seek, as an architectural principle, to leverage prebuilt assemblies in our IS solutions, we use object orientation as a prebuilt set of architectural principles in the conduct of the solution-building process itself. Object orientation amounts to a *pattern* of mutually reinforcing thought, techniques, and supporting technology. A later section will explain which facets of the "architectural way" are embodied in the object-oriented discipline. First, let's find out what object orientation is all about and how it fits into the solution-building process.

3.1 What is object orientation all about?

Object orientation is an approach to system analysis, design, and implementation. The cycle begins with an object model, which can model systems—such as businesses and the information systems that support them. Objects making up the model generally correspond to the real-world things making up the system. Thus, we would model a bank in terms of objects such as customer, account, check, and so on. We would model a restaurant in terms of such objects as customer, table, menu, server, and so on. The objects of an object model represent *abstractions* of the real-world object that are meaningful in the context of the system being modeled. Thus a "table" object in the model of a restaurant would have such attributes as number of seats and status (whether occupied or available). In contrast, a "table" object in an interior-design system would have very different attributes, such as dimensions, material of construction, and color—attributes that are totally irrelevant in the context of the operation of a restaurant.

In addition to its state, which is represented by the condition of its attributes, an object exhibits *behavior.* Thus, a table object in a restaurant model might provide operations such as ReportStatus and SetStatus, ReportNumberOfSeats and SetNumberOfSeats. One of the fundamental tenets of the object-oriented approach is that an object's *behavior*—its black-box appearance as seen by an external client—is completely separated from its *implementation.* Behavior is "what it does." Implementation is "how it works." The decoupling of behavior from implementation is crucial. A client that invokes an object's behavior does so without knowledge of the implementation. That implementation is thus free to change in any way that does not impact the behavior. It is this freedom that provides system flexibility.

An object model consists of the objects making up the system and the relationships and interactions among them. Objects interact by sending each other messages, or stimuli, which invoke operations. Thus a *host* object in a restaurant model might send a message to a *table* object to invoke the ReportStatus operation, thereby discovering whether or not the table is currently occupied or available.

3.1.1   Object orientation compared with functional decomposition

The non–object-oriented approach to systems analysis and design—typified by "structured" design—tackles the divide-and-conquer task through functional decomposition. Functional decomposition is a fundamentally different approach from object orientation. Whereas object-oriented design models the system in terms of abstractions of the real-world "objects" that naturally occur in the system, functional decomposition breaks the system into the pieces the designer imagines will be used to implement the system.

Both approaches have essentially the same starting point: a black-box model of the behavior of the system, as seen by an external observer. In object-oriented terminology, such a black-box model is referred to as a "use-case model" and is expressed in the specialized language and notation of object orientation. In functional decomposition, the black-box model is likely to be called a "functional definition" or "functional requirements statement," and is likely to be expressed in natural language.

The next stage in the analysis, for both approaches, involves deciding on the broad outline of how the system works. In modeling a business, the "system" is the business, and "how the system works" amounts to an analysis of how the business activities fulfill the business processes. It is in the analysis of "how the system works" that the object-oriented approach and the functional decomposition approach diverge.

In the object-oriented approach, we decide what objects are needed in carrying out the use cases. Where the use-case model represents a business, our knowledge of the business helps us identify appropriate objects. Let's use a restaurant as an example. In analyzing the use case "serving a meal," we can quickly identify some objects that we expect to come into play—for example, host, server, cook, table, order, and cashier. How these objects interrelate and interact represents the business process of "serving a meal." Examination of the total set of use cases allows all pertinent internal objects to be identified.

Without trying to be rigorous or comprehensive, the diagram in Figure 3-1 illustrates how these objects are represented in Unified Modeling Language (UML) notation. Each box represents an object class, which is named in the label at the top. Below the line, the object's attributes are listed. Lines joining classes represent associations and are labeled with the nature of the association as well as an indication of whether the relationship is one-to-one, one-to-many, or many-to-many.

In contrast, a functional decomposition involves looking at stated functional requirements and constructing a functional decomposition. A functional decomposition of our restaurant might include such functional areas as those shown in Figure 3-2 (again, without trying to be rigorous or comprehensive).

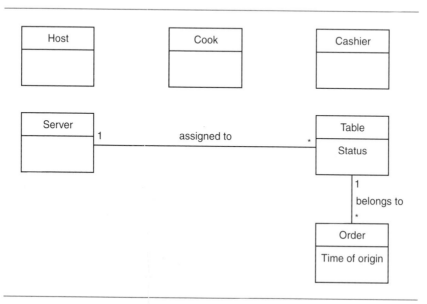

Figure 3-1   Some examples of objects.

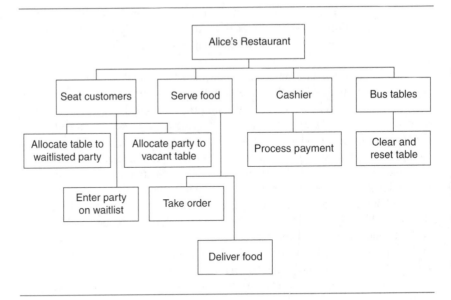

Figure 3-2   An example of functional decomposition.

We'll make additional comparisons between object orientation and functional decomposition later. For now, we're going to look more closely at the role of object-oriented models in architectural solution building.

3.1.2   Models for architectural solution building

The subsequent chapters of this book will refer to these models, which are drawn from Jacobson et al. [1994]. For ease of reference, I'll refer to them as the *OO model set*.

Figure 3-3 introduces and names a number of models. These models are ideally expressed in object-oriented form through the application of appropriate tools. The *business layer* models the business, in terms of business language and business operations. The *resource layer* models the human and automated resources that actually carry out the business processes.

Use-case models

The term "use case" was coined by Jacobson, and use-case modeling has become a cornerstone of object-oriented modeling. A use case describes a service that the thing being modeled provides to an external *actor*. The service results in measurable value to the actor and consists of a related set of transactions. Notice that we have a use-case model for the business as well as for the information system.

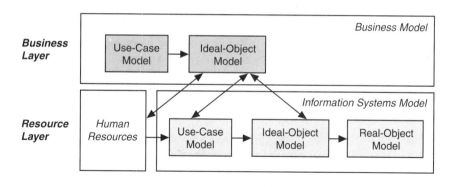

Figure 3-3   Relationship of business models to IS models.

They are not the same. When we model the business, we model it as a black box and construct a use-case model from the point of view of a customer (or other business partner) of that business. The use-case model defines how the business interacts with the outside world. When we model the information system, we model *what it is that we want the system to do*. This is, in general, not the same as what we want the *business* to do, because business behavior consists of human interactions with the customer as well as, or in place of, system interactions with the customer. In contrast, *system* behavior is defined as the black-box view as seen by *its* users. Although these "users" may be true clients of the business, they are more likely to be human users internal to the business, represented in the resource layer of the model structure.

Ideal-object models

The ideal-object model of the business models a "crystal-box" view of the business, which is an internal view of how the business works, in terms of its internal processes performed by people and information systems. We have to make choices about which pieces of which processes are to be performed by the information system and which are to be performed by humans. It is the making of these choices that leads to the use-case model of the information system. Another description traditionally given to this task is *requirements gathering* or *requirements analysis.*

The essence of an object model is that it represents the domain under analysis (which could be, for example, a business or an information system) in terms of real-world objects. We saw earlier how a restaurant might be modeled in terms of objects such as host, server, cook, table, order, and cashier.

The ideal-object model of the resource layer is an abstraction of how the IS solution will work. It models the internal behavior of the IS solution required to fulfill the use-case model.

Real-object model

The real-object model is the basis for the production of the executable software (which Jacobson [Jacobson et al. 1994] refers to as the "Implementation Model"), and as such needs clearly to specify design decisions and technology choices that are below the level of abstraction necessary or desirable in the ideal-object model. Appropriate modeling tools can generate source code from the real-object model, greatly enhancing the intellectual manageability of the solution.

3.1.3   Modeling and requirements gathering

Perhaps looking at the requirements analysis task from the viewpoint of modeling will help throw some light on why requirements gathering always seems harder than we think it should be. IS types get frustrated with business managers and users who don't seem to know what they want, always ask for changes even after they've been given exactly what they asked for, and generally seem to conspire to make IS people miserable. When we look at the situation in the context of our interlocking models, it becomes much easier to appreciate why requirements gathering is so hard.

First of all, business people need to define and articulate the processes that implement their business in order to build the ideal-object model of the business. Having done that, they need to decide which pieces should be automated through an information system and precisely what behavior the human user should require of that system. These two design processes are not independent—both depend on a knowledge of the business and a knowledge of what is reasonable to expect from technology. Thus, IS people and business people need to work together to arrive at a state of mutual understanding—a statement that surely will draw a "Well, duh!" from everyone who's been around the block even once with a software development project.

Traditional approaches to solution building usually don't involve building models of the business. Therefore, traditional approaches to requirements gathering don't have access to the organized knowledge embodied in these models. Rather, business people are *assumed* to have implicitly internalized the knowledge that would be expressed in a use-case model and an ideal-object model defining their business. Furthermore, they're assumed to have decided not only which functions they want the information system to perform but also the essence of what they want the user interface to look like. No wonder requirements gathering is hard. Looked at from a modeling perspective, it's clear that it *should* be hard. From this analysis, it's also clear that IS people generally have had unrealistically high expectations of their counterparts on the business side.

Business modeling gives everyone involved a much better understanding of the business and its processes. Notice that here we're talking about understanding *the business itself,* independent of any supporting information system. Only when we understand the business can we build suitable IS solutions to support it.

The difficult of requirements gathering came home to me personally in a particularly poignant experience. Having had bad experiences with the all-the-money-goes-into-the-same-pot technique in previous marriages, my wife and I decided to use PC power to run our financial affairs in a less strife-inducing way. We used Quicken, with three different environments: His, Hers, and Theirs. On paper, it seemed to be a good solution. When one of us spent money budgeted under Theirs, we "categorized" the transaction as a transfer to the "Reimbursable" account—a virtual account that recorded debts we owed and debts others owed us. We used the same technique when spending money for each other. (Yes, I buy her flowers, but if I put gasoline in her car, then by golly she's going to pay for it!) Once a month, we'd settle up and clear all the debts with a real paper check.

Now, when you actually operate this scheme, what happens is that each "debt" transaction needs to be recorded twice—in the Quicken that's making the loan and in the Quicken that's going to repay it. To make a long story short, getting all the transaction entries entered into all three Quickens at settle-up time—correctly—was an evening-long, manual-labor-intensive epic that produced a lot of frustration and gnashing of teeth. Less-stubborn people would have given up. But hey, we're both computer geeks—we can *do* this stuff, can't we?

All we needed was a program that would mirror the transactions in each complementary Quicken. How hard could this be?

As experienced IS professionals, we drew up a Requirements Statement (corresponding to a use-case model of the program). We both agreed on it. Then we drew up a Design Spec (corresponding to a real-object model) that we both agreed on. Then I cranked out the code, and we eagerly sat down to run it.

It was horrible. It didn't do what we wanted at all. Or, rather, it did exactly what we thought we wanted, but when we saw in action what we thought we had wanted, it was rubbish.

The experience really smacked me in the forehead. Here we were, two IS professionals with years of experience. We were the customers, the executive management, the end users, and the IS designers, developers, and testers *all rolled into one two-person team!* And we'd still managed to repeat the painful experience of large enterprise IS projects, in this tiny microcosm, over an IS challenge of almost mind-boggling triviality.

It was a truly humbling experience that gave me a good dose of empathy for business people and their difficulties in expressing IS requirements.

Epilogue

After some iteration and incremental improvement, the Quicken mirror program has been running smoothly, with only occasional glitches, for more than seven years.

Inevitably, however, the IS solutions we build reveal that we didn't, after all, really understand the business processes. So we go back and revise our business models with the insight gained from the IS solution. This is the familiar iteration cycle of model, implement, review, and then back to modeling to fix things misunderstood the last time. It's a never-ending cycle because you always have things on your to-do list, and while you're busy doing things, the world out there is changing, adding more things to your to-do list. To stop your to-do list from growing to infinity, you have to be able to reuse bigger pieces of solutions, which is what reuse of common components, subassemblies, and frameworks is all about.

3.1.4   Object-oriented development environments

After a long gestation period, object orientation is now a pervasive force in IS solution building. A large body of knowledge and system development tooling now exists to support an object-oriented approach from requirements gathering all the way through to solution deployment. There are software tools to support the building of the object-oriented models we have discussed. The SELECT product suite and Rational Rose are examples. There are object-oriented programming languages (such as Java, C++, and Smalltalk) and supporting development environments. Modeling tools are typically capable of generating program source code directly from models.

There are object-oriented run-time support environments, dominated by product suites based on the big two component technologies (Microsoft's DNA and Sun's J2EE). By another name, these are *component frameworks*. Does something sound familiar? By using one of these component frameworks, we are applying the architectural principle of reuse, by reusing the framework itself. Just as significantly, the framework provides an environment for the development and deployment of reusable components that plug into it.

3.2   Object orientation and the "architectural way"

It's time now to compare object orientation against the principles of the "architectural way," which we summarized in Section 2.5. Table 3-1 restates those principles and notes their relationship to the object-oriented approach. Where object orientation does not materially support a principle, the corresponding comment appears in parentheses.

It is clear that following an object-oriented approach helps us to follow architectural principles. To complete our comparison of object orientation and "architecture," let's assess how an objected-oriented approach supports the requirements we laid out for architecture in Section 2.3.

Table 3-2 reviews the architectural requirements and briefly notes how object orientation helps fulfill each requirement.

Table 3-1   Architectural principles and their relationship to object orientation

Architectural principle	Relationship of the principle to object orientation
Solution fitted to client needs	Object-oriented solution building begins with a model of the business, thus defining its desired externally visible behavior and the business processes that will fulfill that behavior. This model is the basis for expressing the client's requirements.
Empirically validated principles	
– A clear separation of concerns between interface and implementation	A clear separation of interface from implementation is one of the key tenets of object orientation.
– Construction based on a hierarchy of well-defined layers of abstraction	(Object orientation does not intrinsically add value in support of layered construction.)
Implementation principles and guidelines	(Principles and guidelines need to be applied independently of whether an object-oriented approach is being used.)
Conceptual integrity, and elegance in all things	The object-oriented mindset and consistent pattern of expression, from requirements through implementation, inherently promote elegance and conceptual integrity.
Components, patterns, and frameworks	An object-oriented design development environment inherently provides a framework, which forms a consistent pattern for the interaction of components.
	A run-time object component environment provides a standard framework with prebuilt support for component interaction and a consistent set of interfaces into which components can be inserted.
Formal description and recording	Object-oriented modeling and development tools provide for the recording of solution artifacts and deliverables at each stage of solution development.

In light of these comparisons, it is worth considering the question of whether following an object-oriented approach to solution building implicitly means that we're following the "architectural way." The answer is a resounding "yes," "not necessarily," or "it depends," depending on which aspect of the architectural way we're talking about. First of all, let's assume that we're applying object orientation in the proper way and not falling into the traps described later in Section 3.5.2. Given that we're applying object orientation appropriately, some of the architectural principles are indeed implicitly supported. "Solution fitted to client

Table 3-2 Architectural requirements and their relationship to object orientation

Architectural requirement	How object orientation supports the requirement
Ensure that the IT environment is *aligned* with the business's imperatives (its mission, objectives, and processes).	The object-oriented model set clearly represents the business and its processes and allows for straight-forward mapping onto supporting IS models.
Help build an IT environment that can be easily changed and extended, so as to *retain* its alignment with changing business imperatives.	A key tenet of object orientation is that an object's interface (what it does) is completely decoupled from its implementation (how it works). Therefore, object implementations can be changed without breaking functions that rely on them. The standard intercommunication infrastructure model allows components to be reused from other environments or purchased commercially.
Help control the costs of acquiring, developing, and maintaining IT resources.	Standard object-model interfaces and supporting infrastructure make for economical development and deployment.
Communicate appropriate views of the solution to, and among, the various stakeholders.	Object models, expressed in terms of real-world objects, communicate ideas and proposed solutions to stakeholders in familiar terms.
Help keep intellectual manageability of the IT environment and the e-business processes it supports.	Object models expressed in terms of real-world concepts, with object-oriented design and development, minimize the semantic gap between the business domain and the information solution domain. Errors and misunderstandings in the translation between the two domains are minimized.
Provide a framework for making and communicating technology choices.	The object-oriented framework provides substantial infrastructure. This infrastructure provides a foundation for evaluating and communicating specifications for supplementary technology services.
Provide freedom of choice of IT components.	The object framework provides a standardized infrastructure for the development of interchangeable components. The object-oriented discipline of requiring rigorous definitions of component interfaces establishes an environment of interchangeable components.
Maximize efficiency in building and evolving the IT environment through reuse of earlier work.	Components built with proper levels of abstraction can be reused in a variety of different environments, even in completely different business domains.

needs" (see Table 3-1) is in this category. Some of the other principles are outside the scope of object orientation, as noted in Table 3-1; for example, "Implementation principles and guidelines" is in this category. Still other principles are supported indirectly by object orientation, and designers must consciously apply the principles within the object-oriented method rather than assume that merely following the object-oriented path will bring about implicit application of architectural principles. "Conceptual integrity, and elegance in all things" is firmly in this "it depends" category.

3.3   Benefits of an object-oriented approach

We have already seen how object orientation supports the architectural way of solution building. This support is, of course, a benefit in itself. However, the inherent benefits of object orientation are what led to its adoption and the growth of its supporting ecosystem of analysis, design, and development tools and run-time environments. In this section, we'll examine the chief benefits of the object-oriented approach over earlier techniques.

3.3.1   Narrowing the semantic gap

In case you missed it, the narrowing of the semantic gap appeared in Table 3-2, which compared architectural requirements with object-orientation support. The table entry said:

> *Object models expressed in terms of real-world concepts, with object-oriented design and development, minimize the semantic gap between the business domain and the information solution domain. Errors and misunderstandings in the translation between the two domains are minimized.*

It has been found, in analyses of sources of errors in software, that *translation* errors account for a significant proportion of the total. By "translation" in this context, we mean the translation between the requirements of the business domain and the mechanisms of the information solution domain. By expressing the business processes as an object model, we find that the objects of the business domain carry through straightforwardly into the solution domain. In applying object-oriented modeling, we model the business in terms of abstractions of business concepts, and proceed to modeling the supporting information system in terms of real-world objects. Modeling real-world objects in this way helps overcome one of the most troublesome and error-prone tasks of information system design—the translation of the needs of business processes to a cooperating set of IT artifacts that can fulfill those needs. Object orientation helps with this translation when we begin with an object-oriented model of the business, expressed in *the language and terminology of the business,* and proceed to object-oriented models and object-oriented development of the desired supporting IT system. The object orientation of all stages in the process minimizes the conceptual discontinuity—the semantic gap—from one stage to the next. There is thus little or no problem of translation across a semantic gap.

In contrast to object modeling, design by functional decomposition introduces a discontinuity, or semantic gap, between the model of the business process and its supporting information system. The semantic gap leads designers to begin thinking about implementation mechanisms and supporting data structures prematurely. There is thus a focus, too early in the process, on the "how it works" considerations rather than on the "what it does" behavior. Misalignment of the IS solution with required business functionality is the likely consequence.

Referring back to our restaurant example in Section 3.1.1, notice how our functional decomposition has lost track of the human players in the business process. An object-oriented business process model would retain the explicit interactions of the human players, thus making it easier to identify their needs for IS support.

3.3.2   Object orientation and good design

We have already seen that the conceptual integrity of a clean internal structure is an essential attribute of a successful system—one that is intellectually manageable, can be extended and reorganized, and is maintainable and testable. Such systems are simpler, smaller, and therefore more reliable.

A clean structure makes it possible to discover common abstractions and mechanisms. This may sound like a Catch-22, but it's really a bootstrap situation, leading to cycles of positive feedback. The use of common abstractions and mechanisms constitutes a clean structure. The clean structure, being lucidly understandable, allows the discovery of larger-scale common abstractions and mechanisms. Redesign around these newly discovered larger abstractions may lead to the discovery of even larger-scale rationalizations.

The discovery of abstractions is what the object-oriented approach is all about. We model the business, in terms of abstractions of business concepts, and go on to model the supporting information system in terms of real-world objects. Both the business model and the IS model are vehicles for finding higher-level abstractions consistent with standard patterns of behavior known to those familiar with the application domain.

It is worth noting that "architecture," in the sense of the word that denotes *design at the higher levels of abstraction*, effectively equates to an object model. For example, Bass et al. [1998] define architecture thus:

> *The software architecture of a program or computing system is the structure or structures of the system, which comprise software components, the externally visible properties of those components, and the relationships among them.*

—which is a pretty good description of an object model.

3.3.3   Object orientation at the source code level

IS professionals are well aware of the "spaghetti code" phenomenon—code that's poorly and chaotically constructed, whether through inept programming development practice or through years of ad hoc "band-aid" maintenance. The spaghetti-like flow of its convoluted logic is only partly to blame for the difficulty of its maintenance. More significant are the uncontrolled and nonobvious dependencies among different areas of code. Procedures that manipulate global data, and by so doing affect each other's behavior, effectively maintain subterranean connections among them. It is the nature and multiplicity of these hidden interfaces that cause bug fixes to generate new bugs and that cause the infamous "one-line patch" to have such surprisingly widespread effects.

The solution to the subterranean interface problem was first clearly articulated by Parnas [1972]. Parnas realized that decomposing a system along "obvious" functional lines led to the proliferation of subterranean interfaces through interactions realized through global data. His solution was to *hide each significant design decision within a single module.* In particular, the design of a complex data structure is a design decision that should be hidden within a module. The point of *hiding* the design decision within one module is that it can be revisited and modified later, *without impact on any other module.*

How do we hide a design decision? We do so by decoupling the design decision from the externally visible behavior of the module. In other words, there is a clear separation of concerns between interface and implementation.

Did that last sentence give you that déjà vu feeling? It should have. It's one of the architectural principles we saw earlier. And, of course, it's one of the tenets of object orientation.

We saw earlier how real-world concepts are the principal basis for the selection of objects. As we get into building the *real-object model* (discussed in Section 7.5), we will find occasion to invent artificial objects as we design the solution. Whether objects are real-world based or artificial, an object—which roughly corresponds to the "module" in a structured design—is the appropriate place to hide a significant design decision.

We can see a rudimentary example of information hiding in the restaurant example. The table object maintains its state in attributes (number of seats, status), which are not visible outside the object. External objects wanting to interrogate or change the attributes are constrained instead to call the table object's operations. The decoupling of interface from behavior thus allows the representation of the attributes to be changed arbitrarily, without impact on any other object in the system. Obviously, keeping track of *number of seats* and *status* would not involve a complex data structure; however, it is easy to imagine objects in real systems whose states would involve very complex structures. A warehouse would be an example of such an object.

3.4   Objects and components

Before we go too much further, it might be a good idea to try to clarify and distinguish the terms "object" and "component." In the beginning, there were "objects," which lived in "object-oriented" environments. Some time later, there emerged "components," which lived in "component-based" systems of various kinds. What's the difference? It seems that, like "architecture" and "e-business," the "object versus component" question will usually produce as many answers as people you ask. What follows is my subjective and somewhat irreverent assessment, boiled down to a degree of granularity appropriate for the context of this book.

An "object" has a clear individual identity. It provides a well-defined service through a clearly defined interface. Its internal operation is not visible from outside, and thus its implementation may change in any way, so long as the interface—essentially its "contract" with the outside world—remains unchanged.

"Objects" and "object-orientation" are concepts associated with the analysis, design, and development processes. Objects tend to lose their identity at run-time, becoming a constituent of an executable program not visible outside of that program. However, "distributed object" systems provide for objects to retain run-time identity and invoke other objects regardless of location.

As the industry gained experience with the deployment of distributed object systems, annoying pathologies became evident. Technology and practice matured, and these pathologies were addressed. To dissociate these new systems from those of the past, the term "component" supplanted the term "object." "Components" have all the properties of "objects," but they have additional properties that make them viable throughout the life cycle—from build through deployment—of industrial-strength distributed solutions. Furthermore, the term "component" tends to connote a larger chunk of functionality than does "object." Most usefully, "components" provide business process functionality, whereas "objects" provide grain-of-sand-sized pieces of software functionality, such as the listboxes, icons, and similar controls of a graphical user interface.

3.5   Pitfalls of an object-oriented approach

Object orientation is not a silver bullet that will magically eliminate all known IS solution-building problems. Pitfalls await the unwary and the ill-prepared. This section considers those pitfalls.

3.5.1   Large, complex enterprises

A small restaurant is obviously much easier to understand than a large, complex enterprise. In trying to understand the business processes of a large and complex enterprise, we'd probably start with an organization chart, and, using that as our first-level divide-and-conquer device, we'd attempt to discover the business functions one enterprise division at a time. The problem that such an approach presents for an object orientation is that it's inherently a *functional decomposition* of the enterprise. The object-oriented solution builder is thus forced down a path he doesn't want to travel. What should he do?

There are two choices: (1) roll with the punches and accept the functional decomposition as the starting point, or (2) use the organization chart as a people directory and piece together what the enterprise actually wants to do.

Option 2 isn't easy. As Parkinson [1970] observed, people generally have only a fuzzy idea of what it is their enterprise is trying to do—but they can usually tell you how they should go about it, whatever "it" is. The radical approach of option 2 is known as *business process reengineering*. It implies a project of large scope, requiring strong management commitment from the very top of the enterprise. We'll examine the considerations of project scope in Chapter 4.

Going with option 1 effectively means that we will not be tackling business process reengineering. Rather, what we'll be doing is better characterized as business improvement. Rather than trying to discover an idealized picture of what the enterprise is trying to do, we will discover existing business activities without getting hung up on what mission they support. Having discovered the business activities, we'll find ways to improve them, through information technology, in an incremental way.

Of course, for all the reasons we've already explored, we will want to apply object-oriented methods in our building of the IS solution. However, because we're effectively constrained to represent our business requirements through a functional decomposition, there's going to be a discontinuity in the solution-building process. We're going to have to understand the business processes in non–object-oriented terms and yet design the supporting information systems in object-oriented terms.

3.5.2 Inappropriate mindset

One of the greatest challenges in the effective application of object-oriented techniques is to get everyone involved onto the proper mental wavelength. People accustomed to more traditional techniques, such as structured analysis and design, will tend to continue—whether they realize it or not—to think along their familiar patterns. Just as when you use a hammer to drive a screw, the results are less than ideal.

The paradoxical result is that the use of object-oriented design and development tooling does not necessarily imply that object-oriented philosophy is being applied. Designers and developers steeped in earlier design techniques—"structured" methods or their ad hoc precursors—will often have a difficult time getting their brains into the object-oriented groove without substantial education and on-the-job mentoring. Turned loose prematurely on object-oriented tools, unreconstructed designers can totally subvert object-oriented environments and produce old-style designs with all the problems that object orientation was designed to address. Instead of defining objects that correspond to real-world concepts in the problem domain, designers might instead define objects to reflect concepts that their traditional designs might use.

In the limit—and such designs have actually been observed in the wild—the resulting system design amounts to a functional decomposition, with each functional area represented by a single object whose operations correspond faithfully to the procedures that a structured design would have proposed. Alternatively—and equally inappropriately—the design invents an object corresponding to each procedure of a structured design. Each such object then has precisely one operation, which effectively says "do it."

Object orientation is more appropriately thought of as a mindset—a mode of thinking, a philosophy—than as an attribute of software tooling. Object-oriented software tooling—both development and run-time—*supports* this mindset and philosophy but cannot enforce it. To reap the benefits of object orientation, you must have an object-oriented mindset. To make a screw work best, you use a screwdriver, not a hammer. Yes, you can use a hammer, but the results are messy. If you really can't figure out how to use a screwdriver, you should use nails instead of screws. If your staff just can't "get" object orientation, stay with structured methods.

3.6   OO benefits without OO tools

Let's not be too gloomy about whether we can reap the expected benefits of object-oriented tooling. Let's look at things from the flip side. Just as object-oriented tooling can be subverted by an inappropriate mindset, non–object-oriented tooling can be "subverted" by an object-oriented mindset. Thus, there is no implication that an architectural approach to solution building *depends* on the use of object-oriented methods.

For various reasons, in any given solution-building effort you may find it inappropriate to employ formal object-oriented methods and tools. Perhaps the bulk of the components to be integrated are not object-oriented. Perhaps the scope of the project is too narrow to justify the expenditure on the required tooling and education. In spite of such impediments, solution builders can still apply architectural principles.

It is certainly easier to apply the architectural principles within an object-oriented approach. By the same token, it is easier to *describe* architectural solution building in terms of an object-oriented approach. For this reason, the body of this book is written from an object-oriented viewpoint. Adaptation to non–object-oriented environments is an exercise for the reader.

3.7   Where to find more information

Bahar [1996] provides a highly readable introduction to object orientation that requires no prior knowledge. Booch [1994] and Jacobson et al. [1994] are more substantial works on object orientation. Marshall [2000] describes the use of UML in modeling business processes.

The so-called *three amigos* (Booch, Jacobson, and Rumbaugh) of the Rational Software Corporation are steadily producing books that advance the art through the Unified Modeling Language (UML). Object-oriented modeling gained a welcome common platform and focus with the coming together of the three amigos and the subsequent development of UML—a single common language for object modeling—in late 1997. Particular titles are Booch, Jacobson, and Rumbaugh [1998 and 2000].

You can find additional citations to works on object orientation in the Bibliography and References Section.

Examples of modeling tools are

- Rational Rose from Rational Software Corporation
  (http://www.rational.com)
- SELECT Component Factory from Princeton Softech
  (http://www.selectst.com/products/)
- Paradigm Plus from Computer Associates
  (http://www.cai.com/products/platinum/appdev/pplus_ps.htm)

4

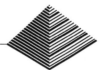

Project Scope
Considerations

The scope of a project has a critical bearing on its probability of success. It is essential to keep the scope constrained to what you can achieve. The implications here are that we need to stay continuously in touch with the real scope of the project—avoiding insidious "scope creep"—and to stay continuously aware of the state of the project's ecosystem. The ecosystem comprises the technical, business, and political environments surrounding the project. The interplay and tension among these environments set the upper and lower bounds on the scope of an IS solution project.

Overall project scope is a function of two dimensions that are analogous to breadth and depth in the physical world. The breadth of a project is a measure of how much of the enterprise is involved in the effort. The depth of a project is a measure of how radical a change the enterprise is aiming to make in its business processes. Truly radical change, which starts with a blank sheet of paper, is what Hammer christened *business process reengineering* [Hammer and Champy 1993, Hammer and Stanton 1995]. A less ambitious, less disruptive approach starts from the enterprise's current state and makes incremental changes.

In a real information solution-building project, breadth and depth are not truly independent. A radical approach to reengineering tends to expand the breadth of the project, because all business processes are, at some level, ultimately interdependent. Similarly, involving a greater proportion of the enterprise tends to expand the depth of the project, as more possibilities for improving the end-to-end process, and the interactions among processes, come to light through the insight gained from a more detached perspective. In work that predated Hammer and Champy [1993], Spewak [1992] termed a wide-scope project *enterprise architecture planning,* although his focus was the application of information systems to business processes rather than the reengineering of the business processes themselves.

In this book, I have tried to embrace both large- and small-scope projects. Whether you go for breadth or depth—or both together—is a function of your business situation, your ambition to succeed, your tolerance for risk, the availability of capable resources, your enterprise culture, and much more. You should look to other sources (for example, Hammer and Champy [1993], Hammer and Stanton [1995], and Spewak [1992]) for guidance on the scope of business process change you want to tackle. My main purpose in this book is to lay out the process of making an orderly, effective, and efficient approach to the application of enabling and empowering information technology to business processes. However, it is inevitable, and not undesirable, for the design of information systems to feed back into the design of the business processes that they will support. Consideration of business process reengineering is, therefore, both necessary and appropriate.

Before getting into a deeper discussion of project scope, we need to establish some terms. I will use the term *business process* (or simply "process" when the context is clear) in almost the same way that Hammer and Champy [1993] use it—as a set of related tasks that add value for a customer. Jacobson [1994] uses the term *use case* for the same idea. There is a slight difference, however, between Hammer and Champy's *process* and Jacobson's *use case*. Whereas Hammer and Champy limit a process to that which adds value for a *customer,* Jacobson considers an interaction with any actor external to the enterprise—such as a supplier or other business partner—to be a use case. This book is about IS solutions and e-business, and in this context Jacobson's more general interpretation of business process, or use case, is more relevant to our needs. The important point about a business process is that it describes a view of the enterprise *as seen by an actor external to the enterprise.*

A *business process* is thus distinct from a *business function,* which describes a set of activities performed *within* the enterprise. Thus "human resources," "marketing," and "sales" are all business functions, not processes. A process, by its nature, crosses functional boundaries. Thus, the process *order fulfillment,* which adds value for customers by allowing them to obtain products or services, would involve the functions *sales, accounts receivable, packing, shipping,* and so on, depending on the internal organization of the enterprise. This said, I have generally tried to steer clear of using the term *function* in the sense of business function, preferring *activity* or *activities,* because "function" has IT connotations that could cause unnecessary confusion.

4.1 Large-scale projects

Building a large-scale IS solution for an entire enterprise—a formidable technical challenge even in ideal circumstances—is at least as much a diplomatic and political endeavor as a technical one. In the context of a medium-size or large enterprise, the dynamics of organizational behavior are almost always a greater challenge than the technical complexity of the effort. Experience has shown, unfortunately, that the majority of enterprises that undertake large-scale projects are not successful. However, the history of bad experiences by no means implies that we should abandon thoughts of comprehensive reengineering in favor of tactical expediency. What it means is that we need to take realistic inventory of the

- organizational climate and culture
- business imperatives and desires
- in-place IT systems
- available enabling technology

From this assessment, we can derive a realistic set of expectations to help us decide on an appropriate scope and level of ambition for an IS solution.

4.1.1   Characteristics of large-scale projects

A project's scale is determined by its breadth across the organization and by its depth, as measured by the extent of its impact on existing business processes. A project that spans an entire enterprise—even if driven by no more ambition than to "clean up" existing business processes—nevertheless implies substantial scope.

A project that selects a single business process, yet is determined to redesign the process from the ground up, also implies substantial scope, because business processes by nature span multiple organizational units.

A full-scale reengineering effort involving both depth and breadth across all of an enterprise's business processes is of course the most ambitious kind of project.

Whether driven by breadth or depth, or by both, a large-scale project necessarily involves multiple organizational units and a large number of people. A large-scale project is therefore a top-down phenomenon. Unless driven from the top of the enterprise, a large-scale project cannot succeed.

4.1.2   Critical success factors for large-scale projects

Experience with large-scale projects has given us an understanding of the factors that make the difference between success and failure. This subject is discussed at length by Spewak [1992] and by Hammer and Stanton [1995], which are required reading for anyone planning to embark on a project of large scope.

Essential success factors are summarized below. After assessing all of these factors, we decide on the scope of the project we want to tackle, making decisions on the trade-offs involved.

Management commitment and support   This is the overriding essential ingredient for success. Unwavering management commitment *from the very top level of the hierarchy,* consistently and explicitly demonstrated through action (for example, consistent personal interest, commitment of resources, and allocation of priorities), not just lip service, is the greatest single predictor of success.

Conversely, the absence of such commitment is an ironclad guarantee of failure. No exceptions to this rule have ever occurred in practice.

End-user and management participation and cooperation   Involvement and buy-in by all stakeholders is essential. Systems designed in detachment or isolation by IS professionals will be rejected or sabotaged.

Effective project leadership and methodology   Success requires a systematic approach. A methodology[1] must be employed in motivating and guiding the project.

Qualified team, and use of both insiders and outsiders   The team must be competent and well respected in their fields of expertise, whether business or IS. "Insiders"—people involved in the performance of the current business processes—provide the knowledge necessary to understand the business as it currently functions. "Outsiders"—either consultants hired from outside the business or personnel from a different area of the business—provide an objective viewpoint, with no emotional investment in the status quo. Consultants bring knowledge from similar engagements—competitors, perhaps—and may have broader knowledge of the industry at large than most insiders.

Productive recording and analysis tools   This factor is equivalent to saying that we have to "do architecture" in the sense, discussed earlier, that "architecture" describes the process and result of applying a design recording and organization discipline in which the design is presented and rigorously documented ("blueprinted") in various views, representing different levels of abstraction as well as the complementary viewpoints of the various stakeholders.

Compatible culture   The solution-building effort must be promoted and performed in a manner consistent with the corporate culture; otherwise, it will be rejected (explicitly, or implicitly by noncooperation or sabotage) by the corporate immune system.

Agile organization   A reengineering project is going to take you into unknown territory. You can't know in advance what to expect when you get there. Cost–benefit analyses are estimates at best. The organization has to be able to adapt as the picture clarifies. Is your organization as nimble as it will need to be?

---

[1]The word "methodology" sometimes carries connotations that are not intended in this context. The specific meaning of "methodology" as it is used here is discussed in Chapter 14.

Effective communication, involvement, and distribution of intermediate deliverables   It is essential to keep all stakeholders fully involved and fully informed about progress and issues to retain buy-in and commitment. In a large-scale project, it is almost impossible to overcommunicate. People feel very threatened by change, and the rumor mill will go into full production if your communication stream leaves any kind of vacuum.

Understand the current system, but don't analyze it to death   Reengineering is about *replacing* the current business processes. If reengineering is our purpose, we don't need to analyze current business processes in great detail because they're going to be replaced anyway. We need only understand current processes in broad outline, and how they support the enterprise business and customer-visible functions.

In areas where business processes themselves are not being actively reengineered, but new IS support—such as e-business enablement—is being considered, more detail is needed. But here again, the focus must be on those business areas where IS support is going to be applied. Business process analysis can easily become an end in itself if not held closely in check.

4.2   Narrow-scope projects

Large-scale business-process-reengineering projects necessarily follow a top-down process, beginning with business modeling from an idealized view of the enterprise and its business ambitions. For all the reasons summarized in Section 4.1.2, it is often not feasible to engage in business modeling on such a grand scale. However, in many situations, dramatic benefits can be realized by approaching the situation from a different angle—through a tactical, bottom-up approach, in the context of a small part of the enterprise.

4.2.1   Characteristics of narrow-scope projects

A narrow-scope project involves an appraisal of the business within the scope of an organization, or of a small number of tightly coupled organizations within the larger enterprise. Business modeling is guided by the realities of "the way things are now" rather than by idealized projections of "the way things should be." These "things" cover human activities as well as the information systems that support them. By identifying the most promising areas of opportunity and critical areas for improvement, high-payoff projects can be quickly identified.

Identification of projects with high payoff potential is not normally difficult. People who work day in and day out in a business usually have a well-developed sense of what improvements in their microcosm could usefully be made and are all too familiar with their daily frustrations.

The essence of this tactical approach is to list the possibilities for improvement and then to pick a small number of well-defined targets to pursue through the next stages. It is very important at this stage firmly to constrain the number of subprojects; otherwise, the effort may bog down under its own weight.

A narrow-scope project—tightly constrained in both breadth and depth—is the least demanding of high-level management support. The goal is to make incremental improvements by building on existing business activities and their existing information systems.

Projects of this kind can show significant benefits in a very short period. They are appealing from both the IT vendor and IT customer points of view. The IT customer gets a meaningful improvement from his information systems in a short timeframe. Conversely, the IT vendor can propose and execute an engagement of this kind without spending a lot of effort and time working organizational issues. The IT vendor can use the exercise as a demonstration of his skills, capabilities, and ability to execute, ultimately setting the stage for engagements of broader scope.

4.2.2　Narrowing the scope to produce repeatable solutions

The narrow-scope, tactical approach has other attractions besides political tractability—specifically, repeatability and predictability. Because many organizations have faced similar needs (for example, "improve customer service" or "Web-enable access to our reservation system to reduce the number of human customer service reps"), information systems consultants have generally accumulated a body of experience in delivering many similar solutions.

Once a business need has been identified in the context of an existing IT system, a knowledge base built from earlier engagements can be applied to deliver a proven solution very economically, very quickly, and at low risk. The entire process can be supported by software tooling and a rich knowledge base, which provides full design documentation and a detailed blueprint, supported by work breakdown structures and resource lists, for the management of the project through implementation. The approach thus conforms to both the blueprinting and common-component senses of the word "architecture" discussed earlier in the book.

4.3　Trade-offs in project scope

Trade-off 1: The wider the scope, the higher the potential benefit　A project of the scope of Business Process Reengineering promises many far-reaching benefits, such as

- total integration of IT systems within and beyond the enterprise
- identification and pursuit of new business opportunities
- rationalization of a wide range of IT systems to eliminate overlap and reduce cost
- enhancement of customer and business partner relationships through automated and value-added interfaces (for example, the Internet)
- reduction of labor cost through automation

Trade-off 2: The wider the scope, the higher the (immediate) cost of the effort
The architecture project itself incurs incremental costs over a continued tactical ad hoc approach. These costs will not be reclaimed unless the project is ultimately successful.

Trade-off 3: The wider the scope, the higher the risk   *The people aspect:* The wider the scope, the more people are involved, with correspondingly higher numbers of interactions and potential for organizational conflict. More people involved means more people who must be convinced of the value of the project and more people who must be prepared to let go of a cherished status quo and move forward into uncharted territory.

The technical aspect: The wider the scope, the greater the potential for intractable complexity. Here are two related extracts from Gall [1986].

A complex system that works is invariably found to have evolved from a simple system that worked.

A complex system designed from scratch never works, and cannot be patched up to make it work. You have to start over, beginning with a working simple system.

Gall notes that diligent search for exceptions to these axioms has yielded negative results.

Trade-off 4: The wider the scope, the higher the required level of management commitment   This is almost a corollary of trade-off 3. As we saw in Section 4.1.2, tackling projects of a wider scope requires the involvement of a larger number of organizations, so that more managers, extending to higher levels of the hierarchy, need to be committed to the effort. If such commitment is not forthcoming (and making this determination can in itself be a significant challenge), then you must scale back the level of ambition and address the problems and opportunities in a more focused area where you can get the support you need. If you're determined to ignore my advice and plow ahead anyway, then at least read Spewak [1992] and educate yourself fully about all the ways you're going to fail.

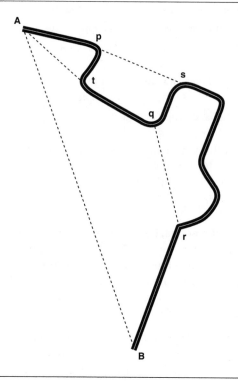

Figure 4-1 Road system improvement.

4.3.1 A scope trade-off illustration

Let's look at an analogy from civil engineering to give us an intuitive appreciation for these kinds of trade-offs. Imagine we have a road, running from point A to point B, which takes a circuitous route through several sharp bends (see Figure 4-1) As an authority responsible for this road, we would want to improve this section. Obviously, the "best" solution would be to eliminate the entire stretch and replace it with a new section of road running directly from A to B. However, tackling a project of that magnitude may prove to be too complex to be feasible within a reasonable planning horizon. There may be difficult technical challenges (swamps, rock barriers, forests, bodies of water); there may be political barriers concerned with environmental management of the impact of the proposed route; and there may be difficulties with property owners and the government jurisdictions over various sections of the proposed highway. There may be difficulty securing funding for a project of such magnitude. All in all, the "best" solution may not be achievable.

However, we can perhaps lower our ambitions and tackle a project yielding significant benefits. Building a new section of road from point p to point s eliminates four sharp curves and reduces the distance, as does building a new section from point q to point r. Clearly, we can see many possibilities for meaningful improvement that stop short of the utopian direct route.

Notice also that the direct A-to-B route is optimum only within the context of the section from A to B. If we consider a larger piece of geography, then the A-to-B direct route may not be so optimal after all—it will depend on the structure of the surrounding system and traffic patterns.

These kinds of questions have direct analogies in the world of IT solutions. The A-to-B microcosm corresponds to a single enterprise; intermediate sections correspond to organizations within the enterprise. While business process and IS optimization across the total enterprise is in some sense "optimal," there are going to be greater optimizations available if we consider the external world, where e-business relationships with business partners, customers, and government come into play. Ultimately, of course, we find every enterprise in the world to be interconnected in some way.

It is worth noting that we can improve the road in Figure 4-1 in two manageable steps by building a new section from A to t and a new section from q to r. This approach offers two benefits: more of the "legacy" system is retained (saving cost), and improvements are made incrementally (heeding the warning from Gall quoted previously, and thereby lowering risk). The revised route is almost as efficient as the direct route and probably has a better cost-to-benefit ratio. This extension of our road analogy again has lessons for IT. It tells us to seek incremental solutions that will be supportive of a larger integration, rather than choose expedient solutions that are likely to be throwaways. Thus, in our road analogy, we can see that a new section connecting p to s is more difficult to include in an ultimately final design. The p-to-s section might correspond, for example, to fixing up an antiquated payroll system—only to throw away the new system a year later when we reengineer the business and decide to outsource the entire payroll process.

4.3.2   Scope, commitment, and risk

Every solution-building project we undertake is going to fall somewhere on a continuum between a narrow-focus, incremental improvement and an enterprise-wide business process reengineering. Figure 4-2 illustrates that the larger the intended scope of the project, the greater the required level of commitment throughout the enterprise.

Operating "above the line" puts the project under high risk, because the level of enterprise commitment is insufficient for the intended scope. Conversely, operating on or below the line represents a conservative approach where enterprise commitment is adequate for the intended scope.

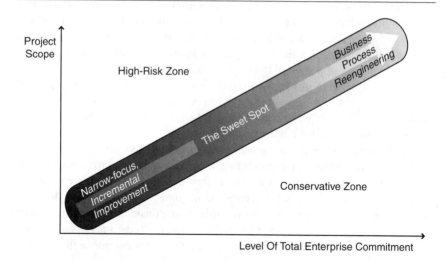

Figure 4-2 The project scope continuum.

4.4 Impact of varying scope on architecture stages

The stages of architectural solution building made a brief appearance in the book outline in the preface. Part II is devoted to a more detailed treatment of the stages, but before we get to Part II we're going to look at the effect that a narrowing of project scope has on the various stages.

The various stages of the architectural solution-building process are necessarily affected by the scope of the project we're tackling. To make things easier to explain as we go along, I'm going to characterize three different project scenarios, which I'll use to explain how each stage is modified, if necessary, to accommodate projects of differing scope. I'm going to give these scenarios descriptive labels, for ease of reference, and elevate them to paradigm status—hoping that such exalted status will make them easier to remember.

4.4.1 The e-business paradigm

Let's pretend for a moment that, with limited aims, we aim to equip current enterprise processes with e-business capability. Here, the emphasis is on discovering exactly what are the enterprise's processes (what the enterprise currently does) and how those processes are fulfilled (how the enterprise currently works). Having made these discoveries, we examine the more important interactions with the external world and make the best use of e-business technology to remove the latency and friction. Thus, we would be changing the business processes only to the extent necessary to apply e-business—a shallow-depth approach, but across a broad scope.

This approach, the *E-Business Paradigm,* is shallow because we're not going to attempt a radical modification of the way the business processes are conducted. Enabling the processes with e-business amounts to replacing the external-interaction infrastructure—it does not, in itself, amount to a radical redesign of the processes themselves. The scope, however, is broad, because any externally visible business process involves, by its nature, multiple organizations within the enterprise.

In practice, it is usually the case that the application of e-business technology inevitably requires that you overhaul business activities as a result. Especially where back-office activities are concerned (as opposed to the consumer interface), applying e-business technology tends to force business activities into new ways of working, thus moving toward the realm of reengineering.

In these situations, you may find yourself in a situation where you need to "bolt on" the e-business technology, and the business activities that surround it, to existing practices. You don't have the organizational commitment to tackle top-down reengineering—otherwise you wouldn't be trying to constrain your scope in the first place—and you can't introduce e-business functionality incrementally because it would take too long. You're left with the "bolt-on," "force-fit" approach, where you insert the e-business technology and let the business environment adapt to it, as if by osmosis. It's far from an ideal approach—although ironically it is an application of iterative and incremental deployment—but in some situations it's the only practical way to make things happen in a reasonable timeframe.

We'll see in Chapter 7 more specifically how e-business tends to stimulate reengineering (with the exception of applying e-business only at the consumer interface, which is what we often refer to as "e-commerce"). For the moment, we'll note that applying e-business usually moves us in a reengineering direction, which, as we've seen, requires a high level of organizational commitment. However, in recognition of the realities of organizational politics,[2] I'm going to retain the E-Business Paradigm throughout the appropriate chapters of the book.

Interestingly, organizational commitment is usually easier to marshal for an e-business-motivated project than for an "ordinary" reengineering project, because executive and middle-level managers are more aware of—or can be more easily persuaded by—the business imperatives driving e-business. If this organizational commitment can indeed be marshaled, then the project becomes an honest reengineering effort rather than one characterized by the E-Business Paradigm.

4.4.2   The reengineering paradigm

The *Reengineering Paradigm* characterizes projects that are of wide scope and radical depth. Our intent is the radical reengineering of processes across a broad range of the enterprise's activities. We will be taking a look at all the enterprise's

---

[2]Here, I am using "politics" in the straightforward sense of Bismarck's "Politics is the art of the possible," rather than in any pejorative sense.

important processes, and, guided by the enterprise's mission and objectives, designing from first principles how those processes should be fulfilled.

Note that the Reengineering Paradigm in no way excludes e-business solutions. The distinction is that the E-Business Paradigm aims for incremental effect on business processes, without radical overhaul, whereas the Reengineering Paradigm fundamentally redesigns them. The fact is that in today's world we expect e-business to be one of the leading motivators of reengineering initiatives.

4.4.3   The incremental improvement paradigm

The *Incremental Improvement Paradigm* is the least ambitious of our project scenarios and lies at the opposite end of the scope spectrum from business process reengineering. A narrow-scope incremental improvement is appropriate when organizational politics and culture place more ambitious endeavors out of bounds. We take on a small part of the enterprise—so as to minimize the political difficulties—and implement the high-payoff improvements.

Normally, candidates for high-payoff improvements are not hard to find. People who spend their workdays immersed in an environment are not short on ideas for improving things. A project of this type, being confined to a narrow part of the enterprise, does not normally involve e-business. By definition, e-business is about extraenterprise interactions. Extraenterprise interactions concern a business *process,* which corresponds to a *use case* and consists of a related set of transactions involving an external actor. By its nature, a business process spans multiple business functions.

Perhaps a real-life example will help in illustrating the importance of considering a complete business process for e-business enablement. I once tried to purchase an item from a Web site run by a certain government agency. Everything seemed to be going fine until it came time to pay for the item. Now, instead of the familiar secured dialogue to enter my credit card details, up came a screen that invited me to print the displayed form and send the printout in the mail with a check. In effect, the agency had e-business-enabled discrete business functions, not whole processes as seen by an external customer. The result was thoroughly unsatisfactory.

4.4.4   Summary of project paradigms

The Reengineering Paradigm is wide and deep, the E-Business Paradigm is wide and shallow, and the Incremental Improvement Paradigm is narrow and shallow. We'll see these various paradigms popping up in the body of Part II, wherever the architectural solution-building process needs to apply different techniques to different project characteristics.

You will notice that the list of project paradigms does not include one that's narrow and deep. Such a project would try to reengineer business processes across a narrow part of the enterprise organization. But because a business process by its nature spans multiple business functions (or departments), a narrow and deep paradigm is a logical contradiction—going deep necessarily implies going wide.

4.5   Where to find more information

Hammer and Champy [1993] wrote the book—literally—on *business process reengineering.* Hammer's later book [Hammer and Stanton 1995] builds on the first work and shows the benefit of an additional two years of practical experience.

Jacobson coined the term *use case* and explains the concept as applied to business process reengineering [Jacobson et al. 1994].

Spewak [1992] explores in depth the political and organizational challenges of taking on a *large-scope project,* as do Hammer and Stanton [1995].

PART II

THE SEVEN-STAGE SOLUTION-BUILDING PROCESS

In Part II, we'll be looking in more detail at the seven stages of solution building. We'll see how they interrelate and investigate their relationships with various object models. We'll consider the roles of the participants needed to carry out the stages, and we'll check back periodically to see how the stages apply to an "architectural" discipline.

5

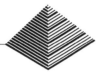

Introduction

5.1 Overview of the architectural solution-building process

The individual stages of the architectural solution-building process were summarized earlier, in the book outline. Figure 5-1 shows how the stages relate to one another. In this seven-stage model, the first four stages help *plan* the enterprise's IS architecture. In these stages, the enterprise focuses on its business objectives and the information technology it needs to support them. The last three stages of the architectural solution-building process help the enterprise *implement* its IS architecture. In these stages, the enterprise applies architectural principles to guide the design and development of its IS solution. The *planning* and *implementation* phases are mapped onto the individual stages of the process in Figure 5-2. The planning phase of architectural solution building corresponds to the model-building activity we discussed in Chapter 3. Figure 5-3 maps the stages of the planning phase of solution building to the models.

The architectural solution-building process, rather than starting with individual applications or information technologies, begins with an analysis of business needs and objectives. Throughout the process, the focus is on designing and implementing systems that unify the enterprise's information resources and support its business strategies.

Architectural solution building is an iterative process. As that process proceeds, the results are subjected to an increasingly detailed level of analysis, always with the assumption that information acquired during a previous stage may need to be revised in the context of changing conditions or new requirements.

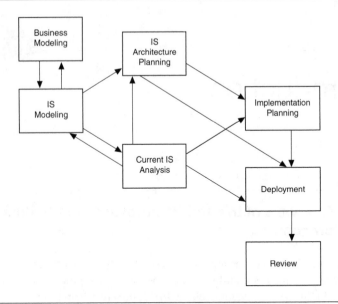

Figure 5-1 Architectural solution-building process.

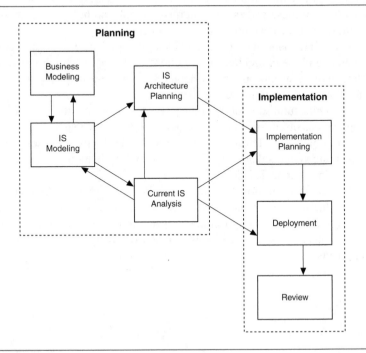

Figure 5-2 The two phases of solution building.

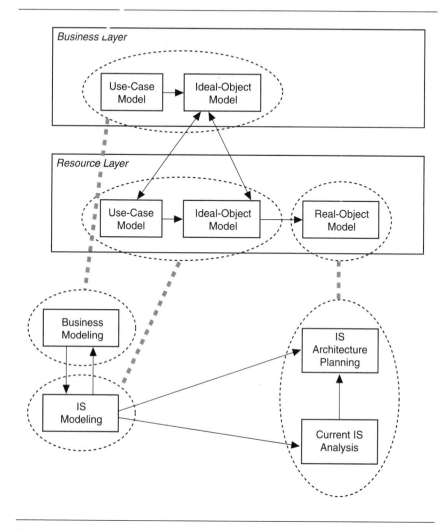

Figure 5-3   Correspondence of solution-building stages with modeling activities.

5.2 Architectural solution-building team

Architectural solution building requires the participation of people with a wide range of skills and experience. This book uses the following generic titles to describe the groups that participate in various parts of the architectural solution-building process.

- **Executive managers.** An enterprise's executive managers are responsible for defining the enterprise's overall mission and strategy as shaped by their understanding of its objectives and the competitive environment in which it operates. Executive managers' participation is also necessary to ensure that the enterprise is committed to the results of the architectural solution-building process.

- **Business managers.** An enterprise's business managers supply detailed knowledge of the enterprise's business operations and of interdependencies among organizations. This knowledge helps the team identify critical business activities, analyze the types of information those activities require, and determine how that information must flow through the enterprise.

- **IS managers.** IS representatives contribute their experience in the analysis, design, and implementation of computer hardware and software systems. Their knowledge of the capabilities of information technologies, both existing and emerging, helps the team identify the opportunities for IS to support business activities that serve the strategic needs of the enterprise.

- **IS professionals.** This group includes analysts and programmers, the technical specialists whose expertise is necessary to design and implement the systems identified by the IS modeling process.

- **Users.** This group may encompass people from all levels of an enterprise: executive, managerial, professional, and clerical. These are the people who actually use the systems that result from architectural solution building, and it is important that their needs be considered in all pertinent stages of the process. Some enterprises have formal end-user departments responsible for workstation and departmental applications. These departments should be represented on the solution-building team.

- **Customers and key business partners.** In the e-business era, where IS solutions interact directly with customers and business partners, the "user" of earlier eras now includes customers and business partners as well as internal staff.

5.2.1   Stages and participants

The matrix in Table 5-1 shows the groups involved in the different stages of the architectural solution-building process. Each of the subsequent chapters of Part II includes a Participants section that highlights the key players in that particular stage of the process.

5.2.2   Team roles

Every team member plays an important part in the success of the solution-building process. Some team members also have special roles as a leader or as facilitators.

Table 5-1　Participants in the seven stages of solution building

Stage	Executive managers	Business managers	IS managers	IS professionals	Users	Customers and key business partners
Business modeling	X	X	X			X
IS modeling		X	X	X	X	X
Current IS analysis			X	X	X	
Architecture planning			X	X	X	
Implementation planning		X	X	X	X	
Deployment		X	X	X	X	X
Review	X	X	X	X	X	X

- **Leader.** For the sake of continuity, the architectural solution-building team should have a leader who works with the team throughout the entire process. This person has a special responsibility for keeping the solution-building process moving and for resolving disagreements. The leader also has responsibility for the overall integrity of the project, ensuring that project deliverables are properly created and maintained in the project repository.
- **Facilitators.** At each stage of the process, the solution-building team must have one or more facilitators with specific skills appropriate to the kinds of information being collected and analyzed. For example, someone with experience in the appropriate modeling and analysis techniques must work with business managers to produce the business model in the business planning stage. Different people could serve as facilitators in the different stages of the architectural solution-building process. The enterprise can enlist the services of an outside facilitator for one or more of these stages.

As a group, IS managers are often the only ones almost certain to be involved in all stages of the process. A manager or other high-ranking person from the IS organization may be a logical candidate for the leader and facilitator roles on the team.

5.2.3 Team size and dynamics

The size of the architectural solution-building team has important consequences for how the team operates. Planners should consider the potential trade-offs between making the team large enough to guarantee that all interests are represented and keeping the team small enough to operate efficiently.

While the exact composition of the team is, of course, subject to the needs and resources of the enterprise, a general guideline is that the team should have a relatively small core of members who stay involved throughout the entire process. To ensure good representation of all interested parties, the team should hold workshops, brainstorming sessions, and interviews with executive managers, business managers, users, and other subject-matter experts as needed. The team can bring in additional people to provide specific expertise needed at different stages of the process.

Regardless of the size of the architectural solution-building team, good communication is necessary throughout the process to ensure that all those with a stake in the process, not just team members, are confident that the results reflect their needs and fulfill agreed-upon objectives. To prevent the solution-building process from becoming bogged down in detail and endless cycles of information gathering and analysis, the team must develop effective consensus-building, conflict-resolution, and decision-making practices.

5.3 Global architectural principles

We encountered the architectural principles in Chapter 2. We'll be going through more iterations of writing and refining principles at appropriate stages of solution building. However, because of the high-level nature of certain of the architectural principles, we need to refine them further at this point. Some of these high-level principles apply to the interactions among the stages of the solution-building process, as well as to the activities within particular stages, which is why we label them "global" principles.

Some of these high-level principles are *axiomatic,* in the sense that they're either inherent in the process of architectural design or well established through substantial empirical evidence. Although the principles may be axiomatic, not everyone coming into the team will have internalized these "best practices," and it's therefore important to have them stated explicitly. It's also important to realize that these principles are idealized and in practice will often need to be bent or broken for pragmatic reasons. However, explicit statement of the principles provides a basis for:

- conducting the project so as to conform to the spirit of the principles as closely as is pragmatically possible.

- understanding how the project bends or breaks the principles, thus forming a basis for assessing likely consequences.

As well as axiomatic principles, it is equally appropriate for each project to write its own specific global principles that apply to the entire solution-building process.

There follows a list of the axiomatic principles. Anticipating the style for stating principles used in Chapter 9, each principle statement is followed by supporting rationale and by the implications of following the principle. Sometimes one or more editorial comments follow for further explanation and clarification.

- **Principle**—All development will be incremental and iterative.
  - **Rationale**
    - ◊ Experience shows that "a complex system that works is invariably found to have evolved from a simple system that worked" [Gall 1986].
    - ◊ Understanding by all participants grows with each stage of the solution-building process. This understanding needs to be iteratively fed back into earlier stages.
  - **Implications**
    - ◊ Output from earlier stages of the solution-building process is subject to revision through the insight gained by applying that output in the development of later stages.
    - ◊ Output from each stage in the solution-building process should be reviewed on a scheduled periodic basis to ensure consistency throughout the architecture.
- **Principle**—There will be a bias toward use and reuse of available components and frameworks (with respect to both application logic and technical infrastructure), so that application development is more akin to *assembly* than to *fabrication.*
  - **Rationale**
    - ◊ Reuse of debugged components is always more cost effective than implementing from scratch.
    - ◊ Application of familiar patterns, components, and frameworks leads to more-repeatable solutions. Project tasks can be more precisely specified, and the effort—in terms of resources and elapsed time—to accomplish the tasks can be more precisely quantified. The result is that projects can be more effectively managed, so that schedules and budgets are attained more precisely.
  - **Implications**
    - ◊ Applications should, wherever possible, be constructed by assembling working components, whether purchased or drawn from existing assets, within established application frameworks.

◊ Where reusable components cannot be found, new application logic should be fabricated so as to create components—and when appropriate, frameworks—that are themselves reusable in future solution building.

◊ The reuse principle will need to be supported by adequate tooling, including a repository, and adequate organizational structure.

– **Comment**—High degrees of discipline and education are needed if software engineers are to produce reusable components and frameworks. It is essential that software designers master the art of *abstraction*. Specifically, the abstraction axis that is most important is the separation of concerns that are independent of the business domain from those that are domain-specific. The capability of defining good abstractions is deceptively difficult and is a thought pattern not easy to teach. For good insight into the problem, refer to Best [1995] and Schmidt [1999]. We'll return to further discussion on the general subject of reuse in Chapter 16.

· **Principle**—There will be a bias toward keeping existing applications intact, running on their existing platforms.

– **Rationale**—Reimplementation of applications merely to move to a different platform is rarely cost-effective and usually causes the introduction of errors and instability.

– **Implication**—Existing applications will have to be surrounded by software wrappers to interface with new applications and to bring their user-presentation interfaces into line with current corporate standards.

– **Comment**—This principle is one that might need to be modified where, for example, the platform (hardware and operating system) supporting the application is obsolescent, with impending withdrawal of support from the manufacturers. However, in the absence of this type of pressure, our preference is always to leave working systems unchanged, consistent with the principle of incremental, iterative development. Development resources are almost always better applied to the development of new functionality rather than to the replication of existing functionality on a different platform.

· **Principle**—All stages of the solution-building process are based on object-oriented principles, specifically supported by component-based development and run-time environment.

– **Rationale**—A component-based environment directly supports the principle of reuse. A component-based run-time environment also provides a coherent middleware structure supporting the interaction of solution components.

– **Implications**

◊ We must select a toolset appropriate to an object-oriented design and development process.

◊ Connectors and wrappers must be developed to integrate existing IS assets.

– **Comments**

◊ Object-oriented design and development are taking a stubbornly long time to gain momentum in the industry at large. The slow uptake is largely due to the influence of the non–object-oriented nature of most existing IS assets, coupled with the paradigm shift in thought patterns that object-oriented development requires. Continued exposure to non–object-oriented IS systems tends to keep reinforcing IS designers' traditional thought patterns. It would be nice to believe that object-oriented design and development will become the norm before this book is sent to that Great Library in the Sky—but I'm not holding my breath.

◊ In spite of the relatively slow uptake of end-to-end object development environments, e-business infrastructural middleware—the class known as "application server middleware"—is strongly component based. As I write this paragraph, the market is coalescing around two competing ecosystems: Microsoft's DNA and Sun's J2EE.

◊ In Incremental Improvement Paradigm projects, object-oriented middleware may not be appropriate. Because of the relatively turbulent emergent state of component-based development and run-time technology, the most pragmatic course may be to adopt, or stay with, earlier-generation middleware rather than hold onto the object-oriented dictum.

6

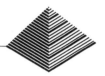

Business Modeling

The purpose of the business modeling stage is to define a business strategy and a business model. The business strategy describes the enterprise's mission and business environment. The business model depicts the important business processes and functions that fulfill the strategy. Building the business model entails both a refinement of the business strategy and a focusing of scope onto those areas where we expect information technology to yield the greatest benefit.

Modeling the business helps us understand it. Companies continuously evolve, and through evolution may become so complex that they can no longer be understood by their inhabitants. Having a model of the enterprise allows the enterprise to understand its functioning in the context of the changing business environment. Models can support analyses of likely scenarios involving customers, competitors, products, suppliers, government, and so on. In effect, the business model is a tool for managing the company's development in a systematic and deliberate way.

In the context of architectural solution building, the business model is the tool that allows us to understand how we can apply information systems to the business processes. And, more than merely applying information technology to business processes we have envisioned, we can, with the aid of the business model, imagine how information technology can create new business processes. Generally, the new processes we're most interested in creating are those that are externally visible, those that result in business innovation that brings added value to our customers and business partners. And externally visible processes are precisely those where e-business comes into play.

The business strategy and business model provide a high-level view of the business, its processes, and its functions, which will be the foundation for the IS modeling stage. The approach we'll take in this chapter is *business-driven,* in that we'll consider an ideal picture of the business and what it can become, rather than consider enabling technology. In business-driven analysis, high-level managers decide on the kind of organization they want to create and on what kind of knowledge they will need to do it. We will see in a later discussion that an equally valid, complementary approach—the *technology-driven* approach—is to find innovative ways to use new technology to create competitive advantage. However, our purpose in this chapter is to approach the solution-building process from a business-driven angle.

Traditional advice on IS solution building was that you should formulate business strategy without *any* regard for enabling technology. This kind of advice is frankly specious, because you need some frame of reference to know what's realistically achievable through technology, what's worth aiming for, and what's outmoded. Aim too high and you'll stall and crash; aim too low and you'll fly into the ground while the competition cruises by overhead.

Realistically, then, taking a business-driven approach does not mean limiting your imagination to what can be achieved with currently available technology. The business-modeling stage is one where imaginations should be given free reign to create the most adventurous, even outrageous, visions of what the company might be able to do. The harsh reality of what's realistically achievable can be left for later. The point of the outrageous imagination exercise is that, as humans, we're all too easily constrained by our knowledge and preconceptions about available technology and our expectations for its linear evolution. The great strides in business strategy come from freeing ourselves from these bounds. As Wayne Gretzky says, you have to skate to where the puck is *going* to be, not to where it is now. For example, planning your business around the telephone in 1876 (the year of its invention) wouldn't have made much sense. But using the

Using crystal-ball technology to skate to where the puck is going to be.

telephone to create competitive advantage—such as providing transaction executions by phone instead of by mail—would have been one of those innovative
leaps if made at the right time, when enough of your customer base had become
telephone subscribers. The planning and positioning for such an innovative leap
would have been like skating to where the puck was going to be.

Seeing the potential of new technology is never automatic—it takes creativity and insight. "I think there is a world market for maybe five computers," said
IBM chairman Thomas Watson Sr. in 1943. "There is no reason why anyone
would want a computer in their home," pronounced Digital Equipment Corp.
founder Kenneth Olsen in 1977.[1] The Times of London's reaction to the invention
of the telephone was similarly nonprescient, when that venerable newspaper
wondered in an editorial how this new instrument would find any useful application, given London's abundance of messenger boys. IBM passed up the chance to
become the world's first entrant into the copier industry, having satisfied itself of
insufficient market potential [Hammer and Champy 1993]. One lesson here is
that supply creates demand—market research on a radically new product is
meaningless. However, the more general lesson is that quantum jumps in business advantage come from the creative application of new technology, and that
ignoring technology while formulating business strategy is neither possible nor
desirable.

In designing business processes, it's important to pay proper attention to the
people side of the business. UUA [1996] observed that sustained successful business performance depends on the harmonious balance of business *processes,* the
people who perform them, and the *systems* that support both processes and
people. This observation is important. It emphasizes that business processes and
IS solutions need to be designed with equal weight given to consideration of the
human side of the triangle. Much of traditional IT addressed automation of
processes—replacing people who performed mundane tasks. More recently, there
has been growing realization that excellence in business process design—and
hence excellence in customer service—involves enabling and *empowering*
people through information systems, rather than merely replacing them through
simple automation of unreconstructed processes. And empowerment starts by
involving the people who will perform the reengineered processes in the design,
development, and deployment of those processes.

Any in-depth discussion of the business thinking behind the exercise of envi-
sioning and redefining enterprise mission and business processes is outside the
scope of this book. Rather, the scope of this book is limited to placing the envi-
sioning exercise in context, so that we can understand its place in the total solution-
building process. The substantial topic of reengineering is the subject of
Hammer's groundbreaking works [Hammer and Champy 1993, Hammer and
Stanton 1995].

---

[1] In the interests of full disclosure, I must reveal that, at the time, I myself heartily agreed with Olsen's
assessment.

6.1 Business modeling in the context of the total process

6.1.1 Relation to other stages

Figure 6-1 illustrates the relationship of the business modeling stage to other stages of the seven-stage solution-building process. The strategic objectives and business functions identified in the business modeling stage provide the focus for the IS modeling stage. Figure 6-2 expands on the contextual picture by showing the deliverables that flow among the related stages, as well as an overview of the principal activities of the business modeling stage.

The deliverables of the business modeling stage provide the benchmark against which results of the final solution are ultimately measured. These deliverables comprise the business strategy and the business model, which is expressed as a use-case model and an ideal-object model. The business model is the primary driving input for the development of the IS model.

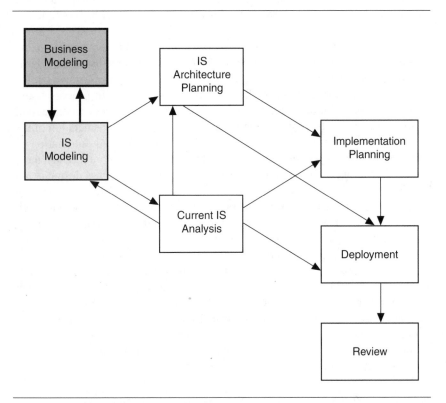

Figure 6-1 Business modeling stage in context.

Figure 6-2 shows an explicit feedback path from IS modeling back into business modeling. In practice, each stage of the solution-building process can cause changes in earlier stages, as the team gains more understanding and insight along the way. This particular feedback path recognizes that the building of the IS model will usually clarify understanding of the business processes and suggest improvements in them.

Ripples in the solution-building process also arise through requirements volatility of the business objectives themselves. One of the major goals of the architectural process is to position the business so that it will be able to respond rapidly to externally imposed changes, and we have to recognize that these kinds of changes are going to come along while our solution-building effort is in progress. We can think of these changes as "feedforward" loops— while their origin is external rather than internal, the resulting ripple-through effect on the solution-building stages is similar to that caused by feedback loops.

Although there is not a strong relationship between the business modeling stage and the current IS analysis stage, information and insights collected during current IS analysis can be useful in developing the business strategy and business model. Because the inventory portion of the current IS analysis has no prerequisites, the team can begin working on it as soon as the solution-building process gets under way.

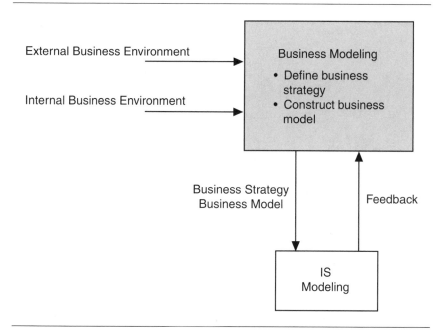

Figure 6-2   Overview of the business modeling stage.

6.1.2   Relation to the OO model set

Figure 6-3 shows the mapping between the business modeling stage and the associated object model in the OO model set, showing that the use-case model and the ideal-object model of the business layer are produced by the business modeling stage.

6.1.3   Participants

The team that produces the business strategy and the business model should bring together high-level knowledge of an enterprise's mission and strategic direction as well as detailed knowledge of its organization and business practices. If reengineering is the intent, the team should include radical thinkers, those capable of thinking outside the box to come up with innovative and outrageous

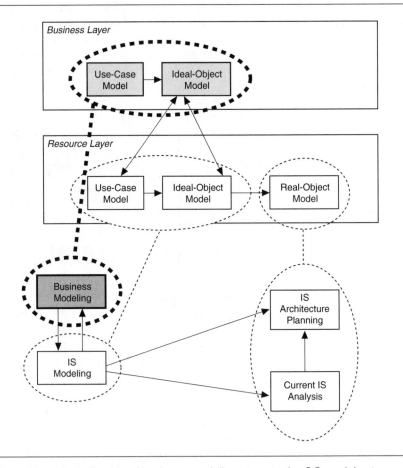

Figure 6-3   Relationship of business modeling stage to the OO model set.

ideas: we can't make discontinuous business breakthroughs by linear incremental developments of the status quo.

To ensure that all viewpoints are adequately represented, and that the necessary mix of skills is available, the team works with the following people during the business modeling stage.

- **Executive managers.** An enterprise's leaders define the enterprise's overall mission and strategy as shaped by their understanding of its objectives and the competitive environment in which it operates.

- **Business managers.** Managers supply knowledge of the enterprise's business operations and of interdependencies among organizations. Ideally, both "insiders" and "outsiders" are represented. "Insiders" know how the current processes work; "outsiders" are unfettered by ingrained assumptions and can see things objectively. "Outsiders" can be external consultants or business managers from other functional areas or business units.

- **IS managers.** IS representatives serve as facilitators or recorders during the business modeling stage and provide continuity throughout the rest of the solution-building process.

- **Customers and key business partners.** Making customers happy is, of course, on every enterprise's wish list (with the notable exception of some monopoly organizations). What better way to capture your customers' needs than to include them in your business modeling stage? Your other business partners, who may be suppliers or government agencies, also interact closely with your business in an e-business world. Electronic interaction with customers and business partners is our very definition of e-business. It is therefore self-evident that these people need to be involved in an e-business solution-building effort from the beginning. There are obvious challenges here. How can you provide a sufficiently motivating incentive for these people to participate? How can you keep the team size down to a manageable number so that interaction is not inhibited?

- **Creative business thinkers.** As we discussed above, we need creative thinkers on the team if our aim is reengineering. These creative thinkers may be represented in the ranks of participants already listed here. However, having a checklist item is worthwhile, so as to make sure that we form an effective team. If necessary, creative thinkers can be recruited to the team to fill the creativity gap. They may be IS professionals, external consultants— indeed, anyone with an appropriate attitude and a fresh viewpoint on the business.

6.2   Information sources for the business modeling stage

Team members can draw on several sources of information when defining the business strategy and the business model.

- existing written material
- experience and expertise of team members
- interviews and brainstorming sessions with executive managers, business managers, customers, and business partners

6.2.1 Existing written material

Planners can use existing mission statements, strategy announcements, business plans, and similar documents for information pertaining to the business strategy. Such documents probably were not written with IS solution building in mind, and in practice they serve as source documents rather than finished deliverables that could support the solution-building process directly.

If the enterprise has a formal business plan, this plan can provide extensive information about the enterprise's mission and business activities. Some of the information found in business plans (financial performance, assets, market surveys, and so on) may not be relevant or may be too detailed for the business strategy. Careful analysis is required to extract the high-level information needed in this stage of the analysis.

Organization charts contain information useful in mapping out business activities and the relationships among organizations. Other valuable information about important business activities can come from process descriptions written for quality assurance programs.

Any information acquired from existing sources should be checked by team members or through the interview process in order to verify its currency and accuracy.

6.2.2 Team experience and expertise

The members of the solution-building team during this stage represent a cross section of the enterprise's executive, business, and IS managers. Team discussions and brainstorming sessions can supply much of the information needed to draw up a first draft of the business strategy and business model.

6.2.3 Interviews

If the team is kept small enough to operate efficiently, it may be too small to include representatives from all parts of the enterprise and from customers and business partners. In this case, the team must fill its information gaps by conducting interviews with the appropriate people. Before conducting individual interviews, team members may wish to hold an orientation meeting to introduce potential interviewees to the process and explain the sorts of information they will be seeking.

It is particularly important that executive management be well represented at this stage to ensure that their business concerns are addressed and to lay the foundation for their support of the results of the solution-building process.

Interviews are well suited to gathering information about the way the enterprise currently operates. Interviewees will also suggest improvements in the way the business operates. More-significant suggestions for improvements and radical innovations are likely to come out of brainstorming workshop sessions, where group participation stimulates everyone's creative idea production.

6.2.4   Brainstorming workshops

Brainstorming leverages the synergy of team interaction. It is a well-known technique for gathering and stimulating ideas. Brainstorming to create initiatives for radical innovation and far-reaching improvement should involve a broad cross section of interested stakeholders, including executive management, middle management, customers, and business partners.

Brainstorming sessions can include quite a large number of people. Studies have found that 16 is the optimum number of participants for a brainstorming session. Remember, the purpose of a brainstorming session is to generate ideas, not to evaluate them. At this stage in the process we are gathering information. Its evaluation comes later, when we formulate the business strategy and build the business model.

6.3   Business strategy

The business strategy is a written record of a variety of information used to guide the rest of the solution-building process. In fact, a properly written strategy transcends the solution-building process. A business strategy is a high-level map that can provide a foundation for strategic business decision making in all its facets.

The essence of the business strategy consists of:

- enterprise mission and objectives
- business environment

An important quality of the mission and objectives statements is that they provide a framework for decision making. While high level, they need to be more than mere platitudes if they are to be of value.

6.3.1   Enterprise mission and objectives

The business strategy begins with high-level statements that represent executive management's vision of an enterprise's mission and objectives. These statements summarize the activities in which the enterprise is engaged and identify the goals

This example of a *mission statement* reflects executive management's commitment to customer satisfaction:

> To be a superior supplier of products through total customer service and support. To determine customers' requirements for products and to deliver the products that meet those requirements on time and free from defects.

To support this mission statement, the executive management identified the following business objectives.

- Focus on customer satisfaction.
- Develop a technically competent, cross-trained, and flexible management team and workforce.
- Provide lifetime product warranties.
- Provide reliable product installation and predictable performance.
- Provide a rapid response to customer queries and problems.
- Develop world-class quality assurance and reporting systems.
- Establish a forum for determining advanced capabilities needed by customers.
- Reduce time between order entry and product delivery.
- Produce cost-competitive products.

by which the success of the enterprise can be measured. Mission and objectives are defined primarily from an *external* focus, in which the enterprise is viewed as a black box providing products and services to its customers.

Objectives encompass both general and specific approaches for fulfilling the enterprise mission. Mission and objectives represent the enterprise's business direction, both for the near term as well as for the medium and long terms. To prepare adequately for changing business and technological conditions, the enterprise's planning horizon should ideally extend three or more years into the future.

In formulating business strategy, beware of confusing means with ends, of confusing strategy with infrastructure. In particular, "doing e-business" has no place in a business strategy statement. If you have "e-business" in your business strategy, you will probably find the need for a knowledge-management strategy, a decision-support strategy, and all kinds of other technology "strategies." All of these "strategies" are not strategies at all in the context of the business—they're the means of pursuing business strategy, rather than the strategy itself. Look at the sample business objectives under the mission statement in the sidebar above. All of the objectives are expressed in terms of the *business*. Although several of these are clear candidates for e-business, including e-business technology considerations in the business objectives is clearly inappropriate. In an architectural sense—as we discussed in Chapter 2—what we're doing is fitting form to function, where the "function" corresponds to the business objectives and the "form" corresponds to the IS solution that will support them.

When we discuss IS strategy in a later chapter, it will be entirely appropriate to talk about "e-business" in the context of an IS strategy. For our purposes in this chapter, however, we're talking business goals, not the IS behind them. This clean separation of ends and means is another reflection of the architectural principles we discussed in Chapter 2.

6.3.2   Business environment

As well as the enterprise's mission, an important element of the business strategy is an assessment of the environment in which the enterprise operates. It is this environment that determines the nature and focus of the objectives that will be needed to pursue the mission. From an e-business point of view, it is the enterprise's *external* environment that's of interest—e-business, after all, is concerned with the interactions of the enterprise with its internal environment.

External environment   The business strategy should answer basic questions about the *external* environment of the enterprise, within the context of the enterprise's planning horizon. The external environment includes the climate in which the enterprise operates, in terms of such factors as:

- competition
- customer base
- customer behavior
- supplier base
- technology influences on products, services, or supply chains
- government regulation

Internal environment   An enterprise's *internal* environment is an equally important influence on the business strategy. The internal environment includes the organizational and cultural conditions underpinning the enterprise's operations and the values the enterprise holds and acts on. A good example of the way internal values shape business mission appears in the philosophy of a large travel agency—Rosenbluth International. Rosenbluth's culture holds that the associates (employees) come first, and the customer comes second. The rationale is that only happy employees can be effective in delivering excellent customer service [Rosenbluth and Peters 1993].

Mergers and acquisitions have a significant impact on the internal environment. A newly completed merger will usually spawn task forces charged with unifying various aspects of the two companies' information systems. As far as more normal-state solution building is concerned, the complexity resulting from incompletely digested acquisitions will inevitably affect the solution-building process. In these situations, the business modeling stage represents an opportunity and a challenge to understand and help harmonize the business processes of the merged companies.

The internal environment has no impact, strictly speaking, on e-business considerations, and is of concern only in the building of internal IS solutions. However, the *technology* of e-business may be relevant in certain areas. A good example is the use of Web interfaces to employee communications and transactions.

6.4 The business model

The business model describes the business processes through which the enterprise fulfills its mission and business objectives. The business model is thus the bridge between the business strategy and the formulation of requirements for an IS solution that will support the business processes and the people who perform them.

6.4.1 Content of the business model

Object-oriented business models are the most natural way of providing the starting material for the creation of an object-oriented IS model, which is the subject of the next chapter. Studies have shown that the discontinuity—or semantic gap—where business concepts are translated into supporting IS artifacts is a source of great difficulty, leading to misalignment between business functions and the capabilities of the supporting IS solution. When we maintain both business model and IS model in object-oriented form, we minimize this discontinuity. This uniformity in the thinking framework is one of the reasons for adopting a principle of object orientation throughout the solution-building process.

As we saw in Chapter 3, we express a business object model in two complementary views:

- a "black-box" view, expressed as a *use-case model,* which represents the business as seen by the external world of its customers, suppliers, and business partners
- a "crystal-box" view, expressed as an *ideal-object model,* which represents a high-level abstraction of how the business works

The black-box view helps us understand the business, and from this understanding we craft a crystal-box view of how we want the business to work. The crystal-box view is the real target here.

The crystal-box view, or ideal-object model, is the basis for the derivation of requirements for the IS systems we'll be developing. The ideal-object model expresses how the objects of the business collaborate to perform the use cases.

A black-box view of the Instant Meals R Us Corporation.

A crystal-box view of the Instant Meals R Us Corporation.

In practice, developing the use-case and ideal-object models is an iterative process. Progress in one model amplifies and clarifies understanding of the other.

The ideal-object model also captures features essential to the business that are not adequately expressed in the black-box view. Be aware that you cannot describe in a black-box view *everything* that you consider essential to the business. Essential company values such as product quality and employee quality of life cannot reasonably be represented in use cases. However, these values need to be captured, where possible and appropriate, in the way the enterprise operates, as expressed in the ideal-object model of the enterprise.

The black-box business model comprises a set of use cases. A use case is essentially an externally visible business process such as purchasing a product or making a reservation. The term *use case* is used specifically to distinguish an outsider's view of a business process from purely internal functions. Use cases are performed by *actors,* a term that abstracts any external entity (usually human, but with increasing possibilities for automated actors in an e-business environment) that participates in a use case. To qualify as a valid use case, performance of the use case must return some value to the actor.

6.4.2   Tools for developing the business model

Business modeling of any serious scope needs adequate tools. No longer is it satisfactory, if it ever was, to use manual techniques to record the emerging design of

Let's return to the example mission and objectives statements and see how they fold into the use-case and object models.

For use cases, we can deduce that *order fulfillment* and *customer service* are going to be important ones. However, the mission statement and objectives are worded with enough generality that we'll need to know much more about the business to do a decent job of completing the list of use cases.

In finding use cases, we need to work at an appropriate level of abstraction to keep the model manageable. Use cases should be relatively coarse grained. *Order fulfillment* is coarse grained. *Selecting an item from a catalogue* and *making payment for purchase* are examples of fine-grained use cases, which will lead to an unmanageably complex use-case model.

Notice that some of the objectives—such as *develop a technically competent, cross-trained, and flexible management team and workforce,* and *develop world-class quality assurance and reporting systems*—are not going to be represented in use cases. Instead, these objectives must be satisfied by business functions that are entirely internal. In modeling terms, these functions are satisfied in the ideal-object model but are not identifiable in the use-case model.

a large-scale model. Development of the business model is best carried out with purpose-built modeling tools. Such tools relieve much of the physical burden of maintaining the model, and maintain the model in machine-readable form that can help automate later stages of system development. The details of processes you use in developing the business model will inevitably be strongly influenced by the assumptions embodied in the tools you choose. However, the ultimate goals of business modeling are the same, regardless of the chosen tools.

The industry has seen an evolution of modeling and diagramming tools. Yesterday's "structured design" and "entity relationship" techniques and tools are being succeeded by the object-oriented paradigm, supported by such products as Paradigm Plus and Rational Rose. Capable tools such as these are much more than mere recording devices. They provide organization and management of the modeling process and greatly assist the application of the business model to the design and production of the enabling IS artifacts. Thus, the process of documenting the model becomes an integral part of the total IS solution life cycle.

While it is true that automated modeling tools are a practical necessity for large-scale projects, such tools will be overkill for smaller-scale, narrowly focused projects. Drawing the models in a tool such as Visio, or expressing them in natural language, will be more appropriate for smaller-scope projects.

A discussion of business modeling tools must mention alternative (non–object-oriented) methods for business modeling. Examples are Adonis [BOC] and Aris [IDS Scheer]. These tools do not require such a radical shift from traditional IS thinking as an object-modeling tool requires, and their models are therefore generally easier for the business-oriented team members to understand. The downside is that we're going to run into the semantic gap, discussed earlier, as we make the transition to object-oriented methods to develop the IS model.

6.4.3   Adjusting the focus—setting the scope

As we saw in Chapter 4, there are trade-offs to be made in deciding how much we are going to try to achieve. Before we set about building the business model, we'll need to have determined the scope of the undertaking in terms of its breadth and depth. The scope indicates what kind of model to build and how to build it.

If reengineering is our aim—the Reengineering Paradigm—then we follow the modeling scheme as described in Section 3.1.2. We'll discuss this route in more detail in Section 6.4.6.

Now suppose our aim conforms to the E-Business Paradigm, where the objective is to apply e-business to our most critical business processes with the minimum of disruption to those processes. In other words, we are consciously *not* going for reengineering, but retrofitting e-business technology onto existing ways of working. In this case, we still need to follow the modeling scheme described in Section 3.1.2. Because e-business is about the interaction of the enterprise with its external environment, it follows that we need to model the enterprise *in terms of* its business relationship with the external environment. It is this relationship that is captured by the use-case model. The difference between this route and reengineering is that the business ideal-object model illustrated in Figure 3-3 substantially depicts *current* business behavior, whereas in a reengineering project the ideal-object model is redesigned from scratch. We will discuss this route in more detail in Section 6.4.7.

When our objective is a narrow-scope improvement of business processes—the Incremental Improvement Paradigm—we're not specifically concerned about e-business. We're more concerned about fixing some areas of pain, or grasping some obvious area of opportunity (which of course may involve e-business). Furthermore, we're not prepared to take on more than a relatively small part of the enterprise. The political climate may be such that we're not confident of being able to shepherd through a project of very far-reaching scope. In this scenario, we would most likely not start with a use-case model of the enterprise. Because we have chosen a narrow-scope project, an enterprise-wide use-case model may not help much. Instead, we may start examining the business functions we want to improve. We saw the business functional model in Section 3.1.1.

Whichever paradigm the project matches, we're going to need to be selective in choosing the areas to pursue. Even within a large-scale reengineering program, we prioritize the business processes and select the most important, rather than attack the entire business all at once. Within the chosen scope, we are able to factorize the total effort into separable initiatives that will help keep the program manageable. In prioritizing and factorizing the total effort into separable initiatives, we build the business model as a set of submodels, which we can use to partition the total effort for manageability in later stages of solution building.

6.4.4 Where we've been, and where we're going

We can build use-case and ideal-object models to describe how the business looks now, and we can build models that describe how we want it to look. Why ever should we do the former? Well, we may need to model the current state of the business so that we can better understand it, and then apply that understanding to build the desired view of the business. Or, we may not want to change the basic way the business operates, except to build better IS support for the way things are now. The models we build and the breadth of the enterprise we consider in their building depend on what we want to achieve.

Table 6-1 shows the roles of the various models in terms of our project paradigms. Models that refer to the current state are referred to as *as-is models*. Models that describe the desired future state are referred to as *to-be-built models*. In this table, YES, of course, means that the model is built, but the scope is always constrained by the breadth of the enterprise's processes and functions that are being considered in the project.

Within the scope of an E-Business Paradigm, we want to change existing enterprise operations only to the extent necessary to apply e-business technol-

Table 6-1   Roles of the object models in the various project paradigms

	Use-case model		Ideal-object model	
	As-is	**To-be-built**	**As-is**	**To-be-built**
Reengineering	NO	YES	NO	YES
E-Business	YES	Same as as-is	YES	Same as as-is
Incremental Improvement	NO	NO	YES	Same as as-is

ogy. The to-be-built models are therefore the same as the current models. The same is true of an incremental improvement, where we would be making improvements in existing business functions through the application of information technology.

Although we are not, in an ideal world, interested in the current state when undertaking a reengineering project—and hence the NO entries in Table 6-1—we may nevertheless need to pursue those models to the extent necessary to understand the business.

You may have been surprised by the NO entries in Table 6-1 in reference to the use-case models for the Incremental Improvement Paradigm. What's happening here is that we're proposing to build an ideal-object model without first building a use-case model. In effect, we're saying "we don't know what it does, but we know how it works." This is surely not an ideal way to work, but it's a pragmatic approach we may find necessary. We'll come back to this idea in Section 6.4.8.

6.4.5   Reuse and the business model

Going about modeling in the architectural way, we would not treat the design of the business ideal-object model as an unconstrained exercise beginning with a blank sheet of paper. Recall from Chapter 2 the essential difference between traditional and "architectural" approaches. Restating these characterizations to fit the business modeling context, we can say that:

- Traditional design follows the sequence:
  - understand the business processes
  - design business functions and activities to support the business processes
- Architectural design follows the sequence:
  - understand the business processes
  - match the business processes to catalogued or standardized business process designs

Following the "architectural way" at the level of business processes is in practice going to be quite difficult, because it demands a wide range of experience on the part of the team members. "Catalogued or standardized business process designs" are likely to be in people's heads rather than in available formal repositories, although consultant companies are likely to amass such repositories, as intellectual capital, in support of their practices. However, it is clear that applying architectural design, through the use of proven business process patterns, carries greater potential payoff than applying pattern-reuse techniques at later stages of the solution-building process. By way of illustration of this architectural approach to business modeling, the workflow example that Best [1995] cites (which is described in Chapter 2 of this book) is as relevant at the business process level as it is at the IS modeling level.

The low-differentiation functions of the business are ideal candidates for leveraging reuse, as we saw in Chapter 2. By adapting these business functions to conform to packaged software, we apply reuse at the earliest stage of the solution-building process.

Against the clear benefits of reuse, we have to balance its countervailing tendency to channel thinking into familiar patterns and possibly divert us away from inspired leaps of creativity. Engaging "outsiders" on the project team is a way of guarding against this effect. It is the "insiders" who will, consciously or not, tend to think in terms of patterns familiar to the business domain, thereby implicitly applying the reuse principle. Insiders' domain knowledge will help ensure that familiar patterns are employed, rather than nonstandard patterns offering no added value.

6.4.6   Models for reengineering

In a reengineering project, the ideal first step in business modeling is to construct the to-be-built use-case model, focusing on selected high-priority use cases deduced from the mission and objectives. In general, we would consider the *current* processes only to the extent necessary to gain an understanding of the business. Understanding the broad structure and flow of current processes gives us needed insight into how the company works. However, we need this insight only at a high level of abstraction. There is no need to investigate and analyze existing processes in depth. In fact, deep analysis is not only unnecessary, it's downright dangerous, because analysts can become immersed in current practices. They are then less able to free their minds to create the breakthrough processes that yield the dramatic results we're looking for.

If we decide that modeling of current processes is indeed necessary to understand the business, then we have to be well aware of the downside—that developing business models is laborious and time-consuming. We must ruthlessly constrain the scope and depth of the modeling activity. The appropriate breadth of scope is just those business processes that we've identified for reengineering. The appropriate depth is just deep enough to understand what's going on so that we

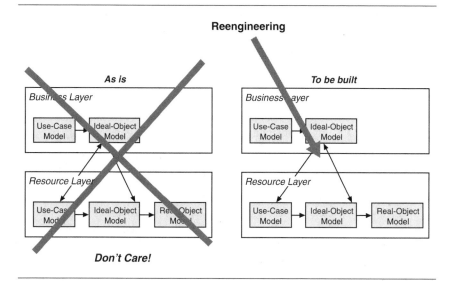

Figure 6-4   Object models for the reengineering paradigm.

can reengineer. We need to enforce the ruthlessly constrained scope with equally ruthless time boxing,[2] to choke off teams' natural tendency to let as-is modeling activity grow into a resource- and time-consuming monster.

The use-case model provides the basis for building the ideal-object model, which describes how the business operates in carrying out the use cases. The goal is an ideal-object model that describes how we want the business to work in the future.

As Figure 6-4 illustrates, we are not concerned with as-is models when our mission is engineering. Focusing on desired models, without regard to the way things currently work, frees the team to build their best business solution, unhampered by the constraints, ingrained and no-longer-valid assumptions, and organizational baggage of the past. As we discussed in Chapter 4, the totally unconstrained reinvention of business processes implies an undertaking of significant scope, requiring high-level sponsorship and commitment.

At this stage, remember that we're building business models, not IS models. A pure business process reengineering approach begins without particular regard for the IS solutions that may be applied—although we always need to be aware of the technological feasibility of the business processes we invent. Conversely, it is possible (although unlikely) that breakthrough business process improvements may be realized with little or no requirement for supporting information systems.

---

[2]Time boxing is the technique of setting an elapsed-time constraint on an activity. It can be a particularly effective technique where the activity in question tends to exhibit the 80/20 rule, with 80 percent of the benefit coming from the first 20 percent of the effort.

Business modeling is an intellectually challenging endeavor, and object-oriented business modeling with UML is a practice still in its infancy. Marshall [2000] explains the technique in detail, and includes guidance on how to leverage reuse.

6.4.7 Models for e-business

An E-Business Paradigm project aims to retrofit e-business technology to existing business processes. We therefore need to understand what those processes are and how the enterprise currently fulfills them. We build the *as-is* model of the business to capture this understanding. The act of building the as-is model is referred to as *reverse engineering*.

The as-is use-case model describes the business processes as seen by an external observer. This model helps us prioritize the use cases as we consider our application of e-business technology. From the use-case model, we derive the as-is ideal-object model for those use cases we decide to focus on.

The as-is business model, comprising the use-case model and the ideal-object model, is exactly what we need for an E-Business Paradigm project. E-business is concerned with external interactions, as described by the use-case model. The ideal-object model describes how the internal business functions fulfill the use cases and therefore indicate where we need to apply e-business technology. Figure 6-5 illustrates the relationships among the various models in the E-Business Paradigm.

As we saw in Section 4.4.1, reengineering is the likely consequence where e-business ambition goes beyond the consumer interface and materially affects

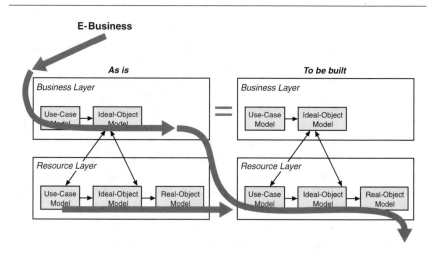

Figure 6-5   Object models for the e-business paradigm.

back-office operations. If we cannot, for whatever reason, realistically pursue reengineering, then the "bolt-on" approach may be the only one practical. In effect, persisting with the E-Business Paradigm in the face of reengineering-type pressures amounts to "bolting on" the e-business solution.

6.4.8   Models for incremental improvement

Incremental improvement is the least ambitious of our project paradigms. We're looking for high-payoff applications of information technology in narrow areas. The aim is to make a big improvement, with minimal impact on surrounding business functions. We're starting with the premise that existing systems will be kept substantially intact and that we'll fix only what is most broken or improve whatever gives the best return on investment.

Building models to support incremental improvement presents some challenges of its own, chief of which is to limit the scope of the model building. First of all, we do not usually need to build a use-case model of the *enterprise*. Because we're aiming for an incremental improvement, we are, by definition, looking at a narrow part of the enterprise. It is therefore not going to be helpful to produce use cases of the enterprise as a whole. It may, however, be useful to produce a use-case model of the business functions we're looking at. By doing so, we effectively treat a department as a miniature business and the rest of the enterprise as the external world. The use-case model then models the behavior of the department with respect to its interfaces with the rest of the enterprise and with respect to any interfaces that department has with the world beyond the enterprise.

In an incremental improvement project, the use-case model serves purely as the means of deriving the ideal-object model and is not an end in itself. In an incremental improvement project, the models we're building are *as-is* models. By the nature of the project, the *to-be-built* models are the same as the as-is models. The incremental improvement comes from the IS support we're going to apply in the IS modeling stage, not from rethinking the business models themselves. Figure 6-6 illustrates the relationships among the various models in the Incremental Improvement Paradigm.

We build the use-case model to help us build the ideal-object model, which is the real target. Yet, ironically, we may find it easier to build the ideal-object model directly, without benefit of the use-case model.

How's that again? The use-case model says "what it does." The ideal-object model describes "how it works." And yet I'm saying that it may be easier to describe "how it works" without even bothering first to state clearly "what it does." This strange-looking advice is attributable to a phenomenon neatly summed up by C. Northcote Parkinson[3]: "For most people it is far more difficult

---

[3]This is the same Parkinson that gave us the infamous "Parkinson's Law."

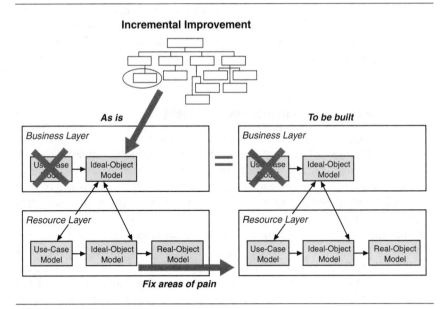

Figure 6-6 Object models for the incremental improvement paradigm.

to decide what they are trying to do than to describe how they propose to set about it" [Parkinson 1970].[4] Particularly in a large and complex business, it may be more trouble than it's worth to analyze precisely what are the interfaces between our target business function and its surroundings. We're better off focusing on what goes on in that department and applying our IS expertise to fix the points of pain that are all too familiar to the people who work there every day.

By definition, an incremental improvement project tackles only a small part of the enterprise. Yet we need to be concerned about scope creep. We need to make some early assessments of which parts of the business functions we will be most closely examining with a view to enhancing IS solutions. We need to develop business models only for those areas. Any improvement or innovation we undertake is going to be more valuable the sooner it is deployed, and speed of implementation versus breadth of scope is a trade-off we're going to face continually.

Depending on the size and complexity of the business function we're taking on, it will usually not be appropriate to build an actual object model in UML. For an incremental improvement project, a less formal documentation in Visio drawings or natural language description is usually more appropriate. In projects of very limited scope, "business modeling" is perhaps better thought of as "business discovery." For example, a city government realized it had a problem with

---

[4]The same phenomenon was observed by Einstein: "Perfection of means and confusion of goals seem—in my opinion—to characterize our age." (*Out of My Later Years,* Chapter 14, 1950)

customer service and staff productivity. The "business model" in this case was adequately documented by describing, at a high level, (1) the information that staff needed to capture and disseminate throughout the organization and (2) the customer service interactions that staff handle.

6.5   Applying the business model

Building the business model is of course a means to an end, not an end in itself. While recognizing its value as a basis for business process reengineering, we're most concerned with its application in building the IS solution. This section discusses several complementary roles that the business model plays.

6.5.1   Alignment of the IS solution with business objectives

The business model is the first building block in the building of the IS solution. It is the primary input to the IS modeling stage, which is where an IS model is built to support the business model. The overriding and ongoing challenge for IS is to *align* the functionality of the IS environment with the mission, objectives, and processes of the enterprise it serves. Misalignment is a very frequently cited problem with IT systems and arises from three primary sources:

- the difficulty of translating business requirements into representative IT artifacts, as discussed earlier
- an inadequate understanding of the business itself
- inflexibility of the IT system, making it resistant to change in response to identified business requirements

We address the first point, difficulty of translation, by use of object-oriented methods. Object-oriented business modeling, followed by object-oriented IS modeling, minimizes the difficulty of translation because the techniques used in each phase are homogeneous. This translation difficulty is the "semantic gap" discussed earlier. Different levels of abstraction are involved in moving from the business model to the IS model, but the lower-level abstraction of the IS model maps more naturally onto the higher-level business model than is the case when using traditional non–object-oriented techniques.

Object-oriented business modeling addresses the second point, inadequate business understanding, by requiring more rigorous documentation of business requirements than is necessary with traditional informal methods, thus forcing the exposure and resolution of ambiguities.

The final point, inflexibility of the IT system, is addressed by taking an architectural approach to the building of the IS system—which is what this book is all about.

6.5.2   Organizational impact of the business model

Building the *desired* business model is all about designing new or improved ways of performing business processes. New processes imply different roles or different behaviors for the people who perform these processes. It is essential to the success of the solution-building effort that end users—the people who will be performing these new processes—be participants in the design of these processes.

There is a world of difference between a *participant* and a *recipient*. A recipient receives processes designed for him by some detached IS person, in the manner of a tablet handed down from the mountain. In contrast, a participant has a personal stake in the success of the new process.

Ambitious overhaul of business processes is likely to require major organizational changes. Specialists in the management of such organizational change are likely to be needed to help the enterprise and its people get through the transition.

6.5.3   Models as monitors of scope creep

A real-world project will generally refuse to be neatly pigeonholed into one of our tidy paradigms. For example, in applying an IS solution for incremental improvement, we will often find it necessary or desirable to modify the business functions affected by the new solution, thus causing a revision of the business ideal-object model. Similarly, in applying e-business technology, we may be forced toward major revisions in the way the business process is carried out, which takes the project toward reengineering.

While it's natural to want to make the solution as good as it can be, we must always be aware of *scope creep*. If our e-business project turns into a reengineering project, we will indeed produce radically better results than we originally intended, if—and it's a very large "if"—we can pull it off. Realize that you need to get the organizational and political support lined up before you plunge into reengineering. If you back into reengineering from a more constrained project, you can expect to fail. If your new insight now helps you make a more compelling case for reengineering, then go back and relaunch the project to get the backing you'll need to succeed.

The models you produce in the course of the project are really quite indicative of the scope you're taking on. You can use them as effective measures of the actual scope of the project, and you can take steps to realign the project if you find that its scope has become misaligned with its mandate, budget, or timeframe.

Make sure that the first pass through the business modeling stage stays within its intended scope. Time boxing is an effective technique for keeping things on track. The real pressure for scope creep is going to come when the later stages—particularly the IS modeling stage—generate creative new ideas that impact on the business functions. It is here that you need to assess carefully the impacts fed back onto business functions to decide if any scope creep may increase project risk to an unacceptable level.

6.6   Where was the "architecture"?

Reviewers of early drafts of this book commented that the chapters in Part II didn't show very clearly how the process being described was "architectural," as opposed to nonarchitectural. In fact, much of the "architectural" approach is embodied in the structure of the process itself. Equally, some elements of the architectural approach are orthogonal to the stages of the solution-building process, representing a more qualitative attitude and way of working. To coin a metaphor, the stages of the process might be teaching you the dance steps, whereas getting you to breathe properly, smile, and move with grace might represent the architectural approach to performing the steps. In the latter case, we have success—an audience-pleasing performance. In the former case, we have mediocrity or failure—some guy stumbling through a routine of awkward-looking footwork.

Rather than clutter the text of Part II with explicit references to architectural treatment, I have elected to end this chapter and Chapters 7 through 11 with a quick review of the facets of "architecture" and how they apply (see Table 6-2). You may want to refer to Chapter 2 for a fuller explanation of the architecture features.

Table 6-2   Where was the "architecture" in Chapter 6?

Architecture feature	Relationship to this chapter
Solution fitted to client needs	In our treatment of the Reengineering Paradigm project and the E-Business Paradigm project, discovering client needs was the first step in the business modeling stage. We analyzed client needs from the highest level, starting with the mission and objectives of the enterprise. An approach less "architectural" in nature might begin with a traditional "requirements gathering" exercise—a subject we discussed in Section 3.1.3. The traditional requirements gathering process puts too great a burden on the business people to understand their business and simultaneously specify the behavior of their ideal IS solution. It's like the bricks-and-mortar architect asking the family "what kind of house do you want?" without bothering to try to understand the family's lifestyle, daily routine, or individual and group needs.*
	In our treatment of the Incremental Improvement Paradigm project, we're also discovering client needs, but at a much less global level. Rather than studying the makeup and needs of the family in order to design a suitable new house, we're looking at the house they're already in and figuring out what their biggest problems and opportunities are. For example, does the roof leak? Are they cold in winter because there's no heat? In a business environment, the equivalent problems might be that the managers are leaking money because they're dealing with too many suppliers and don't have enough

(*continued*)

Table 6-2   Where was the "architecture" in Chapter 6? (*continued*)

Architecture feature	Relationship to this chapter
	leverage with any of them, or that they can't run the reports they need in order to understand the state and trends of their financial position.
Empirically validated principles	Not applicable to the business modeling stage
Design and implementation principles and guidelines	The axiomatic principles apply to the business modeling stage: • Iterative design appears specifically as a feedback loop from IS modeling. • Object orientation is the recommended basis for deriving the business model, in the Reengineering Paradigm. • The reuse principle applies in the retention of existing business processes in the E-Business and the Incremental Improvement Paradigm.
Components, patterns, and frameworks	In the context of the business modeling stage, this feature applies to the Reengineering Paradigm, and less to the other two (because only in reengineering do we start out by redesigning business processes). It means that we design business processes by using activity patterns that are common to the industry in which we're working. It means finding abstract patterns of behavior—workflow is a good example—that can be leveraged in a wide range of business processes regardless of industry segment.
Conceptual integrity and elegance	At its simplest level, conceptual integrity means applying the same patterns to address similar situations throughout the enterprise's activities. We discussed elegance, and Alexander's elusive "quality without a name," in Chapter 2. Like a smiling dancer, both of these concepts apply throughout the solution-building process. They come from creative minds more than from any logical procedural recipe for doing things. We can regard conceptual integrity and elegance as the artistic skill and flair that apply business process components, patterns, and frameworks in the most effective way to address the enterprise's mission and objectives.
Formal description and recording	The body of this chapter discussed tools for building business process models and for recording and maintaining the models.

*Familiarity with Alexander [1979] will help you grasp the full significance of the point made here.

7

IS Modeling

Conflicting views abound on the proper drivers for business IS solutions. Chapter 6 introduced the notions of business-driven solutions versus technology-driven solutions. While apparently conflicting, these two approaches are best viewed as complementary.

Here are two brief samples of what other practitioners have had to say, which nicely illustrate the apparent conflict.

IS information systems planning should be driven by business problems and opportunities, not by technical developments. Participants in the strategic planning process should view IS as a means of achieving organizational objectives. [Moynihan 1988]

Traditional automation begins with a detailed description of existing processes in order to fit technology to them. Reengineering takes the exact opposite position—technology should not be adapted to processes, but processes must be totally reconfigured to exploit the full potential of technology. [Hammer and Stanton 1995]

The goal of business-driven IS modeling is to translate the business strategy and business model into an IS strategy and model that support business processes and activities. The IS strategy explains how the data generated for and by business activities can be organized into useful information and distributed to the locations where it is needed to meet the enterprise's business objectives.

The goal of technology-driven IS modeling is to create innovation in business functions and business processes from new information technology. Innovation of this kind is the stuff of which major competitive advantage is made.

7.1   IS modeling in the context of the total process

7.1.1   Relation to other stages

Figure 7-1 illustrates the relationship of the business modeling stage to other stages of the seven-stage solution-building process. Figure 7-2 expands on the contextual picture by showing the deliverables that flow among the related stages as well as an overview of the principal activities of the business modeling stage.

Relation to the outside world   For convenience in describing the context of the IS modeling stage, I'm going to pretend that the outside world is a stage[1] in the solution-building process.

Information technology industry trends and innovations are the stuff of which business breakthroughs are born. You'll need knowledgeable people on your team to produce breakthrough insights—people who keep up with developing

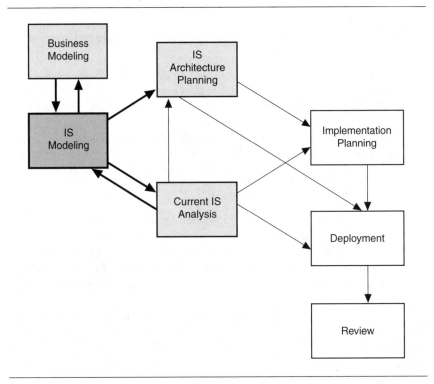

Figure 7-1   IS modeling stage in context.

[1]"All the world's a stage." W. Shakespeare, *As You Like It.*

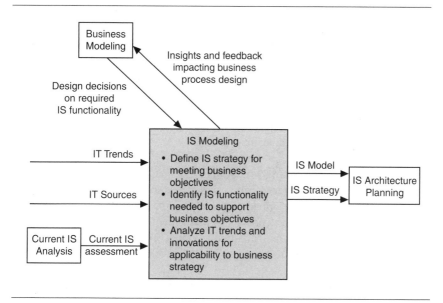

Figure 7-2   Overview of the IS modeling stage

technology trends, absorb information, and understand and evaluate it as they go along. Finding information sources is not difficult. IT publications, journals, conferences, and purchased analyst reports contain information about current industry trends, and the Internet provides limitless opportunity for research and collaboration in depth. What is more difficult is finding people who make it their business to absorb this information continuously. No one can make himself an instant expert to serve on an IS modeling team if technology information absorption is not already a way of life.

Information technology sources include manufacturers and suppliers of information technologies that may potentially be incorporated into the IS architecture. These sources can provide greater detail when researching technologies in greater depth.

Relation to the business modeling stage   The business modeling stage produces a business strategy and a set of business models. Each initiative that the business modeling stage identifies for further development gives rise to one or more business models.

In the IS modeling stage, we consider the business strategy together with the full set of business models. Taking a high-level view from a technology viewpoint, we formulate an IS strategy that best serves the total business strategy through the business processes and the functional areas reflected in the business models. In the process of making these judgments, we generally produce ideas on how consideration of technology can alter the priorities that the business modeling stage has determined from a purely business-driven angle. These ideas feed back into the business modeling stage, perhaps resulting in a reprioritization of initiatives or even changes in the business processes themselves.

The IS modeling stage considers each business model and produces IS models defining the functionality of an IS solution to support the business processes expressed in the business model. The relationship of IS models to business models is not necessarily one-to-one—for example, an IS model may express a utility function that supports several business processes.

Relation to the current IS analysis stage   Planners can begin working on the inventory portion of the current IS analysis stage as soon as the solution-building effort begins. Some of the information collected in that effort is useful in developing the IS strategy for the enterprise. The assessment of the current information system comes into play in an evaluation of how components of the current IS environment can play a role in the solution to be developed.

Relation to the IS architecture planning stage   The IS model and strategy developed in the IS modeling stage serve as the foundation for the analysis done in the architecture planning stage.

7.1.2   Relation to the OO model set

Figure 7-3 shows the mapping between the IS modeling stage and the associated object model in the OO model set, showing that the use-case model and the ideal-object model of the resource layer are produced by the IS modeling stage.

7.1.3   Participants

The team that produces the IS strategy and the IS model needs representation from business interests, IS, and end users. Understanding of both business and IS environments grows as the team works toward discovering the most effective ways to apply information technology to the business. The following interests make up the IS modeling team.

- **Business managers.** Managers supply knowledge of the enterprise's business operations and of interdependencies among organizations. Although the business model is a primary input to the IS modeling stage, business managers need to be involved in the feedback loop that provides for technology innovation to influence the business model. In addition, clarification of the business model itself may be necessary as IS modeling proceeds.
- **IS managers and IS professionals.** IS representatives contribute knowledge of information technologies—both existing and emerging—and their ability

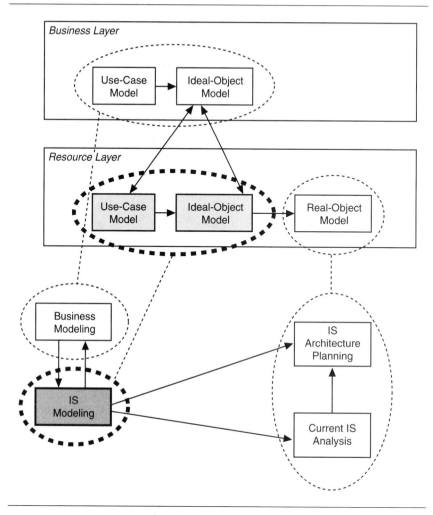

Figure 7-3   Relationship of IS modeling stage to the OO model set.

to support business activities that serve the strategic needs of the enterprise. Skilled IS professionals produce and record the emerging design as the IS use-case and ideal-object models. The specification of IS functionality is one of the most creative tasks in the process of building e-business solutions. Therefore, the IS designers performing this task need to have breadth and depth in the IT industry. Designers must have the imagination to be able to create innovative solutions that deliver business value and competitive advantage through the application of available technology. It is in the IS modeling stage that the strategic direction for the IS solution is established.

It is here that we need our most skilled and creative people—the "architects" we identified in Chapter 2 as those capable of creating elegant designs to fulfill business requirements.

- **End users.** Users supply detailed knowledge of business activities and offer insights about information or services that would improve their ability to do their jobs. End users also provide expert evaluation of impacts on business processes caused by the creative application of IS support.

- **Customers and business partners.** If we can get them to continue their participation, our customers and business partners will be just as valuable as our internal people in generating innovative ideas for using technology to make their experience with our enterprise more enjoyable and effective.

7.2   IS strategy

The IS strategy is a written record of the team's broad assessment of how information systems should be used within the enterprise. It includes high-level information about how existing IS resources and new and emerging technologies can be combined to meet the enterprise's information requirements and promote its business objectives. More tellingly, the IS strategy includes the team's creative insights into how new and emerging technologies can expand the enterprise's business objectives and allow the enterprise to pursue its existing objectives more effectively or at reduced cost. In later stages of the solution-building process, planners develop the strategy into a more detailed plan for the information systems the enterprise needs to implement.

7.2.1   Five-Era View

One way of thinking about the role of IS within an enterprise is the five-era view (Figure 7-4). This approach divides IS functionality according to the changing purposes that IS resources evolved to serve.

- The data processing era, beginning in the 1960s. Systems were used to improve the efficiency of activities that supported the enterprise, such as payroll, inventory, and other data-intensive applications. The expenses associated with these activities were typically seen as overhead, a part of the cost of doing business.

- The management information systems (MIS) era, beginning in the 1970s. Systems were used to increase management effectiveness by providing information to support decision making. The focus was on collecting timely and accurate information and abstracting it and organizing it in ways that enabled managers to make informed decisions.

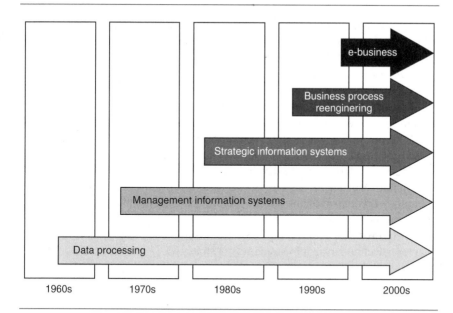

Figure 7-4   Five-era view of information systems.

- The strategic information systems era, beginning in the 1980s. Systems began to play a critical role in improving an enterprise's competitive position. Many strategic business activities would not even be possible without computers: automatic teller machines, instant credit checks, and global airline reservation systems are examples of technology-based services that define the competitive environment in which many enterprises operate. In such industries, strategic use of information systems can be essential.

- The business process reengineering (BPR) era, beginning in the 1990s. BPR represents the apotheosis of the strategic information systems era, taking the strategic systems era to its logical conclusion. Like the strategic systems era, BPR is primarily technology-driven. BPR applies technology through a top-down and systematic examination of business processes.

- The e-business era, beginning in the late 1990s.

Clearly, the activities of earlier eras did not come to an end when new eras began. Just as agriculture continued through the industrial age and the information age, and the manufacturing industry continues through the information age, earlier IS eras continue through the birth and growth of later eras—because, obviously, the services those earlier eras provide continue to be needed. Here, however, is where the analogy diverges. Later eras of human endeavor dramatically reduced the amount of labor needed for earlier-era pursuits—for example, the ability of the industrial age to mass-produce farming equipment led to a much-reduced labor requirement in agriculture. For a variety of reasons, we have not been very successful in applying our progress in information systems to improvements in the efficiency of our development and management of earlier-era IS capability. Thus, data processing still consumes more resource than management information systems, which consume more resource than strategic information systems, which in turn consume more resource than e-business systems.

Here we can revisit the apparent conflict between the business-driven and technology-driven approaches. Clearly, the business-driven paradigm applies largely to the "older" eras (data processing and MIS), whereas the technology-driven paradigm is more appropriate in the strategic information, BPR, and e-business eras. Given that IS developments will continue to embrace elements representative of all of these eras, we can see how the business-driven and technology-driven paradigms are indeed complementary, rather than conflicting.

In this context, it's worth repeating that technology-driven IS makes sense only in terms of an overarching business mission and strategy. As we saw in Chapter 6, technology is infrastructure, not strategy.

7.3 Developing the IS strategy

A sound IS strategy is a judicious balance of business-driven and technology-driven influences. You need to look at your enterprise's situation from both angles. The following sections present some guidelines from each viewpoint. In practice, there will be a blurring of business-driven and technology-driven considerations because competent planners will usually be keenly aware of both business objectives and the capabilities and viability of available technology.

7.3.1 Guidelines for business-driven IS strategy

In developing a business-driven IS strategy, the team builds on the business strategy and business models to make preliminary judgments about the enterprise's information and technology needs. From the business model, team members analyze how information flows among people and functional units in support of business processes. The goal is to identify how best to apply information technology in support of the business model and business objectives.

If, for example, a key business objective of an enterprise is to improve customer access to their accounts, planners will need to analyze the implications of providing information and transaction executions through the Web, and perhaps also via automated telephone access.

The following are general guidelines for creating the business-driven aspects of a useful IS strategy.

- Identify only generic IS requirements during this stage. Specific technology choices should normally wait until later in the solution-building process.

- Concern about limited resources should not prematurely limit consideration of potentially valuable IS uses. Defer more thorough analysis of costs and benefits until later, when more is known about the systems being planned.

- The information strategy should identify promising technologies, together with information and references to support evaluation of suitability for the IS solution being planned. Final decisions about which technologies to use and where to acquire them are usually made later in the process.

- The IS strategy should be forward-looking, but it should not normally pre-suppose a solution based on a new technology until the business case for that solution has been explored. A basic goal of an IS architecture is to build in the flexibility to respond to changing business requirements and new advances in technology.

7.3.2   Guidelines for technology-driven IS strategy

The technology-driven aspects of the IS strategy are the more likely sources of major breakthroughs in business performance. Introductions of technologies that cause widespread impact on the business landscape—such as the World Wide Web—occur relatively infrequently. However, less earth-shattering technologies emerge on a continuous basis. Performing a systematic examination of the technology landscape can provide a useful checklist as you develop your IS strategy. You may not have the luxury of keeping sufficient technology expertise on staff, and without a systematic periodic review, new technologies may be helping your competitors before they've appeared on your radar screen. If your corporate culture has an appetite for being an early technology adopter, you need to stay abreast of the technology landscape. Your technology-driven IS strategy will involve

- researching what new technologies are emerging, and updating (or creating) your list of technology candidates

- matching the list of technology candidates to the business model, business strategy, and business objectives, to discover how technology can produce business breakthroughs

7.3.3   Content of the IS strategy

The five-era view provides important clues for developing the IS strategy. By analyzing the roles information systems play in an enterprise's business activities, planners can determine the extent to which the different needs of the enterprise are met, and what opportunities exist for developing strategic IS solutions.

Not all IS uses are equally critical to the success of the enterprise, and higher net values tend to come from the later-era applications. For example, a new system purchase that results in a 10 percent increase in the efficiency of payroll operations (a data processing era application) could be very expensive but would do little to improve an enterprise's profitability. On the other hand, a comparable investment in Web-enabling technology that makes important account information available to field personnel and customers could give the enterprise a significant competitive advantage over rival enterprises that have not yet implemented such a system.

In the IS modeling stage, the team draws on the business strategy produced in the business modeling stage, which identifies which business functions have been selected as high priorities. The team focuses on these areas when developing the IS strategy. While the business modeling stage prioritized its business functions on the basis of business considerations, the IS modeling stage applies IS considerations to the determination of strategy.

In the IS modeling stage, we want to formulate IS strategy in very broad terms. We will be drawing up a more detailed set of principles in the architecture planning stage. The kinds of principles appropriate for an IS strategy at this level are those that are important to the enterprise's business management and those that will shape the enterprise's overall approach to its IS environment. Principles are as likely to be driven by political and historical considerations as they are by technology and financial considerations.

E-business drivers   In discussing the business strategy in Chapter 6, we saw how e-business is properly viewed as *infrastructure,* not strategy. Now, in this chapter, we're talking about *IS* strategy, not business strategy, and here it's entirely appropriate to consider e-business as part of that strategy. By examining the objectives of the enterprise business strategy, we will usually see obvious areas where we can profitably apply e-business technology—as indeed we did when considering the sample mission and objectives in Chapter 6.

In the e-business era, it's more than likely that the availability of e-business technology, reinforced by competitive pressure, is the impetus that brought us to this stage of the solution-building process. We therefore arrive with an expectation of applying e-business technology. Put another way, we already know what the technology is—the challenge is to find the best ways to take business advantage of it. With this mindset, we're operating in technology-driven-IS mode.

Let's look at some of the principal business drivers of e-business solutions and characterize them in terms of our project paradigms.

E-commerce generally refers to the Web enabling of the human interface to the enterprise. Customers are attracted, can make purchases directly, and can interact with the full range of customer service facilities. The commerce scenario clearly applies to the business-to-consumer (B2C) relationship. However, the "consumer" may be acting as an agent of another enterprise, which gives the relationship a business-to-business (B2B) flavor. In particular, B2B interactions elsewhere in enterprises' business processes may be intertwined with the B2C interface.

Relating e-commerce to our project paradigms, we can see that it best fits the E-Business Paradigm. Web enabling of the human interface need not have significant functional impact on back-end business operations.

Supply-chain integration aims to take the latency and friction out of supply-chain management. Electronically integrating supply chains with those of your business partners allows you to

- reduce inventory levels
- reduce obsolescence—an issue of increasing concern as product life cycles grow ever shorter
- speed new product introductions—also vital in the context of short product life cycles
- decrease cycle time in responding to upstream requirements, and adjusting downstream requirements

In the context of our project paradigms, supply-chain integration could fit the E-Business Paradigm. However, altering the interactions with the supply chain represents change at a rather deep level of the business process. It is likely that impact on the business processes will be necessary. The implication is that supply-chain integration may take on the characteristics of the Reengineering Paradigm.

Trading communities are an extension of the theme of supply-chain automation, where a many-to-many marketplace is provided by an intermediary company. These communities provide for opportunistic buying, including auction or reverse-auction buying, and are more suited to the trading of commodity products by business partners engaging in short-term relationships. The intermediary provides catalogue services, in which all suppliers' products are represented in standard form to facilitate buyer comparison. These trading communities typically require unique client software in order to interface to the service.

Introducing trading communities into the supply chain will cause an impact on the business processes. Unless we handle the introduction by the expedient "bolt-on" method described in Section 4.4.1, we will find ourselves moving toward the Reengineering Paradigm.

Business process integration (BPI) is a more generalized integration of trading partners' business processes, beyond supply-chain integration. This category effectively amounts to business process reengineering across a group of business partner enterprises. In the most highly evolved form of BPI, enterprises forge and just as easily dissolve business relationships as active projects turn over and business conditions change. These kinds of low-inertia relationships result in what we might regard as *virtual enterprises,* loosely coupled associations of business functions cooperating to do business together for a limited time and a specific purpose. The economic and social forces behind these kinds of arrangements were anticipated as far back as 1990 by Handy [1990, 1998]. With e-business and the Internet, we now have the technology to implement these low-inertia arrangements. A BPI project necessarily puts us into the realm of the Reengineering Paradigm.

This discussion of e-business drivers leads us to the conclusion that e-commerce is the only major e-business driver that closely conforms to the

E-Business Project Paradigm. Motivated by the other e-business drivers, the introduction of e-business technology to back-office processes tends to demand change in those processes, moving the project toward the Reengineering Paradigm.

Outsourcing, packaged software, and existing IS assets   Particular considerations that you should evaluate as candidates for inclusion in the IS strategy are your positions on outsourcing and packaged software. These considerations are important because the principal activity in the IS modeling stage is development of IS models of the functionality that we choose to support the business processes. If we are going to be outsourcing or using packaged software, then the task becomes radically different in nature. Rather than using our creativity and technology knowledge to design IS functionality from scratch, we're going to be using our knowledge of the capabilities of outsourcers and packaged software and assess where they can support our business processes.

Recall from Chapter 2 that using outsourcing and standard packaged software is realistically a viable option only for those aspects of the business that represent low differentiation. In the higher-differentiation areas of our business processes, we're going to develop, or at least customize, our own unique software to make sure we maintain that differentiation.

To address this kind of decision, the IS strategy might include a statement to the effect that the enterprise has a bias toward supporting low-differentiation business processes through outsourced services and packaged solutions, even at the expense of making changes in business processes, where changes are required to adopt these services.

The IS strategy also needs to consider the use of existing IS assets. In general, there should be a strong bias toward retaining—intact, on their current platform—existing IS assets. This subject is explored elsewhere in this book, and we won't go into it here in any depth. However, for the purposes of the IS strategy, the policy on reuse of existing assets needs to be stated explicitly—a bias toward retaining existing assets will not be obvious, or desirable, to everyone on the project. The history of our industry has no shortage of war stories about (usually unsuccessful) attempts to convert—with no value-add—existing applications to the new CIO's pet platform.

Application integration   The decisions described in the preceding subsection are going to lead us to the need to integrate application components from diverse sources. Application integration will represent a significant undertaking and is an appropriate consideration at a strategic level. We discuss application integration in Chapter 9.

Infrastructure   At least some aspects of technology infrastructure will be sufficiently important to warrant inclusion at the strategy level—especially the technologies of e-business. As we saw in Chapter 2, the middle ground of the technology stack is always undergoing turbulence. In this middle ground, the value of interoperability between competing products is beginning to challenge the competitive advantage of differentiation. It's somewhat ironic that e-business technology has taken the interoperability versus differentiation trade-off full circle—the degree of interoperability of an e-business product suite *itself* is a differentiator.

You, the user and buyer of the technology, must take your pick from among the combatants. Did you pick VHS over Beta back in 1983? Good choice. Microchannel over ISA? Oops. What are you going to pick for your application server infrastructure in 2001? Microsoft's DNA? Sun's J2EE? Whatever you decide, it's likely to be a strategic-level decision, because it will set the scene for the more tactical decisions lower down the food chain of your IS organization.

New technology   The really big business breakthroughs come from applying technology in a radically new way. But you don't have to be among the first group of technology adopters to profit from the application of technology. If you're late, and realize you have to play catch up, plan accordingly. If it's 2001 and you're still not letting your customers buy your products through the Web, you'd better put a statement in your IS strategy about leveraging the Web to deliver to your customers all the services they can get through other channels.

Preferred vendors   In addition to technology considerations, political and business relationships may dictate that preferred vendors appear as a principle in the IS strategy. To support your selection of a preferred infrastructure technology in the "turbulent zone," the choice of a preferred vendor might be a wise move if that vendor has a reputation and stake in your chosen technology.

Name your strategy   The considerations in the previous sections are representative of the kinds of decisions that may be appropriate as strategic IS principles. There may be any number of dimensions that affect any particular enterprise's strategic decision making. Decide for yourself what belongs in the overarching IS strategy.

7.4   The IS model

The IS model expresses the desired functionality of the information system to support the business processes. Developing this model is a highly creative exercise that we'll discuss in later sections. For the moment, we need to understand the place of the IS model in the overall business context.

What we're doing by building information systems is enabling and supporting *people* in their performance of business *processes*. If our solution-building exercise is to be successful, these three elements must work harmoniously together with mutual support as illustrated in Figure 7-5. As UUA [1996] puts it:

> *To achieve successful, sustained performance, and to differentiate a business from the competition, the three key elements of **processes, people, and systems** must be kept in balance.*

As we develop the IS model, we're in general going to be causing impact on the target business processes—perhaps even reengineering them completely—and thereby delivering feedback to the business modeling stage. At the same time, we're going to be affecting the way people do their jobs—and often changing the fundamental nature of their jobs—through changes in business processes made possible by new IS support. It is therefore essential that end users and business managers be involved in the IS modeling stage. Only through the direct participation of these affected stakeholders can we reasonably expect to arrive at the right balance and synergy among processes, systems, and people.

7.4.1   The IS model for large-scope projects

The IS model fulfills an essential role in architectural solution building, serving as the blueprint that allows the information system to be built. To quote from the UML specification [OMG 1999]:

> *Developing a model for an industrial-strength software system prior to its construction or renovation is as essential as having a blueprint for a large building. Good models are essential for communication among project teams and to assure architectural soundness. We build models of complex systems because we cannot comprehend any such system in its entirety. As the complexity of systems increase, so does the importance of good modeling techniques. There are many additional factors of a project's success, but having a rigorous modeling language standard is one essential factor.*

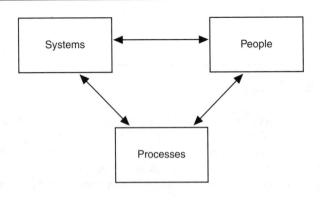

Figure 7-5   The harmonious balance of people, processes, and systems.

The preferred form of the IS model is a UML model, developed and maintained with a suitably capable software tool that stores the IS model in the enterprise repository. Investment in this kind of tooling and development infrastructure is, as a practical matter, feasible only in the context of a rather large-scope project. A necessary supporting condition is that management has bought in to the concept that IS reengineering and revitalization is a permanently ongoing and iterative activity. In terms of our three project paradigms, the Reengineering Paradigm is the only one of the three that would warrant the investment in a UML model.

If we're tackling projects of the more constrained scope of the E-Business Paradigm or the Incremental Improvement Paradigm—those toward the bottom left-hand corner of the project scope continuum in Figure 4-2—then modeling in UML is going to be overkill and a disproportionate overhead for the task at hand. In projects of smaller scope, we tend to keep the bulk of the current information system in place, making well-defined incremental changes or additions. UML models of the current system are unlikely to exist, and creating them amounts to a full-scale reverse-engineering exercise. For these reasons, we prefer to keep the concrete form of the IS model of narrow-scope projects consistent with existing IS documentation—which, in practice, usually means a natural-language document.

Whatever the scope of the project, it's important to focus the modeling effort on those areas targeted for IS solutions. It is all too easy to allow the modeling process to creep outward and bog down by extending its tentacles beyond the bounds of relevance.

Another case in which a UML model may be overkill is where we've outlined—in the IS strategy—a substantial role for packaged software systems and current IS assets in our new solution. Here, we want the IS model to indicate, at a broad high level, how and where the available software supports the affected business activities and what supporting IS functionality may need to be created. Refinement of the design is performed in the implementation planning stage.

For projects of any appreciable size and scope, computer-based modeling tools are a practical necessity. The process you use in developing the IS architecture model will therefore be inevitably influenced by the assumptions embodied in the tool. With this caveat in mind, we will now work through an overview of the IS model development process, abstracted from Jacobson et al. [1994].

As illustrated in Figure 7-3, the salient feature of the business layer as far as IS modeling is concerned is the ideal-object model, which we developed in Chapter 3. Recall that the ideal-object model is an abstraction of how the business operates and thus represents the how (the business activities) that implements the what (the business processes) of the enterprise.

Business activities are performed by human resources and information systems. Information systems support human resources in the performing of business processes, but may also act autonomously, as would, for example, a self-service Web application or an automated supply-chain management process.

We use the business model to derive the IS model. Just as we derived the business model by constructing a set of use cases to represent business processes, we use our knowledge of the business processes and supporting activities to construct a set of use cases for the supporting information system. In this way, we build an object model of the information system. Using appropriate software tooling, this model becomes integral to the automated development of the software itself. Rational Rose is an example of an information modeling tool that can be used for this purpose.

Did that last paragraph strike you as perhaps a little oversimplified? You're right. "Deriving the IS model" is not simply some mechanical process, or even a process needing purely left-brain deductive intellect. Rather, it's an intensely creative exercise. You need your best people for this job, from both the business side and the IS side. It's here that the application of technology can have a major impact on your business processes and ultimately on the service you provide your customers. Creative minds will easily think of ways to apply technology to generate customer value and business value. The impact of technology appears as a feedback loop into the business process definition. During this creative process, the team should be aware of the strategic principles in the IS strategy, because that strategy provides a context—a set of constraints and guidelines—for their decision making.

7.4.2   The reuse principle and the IS model

Although building the IS model is an intensively creative exercise, we'll need to temper our enthusiasm and idea generation with some practical considerations once we've got all our brainstorming ideas safely captured. The practical considerations we're concerned with here are—surprise!—the architectural principles. Specifically, we need to be concerned with the architectural principle of reuse of available components. Rather than building an IS model that assumes we'll custom build IS functionality from scratch, we try to find ways to reuse existing IS assets.

We should already have broached the reuse issue at a strategic level during the development of IS strategy. Here, while developing the IS model, we're concerned with reuse at a more detailed level. We need to find precisely which functionality we can reuse from the enterprise's existing IS assets, from packaged solutions, from outsourced solutions, or from other available sources of reusable components. This examination will generally result in changes to our idealized view of supporting IS functionality, and may consequently cause impact on the business processes.

Going about modeling in the architectural way, we would not treat the design of the IS model as an unconstrained exercise beginning with a blank sheet of paper. Recall from Chapter 2 the essential difference between traditional and "architectural" approaches. Restating these characterizations to fit the IS modeling context, we can say that:

- Traditional design follows the sequence:
  - understand the business processes
  - design information systems to support the business processes
- Architectural design follows the sequence:
  - understand the business processes
  - match the business processes to catalogued or standardized IS components, prebuilt subassemblies, frameworks, and applications

This expression of the architectural approach is subtly different from the one we saw in Section 6.4.5. We're now looking for catalogued or standardized *IS components* rather than business processes. If we were successful in finding standardized business processes, then the matching of standardized IS components will tend to be more straightforward. If, however, the business model created innovative business functions, finding standard IS components to support them will be more of a challenge and will likely need to deal with finer-grain functionality.

The first approach—understanding the business and then designing the supporting IS—is characteristic of a lets-build-it-ourselves mindset, with a bias toward a belief that our business is unique. However, this approach leads to inefficient information systems in the sense that systems built this way cost more to build and operate than their unique benefits are worth. We can draw an analogy between business processes and IT systems (refer to the discussion of standards and their evolution in Chapter 2): it is desirable to standardize business processes that represent low differentiation, because, for these processes, conformance to industry norms and interoperation with other businesses are more valuable than discriminating features.

In the second approach—understanding the business and then matching its processes to standardized IS components—we look for available components, subassemblies, and frameworks that we can leverage and adapt to meet our requirements. Using existing parts of the IS solution—the legacy system—is a particular application of this philosophy.

In general, we may want to modify the business requirements, imposing different processes on the business, to make for a more harmonious fit with the components we want to reuse. In an extreme application of this philosophy, we would buy an off-the-shelf package (for example, SAP R/3) and modify our low-differentiation back-office business processes to conform with the software. The right balance is where low-differentiation processes are supported by low-cost IS development through reuse of standard packages, components, and subassemblies, and where the unique discriminating product and service offerings of the enterprise are supported by custom-crafted software that the competition cannot easily replicate. In light of this philosophy, it is easy to appreciate why a packaged software approach makes sense where the affected processes are of low differentiation, even at the expense of dictated changes in business processes.

The reuse principle also applies to patterns of construction as well as to the functional components that we assemble into a solution. We should try to match our IS solution to known patterns that can be purchased and populated with our domain-specific components, in preference to building a framework from scratch. A workflow pattern is a good example of a framework that can be reused in this way. However, as a practical matter, repositories of reusable patterns exist mainly as the intellectual property of the organizations that built them.[2] To benefit from such a repository, you'll need to engage that company in a professional services contract. The quality of a consulting company's knowledge base and repository will be one of your criteria in deciding whether or not to engage that company

There is a dilemma here, in that we cannot reasonably expect to reuse existing IS assets unless we know what and where they are. Finding out what IS assets are available is what happens in the current IS analysis stage, yet that stage comes after IS modeling. Practically speaking, we need to allow some iteration and parallelism between these two stages. Although we can theoretically conduct the current IS analysis without satisfying any prerequisites, it's not a good idea to perform the analysis in isolation. We need insight from the business modeling and IS modeling stages to help focus on the areas of the current information system that are most likely to be of interest in the new solution. Without this focus, the current IS analysis can waste a lot of effort on areas that will be of no interest later on. The solution to this dilemma, then, is to perform the IS modeling and current IS analysis substantially in parallel so that relevant reusable assets can be leveraged in the new solution, and so that the analysis of potentially reusable assets can be focused through the knowledge of the requirements of the new solution.

7.4.3   Content of the IS model

The IS model comprises two types of models—the use-case model and the ideal-object model. Recall from Chapter 3 that a use-case model amounts to a black-box, what-it-does view of the IS applications, whereas an ideal-object model is a crystal-box, how-it-works view.

In spite of having the same name as the ideal-object model of the business model, the IS ideal-object model is a different model, representing the IS functions only. In contrast, the business model portrays the complete set of business processes, some of which are implemented through activities other than IT (for example, purely human interactions). The IS ideal-object model expresses how the information system will fulfill the requirements of the business activities.

The business model versus the IS model—an example   At this point, we're going to work through a simple example of a business model and a derived IS model. This exercise will give us a better appreciation of the character of the two models and will clarify the difference of scope between them.

---

[2]The open source movement has made some contributions of freely available reusable artifacts. See Schmidt [1999] for references.

The business we're going to model is a restaurant. For simplicity, we're going to consider only one use case: serving a meal. (Recall from Chapter 3 that a use case is a series of transactions performed in a system that yields a result of value to an *actor*.) There is only one actor, which is the party being served the meal.

The use case "serving a meal" proceeds roughly as follows.

1. Party enters restaurant.

2. Host greets party and shows them to a table.

3. Server appears at table and takes orders.

4. Server brings food.

5. Server brings check.

6. Party takes check to cashier, settles up, and leaves restaurant.

Note that in constructing this use case, we have drawn the boundaries around the restaurant as a whole. In other words, we have described an external actor (the party being served) and the benefit provided to the actor by the processes (the restaurant) residing inside the boundary

From this use case and our inside knowledge of how our restaurant works, we can derive the business objects and their responsibilities shown in Table 7-1. Remember that what we have here is a *business* model, not an IS model.

If we look at this object "model" of the business, rudimentary as it is, and look to see how an IS solution may be effectively applied, we can immediately see many possibilities. Here are a few examples:

TABLE 7-1   The restaurant example: objects and their responsibilities

Object	Responsibility
Host	Seats incoming customers
Manager	Assigns servers to tables
Server	Takes food orders from customers; submits food orders to cook; collects prepared food from cook; delivers food to customers; delivers check to customers; delivers copy of check to cashier
Cook	Collects food orders from servers; delivers prepared food to servers
Cashier	Collects payment for check
Busboy	Cleans vacated tables; notifies host that table is ready for new party
Table	Accommodates customer

- System automatically selects a table for newly arrived party, based on server allocation to tables and current servers' workloads.
- System places newly arrived party in wait queue if no table is available, issues pager to party, and gives wait-time estimate.
- System automatically allocates a newly available table to first waiting party and activates pager.

To be able to provide these functions, the information system will need to keep some information:

- status of all tables
- list of parties waiting to be seated
- allocation of servers to tables

Our purpose here is to understand what are the salient features of an IS model as distinct from a business model, not how to build the world's most IS-enabled restaurant, so we're going to limit our investigation of the IS solution to the modest scope of the activities listed above. As our illustration, we're going to define a use case we'll call "allocate party to table." Remember that we're now describing a use case of the information system, *not* of the restaurant.

The use case "allocate party to table" proceeds roughly as follows. Host asks information system to allocate a table to a party comprising a given number of people. Information system allocates a table if available, else asks host for party name, places party in wait list, and delivers wait-time estimate. Host may ask system for specific table, or may reject system's allocation and request another choice.

Notice that in the use case "allocate party to table," the actor is the host. The use case is a use case of the information system, not of the restaurant itself, and the host is (obviously) external to the information system. In deriving use cases for the information system, we draw the boundaries around the information system and regard users of the system as actors.

Analyzing the "allocate party to table" use case, we can derive some required internal behavior of the system. The system should only allocate tables with associated servers, so we'll need the manager to tell the system when servers come on duty, the lengths of their duty periods, and the tables they're responsible for, before the use case can run. We'll need the busboy who clears tables to notify the system when he has done so. We'll need the system to know how long the average party takes from placing their first order to vacating the table, so that the wait-time estimate can be given. This requirement also means that the system will need to capture the time that the first order at each table is placed.

From the description of required behavior, we can construct an object model. We have the classes *server* and *table,* with a one-to-many relationship. *Server* has such attributes as begin duty time and end duty time. *Table* has such attributes as number of seats, status (occupied, vacant), and time first order placed. Notice that the object classes, while being objects of the information system (as opposed to the restaurant itself), map directly onto objects in the object model of the restaurant itself.

In this example, I have tried to give the flavor of what goes into the business model and the IS model, and to demonstrate the essential difference between them, without getting into depth on how to do object-oriented modeling. Object-oriented modeling is a substantial topic beyond the scope of this book, and references for further reading appear in the Bibliography and References section.

7.4.4   The IS model for narrow-scope projects

If the project we're undertaking matches the E-Business Paradigm or the Incremental Improvement Paradigm, we will not develop the IS model in the same way as for a reengineering project. In both of these narrow-scope paradigms, our intent is to make incremental changes to the existing IS assets. The main driver is therefore the current IS analysis.

The IS model for e-business   In setting out to tackle a narrow-scope e-business project, we are—by definition of the E-Business Paradigm—seeking to minimize the impact of e-commerce technology on existing business processes.

In planning such a project, we need to prioritize the business processes— defined by the use-case model of the business—in terms of which ones we want to retrofit with e-business technology. We examine the current IS inventory and assessment to understand how the current IS environment supports the target business processes. As with the Reengineering Paradigm, there is again an iteration and a parallelism between the IS modeling stage and the current IS analysis stage. We need to focus our efforts in IS analysis according to which business processes we have identified for e-business enablement. Having compiled a focused current IS inventory and IS assessment, as described in Chapter 8, the IS model for e-business can be expressed as the set of modifications to the current IS environment required to implement the identified e-business functionality.

Let's look at a couple of examples to see how these ideas might work in practice. First of all, let's e-business-enable our restaurant. We'll assume that the restaurant already has a take-out food business in the traditional business world. Customers call in their orders and then either come in to pick them up or request delivery. (The preceding sentence amounts to a rudimentary expression of one of the enterprise's use cases.) The e-business initiative we want to pursue is to add a Web customer interface, in addition to the telephone. We perform a current IS analysis and discover that there really isn't anything there that qualifies as an information system—the restaurant is run by humans moving paper notes and talking to each other. We decide that the least disruptive way to introduce e-business is to build a Web site that does all the usual marketing stuff and lists the menu items, allowing them to be clicked for placement in a Web shopping cart. When a customer checks out her shopping cart, she's asked whether she's going to pick up her order or whether she wants delivery. The completion of the checkout results in the order being printed on a printer located in the kitchen, where the kitchen manager tears it off and places it in the queue of waiting orders, along with the paper orders being taken from the phone and from live customers in the restaurant itself.

Once the system is in place, it doesn't take much imagination to start inventing ways to improve restaurant operation. By supporting all restaurant operations with an information system, we can replace the paper flow with an electronic flow and thereby gather information on what we're selling, how much of it we're selling, and who's doing the buying. We can make wait-time calculations on incoming orders and give our customers the choice of canceling their orders if they'd rather not wait that long—thus raising customer satisfaction levels.

This scenario illustrates the application of e-business to an existing set of business processes, building incrementally and nondisruptively on an existing information system. The scenario also shows how the introduction of e-business tends to stimulate reengineering of existing business processes, even in this simple e-commerce example.

As our second example, let's look at a local bookstore chain. The bookstore decides to capitalize on its good local image to compete with the national Web-based heavyweights. Like the restaurant, the bookstore puts up a Web site, from which customers can buy books from its catalogue. There, however, the similarity with the restaurant ends. It's obvious that the experience of buying a book through a Web site for home delivery, is radically different from visiting a bricks-and-mortar bookstore and buying a book. The business activities that support the Web buying process are therefore different from those that support the in-store buying experience. Clearly, it would make no sense for orders to be printed up on in-store printers, as they were for the restaurant, and for store clerks to go and pick book volumes from the shelves, put them in mailers, and dispatch them. What's needed is a specialized fulfillment service to which the Web system directs orders for physical dispatch.

The need for a specialized fulfillment service is significant, because it implies a new set of activities not previously seen in this bookstore. In effect, the Web purchasing facility represents a new business process, not simply a minor variation on an old one. In terms of the solution-building process, we're forced to revise our business model. Like it or not, we're being backed into a reengineering project, and we need to treat it with all the respect it deserves. The business model needs to be thought through thoroughly in light of the new processes and the activities needed to support them.

We have real-world examples of the consequences of paying insufficient attention to the impact of applying e-business to an existing business model. During the seasonal heavy buying of the December 1999 holiday period, several high-profile retailers suffered Web-induced embarrassment. They had paid insufficient attention to the scalability and flexibility of their operations. It is arguable whether more extensive research and projection analysis on likely sales volume would have helped. As we've already seen, projections of market size in radically new fields are likely to be off by orders of magnitude, as supply fuels unprecedented demand. As a result of insufficient capacity, these retailers' Web sites were overloaded to the point of denying access to frustrated online shoppers. Worse, however, was their inability to deliver purchases in time for Christmas. In line with the inadequate capacity of their Web servers, their physical order fulfillment was similarly overloaded.

When the application of e-business technology starts to expand into reengineering, there are some challenging trade-offs to be made. E-business can bring significant benefits to the enterprise, even if they're "bolted on" to current processes. The quicker you can realize those benefits, the better off you'll be. Or, in a more brutally competitive environment, the quicker you can realize those benefits, the better chance you'll have of staying in business. You simply may not have the luxury of taking on a reengineering project before deploying e-business on top of current processes. You may be able to buy time by bolting e-business onto current processes and replacing the bolts by neat welds while your business continues to function.

What general lessons can we draw from these examples? First of all, even a relatively straightforward-looking venture into e-commerce may push an enterprise toward reengineering. The closeness of fit between the e-commerce scenario and existing operations determines the severity of the impact. Adding e-commerce to an existing mail-order or phone-order operation need not change the processes drastically in a functional sense, although scalability and availability of the supporting systems are going to be important. On the other hand, adding e-commerce to pure bricks-and-mortar retailing will clearly change the business processes, taking the project toward the Reengineering Paradigm.

The IS model for incremental improvement   Where the project fits the Incremental Improvement Paradigm, we focus our current IS analysis on the IS functions relating to the business activities most in need of improvement.

By way of example, let's return to the city government with problems in customer service and staff productivity, which we encountered briefly in Chapter 6. The solution-building team identified standard office productivity tools (specifically e-mail) that were available to all employees as one part of the solution. Another part of the solution was Web technology, with a browser interface giving access to the information that staff needed to access. It was a straightforward step to extend this Web interface to customers (that is, citizens), thus simultaneously addressing the customer service issue. Finally, an automated telephone voice response system was proposed to handle citizen inquiries, many of which were found to be "frequently asked questions" that could be answered automatically.

Having made these strategic decisions ("strategic" at least in the context of an incremental improvement project), we need now to develop the IS model. What form should it take?

How the IS model is represented will depend on

- the comfort level of the project team with various techniques.
- the form of documentation for any existing models.
- the complexity of the functionality being added.

Most incremental improvement projects will choose a natural-language description. Such a description is usually known as a "Requirements"[3] definition and defines IS functionality (that is, what the system must do) in terms of:

- user interface
- interface to other applications
- user tasks and roles

A UML description for the IS model is appropriate if the project team has a high level of comfort with the technique and is supported by appropriate software tooling that will carry forward through deployment. The more complex the functionality being added, the more appropriate is a UML-based IS model.

7.4.5   Forks in the road: solution alternatives

Sometimes, the building of the IS model may generate more than one alternative, which all look equally attractive in light of evidence available at this stage of solution building. For example, should we use an ERP package? If using an ERP package is already a recorded decision for some business functions, should we force-fit it to other areas, altering our business activities to do so? Or should we maintain the status quo in those areas and adapt our existing IS assets to integrate with the new environment?

Although it's expensive and time-consuming to do so, it may be necessary to develop both alternatives to greater levels of detail, through later stages of solution building, before making a decision. We'll encounter more forks in the road in IS architecture planning in Chapter 9, and we'll resolve them all when we do implementation planning in Chapter 10. That said, you should really try to make these kinds of decisions at a high level—analysis paralysis is a real danger here. Especially where e-business is concerned, speed is of the essence.

7.5   The IS real-object model

The real-object model, which we discussed in Chapter 3 and which is the subject of the IS architecture planning stage, reflects the impact of practical considerations on the building of the information system:

---

[3]In fact, "Requirements" specify nonfunctional requirements in addition to functional requirements. Nonfunctional requirements are discussed in Chapter 9.

- real-world (such as organizational and political) constraints
- integration of legacy systems
- lower-level architectural design decisions
- capabilities and characteristics of the development and run-time environment

When we derive and analyze the IS object model purely in terms of its desired behavior, we will probably idealize it in the sense that we invent objects meaningful in the business domain (such as server and table in our restaurant example). However, to realize the model, we will generally have to make concessions to the real world by inventing classes that reflect real-world constraints on our solution. For example, if we find we need to get the number of seats at each table from a relational database, we may find it necessary to invent objects corresponding to the database itself.

We'll come back to the IS real-object model in Chapter 9, where we discuss the IS architecture planning stage.

7.6   Where was the "architecture"?

As in the preceding chapter, we'll conclude by reviewing how the elements of architecture apply to this chapter (see Table 7-2).

TABLE 7-2   Where was the "architecture" in Chapter 7?

Architecture feature	Relationship to this chapter
Solution fitted to client needs	Primary input to the IS modeling stage is the business model, which, as far as IS modeling is concerned, is an expression of client needs. The IS modeling stage defines the functionality required of the IS solution in supporting the business model.
	An approach less "architectural" in nature would tend to skip over the business modeling stage and start with "requirements gathering" based on business managers' tacit understanding of their business processes. In effect, the primary burden of specifying IS functionality rests on the business side of the house. In contrast, the "architectural" approach takes a balanced view, with the business modeling stage serving to document the business functionality, so that the design of the supporting IS functionality is shared between business and IS interests in a much more balanced way.
Empirically validated principles	Empirically validated principles are supported through:
	• applying an object-oriented discipline—thus separating implementation from interface.

(continued)

TABLE 7–2 Where was the "architecture" in Chapter 7? (*continued*)

Architecture feature	Relationship to this chapter
	• constructing the solution in well-defined layers—which is a mindset and principle to be applied in IS model design, rather than an inherent quality of the process itself.
Design and implementation principles and guidelines	Strategic-level principles and guidelines are defined in this stage. In addition, the axiomatic principles apply throughout this stage.
Components, patterns, and frameworks	Rather than treat IS solution design as an unconstrained exercise in the creative application of information technology for business advantage, we search for available functionality—whether packaged software, existing enterprise IS assets, or commercially available components and frameworks.
Conceptual integrity and elegance	Conceptual integrity and elegance are recurring themes throughout this book. The themes represent a pervasive mindset and attitude applied throughout the solution-building process. In the particular context of IS modeling, these qualities mean that you don't violate principles defined in the IS strategy. Conceptual integrity means that the common patterns you pick in defining the IS model are used consistently. For example, it would be a violation of conceptual integrity to use a standard workflow engine in one part of the solution while building an ad hoc workflow functionality in domain-specific logic in a different part of the solution. And, even more clearly, it would be a violation of the component–pattern–framework architectural principle to use ad hoc workflow in either or both situations.
Formal description and recording	In a reengineering project, we use fully featured modeling tools. In the narrow-scope paradigm projects, we compromise and use less formal methods. However, the state of the design needs to be recorded in a controlled way, whether the tools are sophisticated and special purpose or are general-purpose productivity tools such as Microsoft Visio and Word.

8

Current IS Analysis

This chapter describes the current IS analysis stage. This stage consists of an inventory of the components in the current IS environment and an assessment of the strengths and weaknesses of each component in the IS inventory.

8.1 Overview

If there is a single principal theme, it is that practical distributed systems, and thus practical open systems, must be developed in an evolutionary manner from current systems rather than in a revolutionary way; that is to say, we cannot simply discard existing systems. [Slonim 1987]

A complex system that works is invariably found to have evolved from a simple system that worked . . . A complex system designed from scratch never works, and cannot be patched up to make it work. You have to start over, beginning with a working simple system. [Gall 1986]

(Yes, we've seen this one before, but it's so perceptive and so relevant that it bears repeating.)

During the current IS analysis stage, the enterprise completes a current IS inventory and a current IS assessment.

- **Current IS inventory**. The current IS inventory is a catalogue of the components in the current IS environment. To contain the scope of the effort to manageable proportions, the team needs to include only those components that are relevant to the IS strategy.

- **Current IS assessment**. The current IS assessment is an evaluation of the strengths and weaknesses of the components in the IS inventory. This includes an evaluation of the technical, functional, and nonfunctional characteristics (such as performance, scalability, and reliability) and economic aspects of each component.

The purpose of the inventory and assessment is twofold:

- to define the starting point for the migration to the new information system
- to understand the functionality and capabilities of existing IS assets with a view to their reuse in the new system

8.2   Current IS analysis in the context of the total process

8.2.1   Relation to other stages

Figure 8-1 illustrates the relationship of the implementation planning stage to other stages of the seven-stage solution-building process. Figure 8-2 expands on the contextual picture by showing the deliverables that flow among the related stages, as well as an overview of the principal activities of the current IS analysis stage. The deliverables from the current IS analysis stage are the current IS inventory and the current IS assessment.

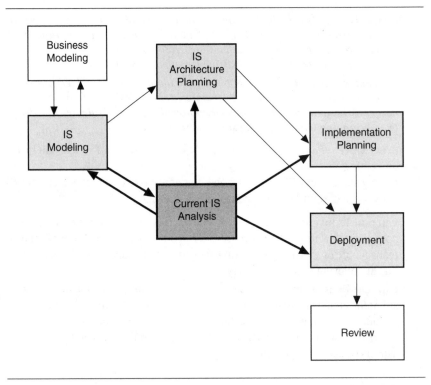

Figure 8-1   Current IS analysis stage in context.

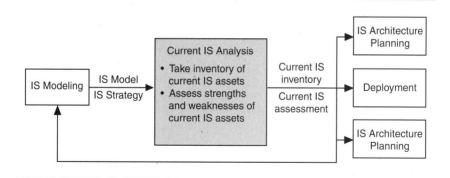

Figure 8-2   Current IS analysis stage.

Relation to business modeling and IS modeling   The current IS inventory needs to be started as early as possible in the project, because it always turns out to be a lengthy process.

The current IS inventory and the IS strategy are the basis for the current IS assessment. The IS strategy helps define which components in the current IS inventory are part of the long-term plans of the enterprise. Consequently, before the team conducting the current IS assessment can begin, the IS strategy of the enterprise must be substantially defined and the current IS inventory substantially completed. However, the current IS inventory need gather information on only those IS components relevant to the IS strategy and relevant to the direction being taken by the business modeling activity. It is important that the team constrain the scope of the IS inventory to keep the effort manageable and consistent with the scope of the total solution-building effort.

The assessment of the strengths and weaknesses of the current IS environment is valuable feedback to the IS strategy. One of the tasks of IS modeling is to identify that functionality of the current IS environment that can usefully play a role in the new environment. The IS modeling stage and current IS analysis stage are thus mutually dependent, like a pair of programming procedures that call each other recursively. This mutual recursion makes up one of the many loops in the iterative whirlpool of the solution-building process.

Relation to IS architecture planning   In the IS architecture planning stage, the current IS inventory and assessment help the team establish the foundation for the IS architecture.

Relation to implementation planning   In the implementation planning stage, the current IS inventory and assessment help the team refine the role of the current IS assets in the new system, a process that began in the IS modeling stage. The greater detail produced in the implementation planning stage flows into the transition plan that identifies projects and their priorities.

Relation to deployment   During the deployment stage, the enterprise acquires or develops new assets, such as hardware, software, applications, development methodologies, policies, and personnel. These new assets become part of the current IS inventory that future projects can use in their implementation and deployment. Consequently, the current IS inventory continues to evolve as new projects are implemented and deployed.

8.2.2   Participants

To complete the current IS analysis stage, the team needs an understanding of what components are in the current IS environment and how well they are working. Since the IS managers and professionals on the team are most familiar with the current IS environment, they can either complete the current IS analysis themselves or organize a task force to complete it.

To complete the current IS inventory, the following people need to be consulted to determine what hardware, software, and IS resources they use:

- business managers
- IS managers
- IS professionals
- end-user departments or end users

Once the current IS inventory is complete, a smaller team can assess the strengths and weaknesses of the components in the current IS inventory. Experienced IS professionals are needed to conduct this assessment, because they will need to make informed judgments, involving many criteria, in the evaluation of current IS assets in the context of the desired solution.

8.3   Introducing the architectural framework

Whenever we travel, it's helpful to refer to a map. A map tells us where places are in relation to each other, and how they're interconnected in terms of natural geographic features and man-made artifacts such as roads and railway lines. Without the two-dimensional visualization a map provides, navigation in the real world is very difficult and hard to conceptualize.

Two-dimensional visualization is a powerful tool that works well for human brains, an observation summed up nicely by the old saw "a picture is worth a thousand words." In designing and building IS solutions, we find the visualization technique helpful in many areas. We've already seen visualization in action in earlier chapters, in the form of object-oriented modeling. Now we're going to look at another visualization device, which we'll find useful in the IS assessment stage and also in some of the solution-building stages that follow. This visualization device is the *architectural framework*.

We met the concept of an architectural framework briefly in Chapter 2, where it came up as one of the several meanings of the word *architecture*. A framework is helpful in thinking about our total IS environment because it classifies the various types and levels of IS components and sketches pictorially how the various building blocks relate to one another. It is a conceptual picture that assists intellectual manageability. It's a divide-and-conquer device that lets us focus our attention on one area at a time. The conceptual picture itself amounts to a reusable pattern, which additionally qualifies it as "architecture" in the *common-component* sense noted in Chapter 2. Furthermore, the structure of an architectural framework reinforces our application of the "best practices" in design that we first saw in Chapter 2. To recap, these best practices are:

- construct systems in well-defined layers of abstraction
- maintain a clear separation of concerns between the interface and implementation of each layer
- realize common behavior through common abstractions and common mechanisms

Finally, it's not stretching too far to point out that the representation of major building blocks in a framework qualifies as architecture in the *blueprinting* sense of Chapter 2, in that the pictorial representation can indeed serve to communicate the high-level view of the emerging design to certain of the interested stakeholders.

There are interesting and instructive parallels between the use of an IS architectural framework and the way architecture is conducted in the physical world of buildings and communities. Architects employ a range of building blocks in practicing their art. Individual buildings consist of walls, roofs, doors, windows, and so on, arranged in well-established patterns. Towns and communities consist of houses and apartments arranged in established residential patterns with commercial districts and their constituent business premises all interconnected and serviced by common infrastructural elements. Architectural rules and "best practices" define how the building blocks interrelate and cooperate in working together to form the larger community.

The IS architectural framework serves a parallel purpose in the world of information systems building. It's a framework that helps us think about, communicate about, and collaborate on the design and building of our information systems. It's a knowledge-management device that provides a taxonomy for classifying and referencing our accumulated technology knowledge resources. It's an organizing device around which we can build architectural rules and best practices to help guide our IS solution-building efforts. It's a framework for technology decision making, and for keeping intellectual control of the ramifications of those decisions. While intrinsically vendor-neutral and unbiased in its view of technology, the framework nevertheless serves as a vehicle for *comparing* technologies of similar scope. The preferred set of technologies can then be more cogently described when expressed in terms of the framework.

Figure 8-3 is an example of an architectural framework that features all the important areas of an IS environment. In practice, each solution development organization—whether a consulting firm or a business enterprise building its own solutions—tends to develop its own framework. Although all frameworks are very similar in character and identify substantially similar sets of building blocks, the differences in emphasis and focus areas are enough to make the details of each organization's framework slightly different. You can find a concrete example of a framework in The Open Group's *TOGAF* [The Open Group 1998], which is promoted to be used freely—by end users—without payment of royalties. Figure 8-3 shows only the top level of an architectural framework. To be really useful, each category (functional layer or vertical capability) needs to be expanded to the next level of detail, which can serve as a checklist in constructing the IS inventory.

The remainder of this book assumes that the solution-building process will be structured around an architectural framework. In keeping with the high-level scope of the book, I am not going to be prescriptive about the details of the architectural framework. Rather, I will use *as an example only* the framework of Figure 8-3.

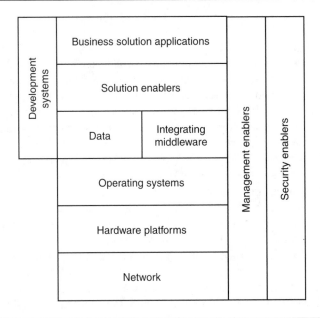

Figure 8-3   Example architectural framework.

8.4   Conducting the current IS inventory

The purpose of the current IS inventory is to document the components in the current IS environment. The components include applications, infrastructural software, data, hardware, policies, procedures, personnel, and any other resources that are part of the enterprise's current IS environment. The compilation of the current IS inventory can be very laborious and needs to be conducted with sharp focus if it is not to take on a life of its own and consume disproportionate amounts of time and resources. The required focus comes from the IS strategy and the IS model that describe the new solution. We are interested in the existing assets only to the extent that they have implications for, or can usefully play a role in, the new solution we are building.

An architectural framework, as described in the preceding section, is most helpful here. In addition to all the benefits discussed earlier, the framework fulfills the very basic function of a *checklist*.

Input to the current IS inventory includes materials from any existing IS inventories. Existing materials might include

- diagrams and models of the enterprise's data, applications, processes, and network
- hardware configuration diagrams
- application documentation—both for end users and for IS development and maintenance staff
- descriptions of business processes
- policies and procedures

The current IS inventory does not need to be an exhaustive listing of every component in the IS environment. The team must always keep the level of detail appropriate to what is needed to support IS architecture planning and implementation planning.

To help make sure the process does not get bogged down in this stage, the team should

- time box the effort by setting time limits for the current IS inventory.
- ensure that the team completing the IS inventory focuses on the components that support the major business functions targeted by the overall solution-building effort.

For this IS inventory, it is better to have a little information about all the components in the current IS environment that support the major business functions than a lot of information about a few components. If needed, additional detail can be added later.

The inventory is constructed around the architectural framework you choose to adopt. For example, referring to the example framework of Figure 8-3, the following categories of IS building blocks are likely to be represented:

A novel approach to taking current IS inventory.

- business solution applications
- solution enablers
- data
- middleware integration software
- operating systems
- hardware platforms
- network
- development environments
- management enablers
- security enablers

In each of the categories indicated by the architectural framework, we include, where applicable, elements of *current* IS strategy (that is, the strategy in force when the current technology selections were made), including associated standards. The following section discusses these framework categories in greater detail.[1]

---

[1]I reiterate here that the framework categories are *examples,* and may vary depending on details of the particular framework you choose to adopt. The text expands on the level of detail of those categories that are likely to appear, or have obvious counterparts, in any viable framework.

The IS inventory should also include the following kinds of organizational information:

- IS department organization, human resources, and skills
- policies and procedures

The output of the current IS inventory is a document that lists the components in the current IS environment. The document provides input to the current IS assessment.

8.5   Inventory of IS components

This section contains *suggestions* for the types of information the team should gather for the current IS inventory. The important word here is "suggestions." The detailed categorization of the IS inventory is determined by the architectural framework that you adopt. Therefore, a prerequisite for completing the IS inventory is to settle on the makeup of the architectural framework and list the functional categories and services provided by each of the framework's layers.

The examples and suggestions that follow are based on the example framework shown in Figure 8-3 and serve to characterize the various information technology categories represented in the framework.

8.5.1   Business solution applications

To begin the application inventory, the team should check for the following applications in each department:

- applications currently in use
- applications currently in development
- planned applications
- references to business process descriptions that these applications support

The team should include both internally developed and vendor-supplied applications in their inventory. For each application, the team can gather the following information:

- Specifications or design documents
  - function of the application and its major attributes
  - any planned enhancements
- Interfaces
  - user interface
  - interfaces to other applications
  - available APIs (application programming interfaces)

- Interdependencies (the following checklist is generated from the architectural framework)
  - solution enablers
  - supporting infrastructure (middleware)
  - databases or data warehouses that the application uses
  - supporting operating system
  - development environment and tools
  - management and administration facilities
  - security enablers

Outsourced services   Services provided by outsourcing vendors should be included in the inventory of the current IS environment—for example:

- payroll
- backup and off-site storage
- auditing
- maintenance
- help desk

These kinds of services imply the existence of interfaces for exchange of data and management of the services and therefore imply impact on any planned solution.

8.5.2   Solution enablers

Solution enablers may include such assets as horizontal business components and high-level information interchange facilities.

The workflow pattern discussed in Section 6.4.5 is an example of a horizontal business component—it is at the application level but is not specific to a particular business domain.

Information interchange facilities are needed, in principle, whenever complex application data needs to be exchanged. The need is most usually felt where the applications concerned were originally designed without their cooperating applications in mind.[2]

Interdependencies should be listed for each solution enabler (the following checklist is generated from the architectural framework).

- dependent applications
- supporting infrastructure (middleware)

---

[2]Discussion of these information interchange features takes us into the realm of enterprise application integration (EAI) which we'll discuss in Chapter 9. As a result, it may be more appropriate to consider information interchange in the context of application server middleware, under *integrating middleware*. That choice depends on your IS strategy and specifically on your approach to application integration.

- databases or data warehouses that the application uses
- supporting operating system
- development environment and tools
- security enablers

8.5.3   Data

The data inventory lists the enterprise's data assets, including databases, data warehouses, directories, and repositories. The inventory briefly states the purpose of each asset and notes the relevant interdependencies, as indicated by the architectural framework:

- underlying technology and associated vendor
- dependent applications
- associated middleware
- supporting operating system
- development environment and tools
- management and administration facilities
- security enablers
- supporting platform

The inventory could usefully contain references to more-detailed information—such as database schemas—to ease rapid access to that information, should it be required in later stages of solution building.

8.5.4   Middleware integration software

Middleware integration software is the software glue that holds applications together and provides common services. It includes

- interprocess communication facilities
- transaction-processing monitors
- object component frameworks
- application server middleware (Microsoft DNA, J2EE, CORBA, and associated functionality)
- message-oriented middleware

Each middleware environment in use needs to be catalogued, along with its interdependencies, as indicated by the architectural framework:

- dependent applications
- dependent solution enablers
- supporting operating system
- supporting network facilities

- development environment and tools
- management and administration facilities
- security enablers

8.5.5 Operating systems

Like middleware, operating systems in use need to be catalogued against the applications that depend on them. It is also necessary to know the number of installed instances of each operating system.

For each operating system, the interdependencies need to be listed, guided by a checklist generated from the architectural framework:

- dependent applications
- dependent solution enablers
- dependent middleware
- dependent databases or data warehouses
- dependent development environment and tools
- supporting management and administration facilities
- dependent management and administration facilities
- supporting security enablers
- dependent security enablers
- supporting network facilities

8.5.6 Hardware platforms

For the current platform inventory, the team can gather the following information:

- type and number of mainframes, servers, and workstations
- utilization and capacity overview

For each platform, the interdependencies should be listed, guided by a checklist generated from the architectural framework.

- dependent solution enablers
- dependent middleware
- dependent databases or data warehouses
- dependent development environment and tools
- supporting management and administration facilities
- dependent management and administration facilities
- dependent security enablers

8.5.7   Network

In earlier days, network engineering was an exacting task, highly interrelated with the applications running over the network. In the e-business era, standardization and vast available bandwidth have taken over. These two forces have combined effectively to decouple network engineering from the need to assess network needs on an application-by-application basis. Rather, network engineering is now the bailiwick of specialist network engineers, whose task is to provide what amounts to "IP dialtone" for the enterprise. IP is the overwhelmingly dominant network protocol, and bandwidth requirements are now effectively addressed through broad assessments of the communications characteristics and quality-of-service requirements of the application mix and through statistical observations of user populations and their behavior.

The implication of the commodity-network situation, for the IS professional assembling a current IS inventory, is one of simplification. The IS professional needs to note any unusual network protocol requirements of legacy systems that must be preserved in the new solution. The expectation is that all new applications and their supporting platforms will run on a standard network supplying IP dialtone designed by specialist network engineers. The IS professional's role is to design whatever interfacing arrangements may be needed to join the IT environment to the IP dialtone utility.

Interenterprise interfaces   Interenterprise interaction is, of course, what e-business is all about. However, businesses have been engaged in limited forms of electronic interenterprise cooperation for decades—EDI, for example.

Interenterprise network links forged before the e-business era are most likely based on private VANs (value-added networks). It is important to identify such existing links and the applications that ultimately make use of them. Sooner or later, we can expect our new e-business solutions to subsume these applications. However, our new solutions may choose to make use of VAN connectivity rather than the raw Internet, and it's therefore important to know what VAN connectivity currently exists.

8.5.8   Development environments, tools, and methodologies

The enterprise will generally have an installed base of tools to support IS development. It may be the case that multiple competing tools have been installed as separate organizations exercised their autonomy or as the result of enterprise mergers and acquisitions.

If outside consultants are involved, the team performing the solution building can ideally be flexible enough to adopt the enterprise's preferred toolset. The discovery of the components of that preferred toolset is the first step in that direction.

Tools used may range from simple automation—for example, drawing programs such as Visio—to fully featured modeling tools—such as Rational Rose—capable of interfacing to a repository through XML to share data with other tools in a cooperative total development environment. Tools may be employed in business modeling, IS requirements gathering, IS modeling, and through all phases of the process of software development.

A methodology is a set of practices and procedures, with supporting templates and knowledge bases, that systematically organizes the development process. Methodologies generally prescribe or recommend the tools to be used. It is helpful, therefore, in the current IS inventory, to assemble references to the methodologies in use in the enterprise.

As far as the current IS inventory is concerned, all development environments in use, and their associated tools and methodologies, should be listed. Their interdependencies should be noted, as guided by a checklist drawn up from the architectural framework:

- dependent applications
- dependent solution enablers
- supporting middleware
- supporting repositories and databases
- supporting management and administration facilities
- supporting operating systems
- supporting hardware platforms

8.5.9   Management enablers

All aspects of an information system need to be "managed" in various ways. The pervasive nature of management is the reason why the framework depicts the management capability as a vertical bar, spanning the horizontal functional layers.

Management includes such considerations as:

- centralized management platform (for example, CA UniCenter or HP Open-View) and associated products
- management protocols (for example, SNMP)
- configuration management and maintenance
- performance and capacity measurement and planning
- policy management
- management data gathering, reporting, and presentation
- alert and alarm monitoring and reporting
- trouble ticketing, tracking, and service dispatch

In addition to listing each management capability, it is necessary to know which of the elements of the IS environment are managed by, or are capable of being managed by, which management capabilities.

8.5.10 Security enablers

Discussion of security is shaped entirely by security policy, which in turn is dictated by enterprise requirements. Many security services are built into operating systems and middleware; how, or even if, they are used depends on the security policy. Where more comprehensive or specialized security services are needed, additional security software or hardware facilities may be in place.

The important principle concerning security enablers is that the inventory listing of installed capability must be structured around the stated policy objectives if it is to be meaningful.

The principal security services are:

* *authentication*—proof of claimed identity
* *access control*—enforcement of the security policy that says who can perform which operations on which resources
* *confidentiality*—keeping data from being seen by unauthorized persons
* *integrity*—preventing undetected deletion of, insertion of, or tampering with data

8.5.11 IS organization

The capabilities of the IS organization have implications on the enterprise's ability to deploy and operate the new IS solution, while coping with the organizational changes that the deployment inevitably implies. The IS inventory should note

* size and structure of the IS organization
* expertise and experience of personnel, expressed in terms of the categories of the architectural framework
* available training and education
* functions the IS organization provides
* policies and procedures applying to the IS environment

8.6 Assessment of current IS environment

The purpose of the current IS assessment is to position the current IS assets in the context of the new solution being built. We need to understand the relationship of existing components to the new solution so as to plan the adaptation and integration of those components in the deployment of the new solution.

We assess the current IS environment along the following dimensions:

* functionality
* nonfunctional attributes

- human resource capabilities
- outsourced services

8.6.1 Functionality

Existing IS environments that have been growing for decades tend to have a very large spectrum of functionality—much of it convoluted and obscure—that no single person in the organization can comprehend. It is very laborious to try to compile a complete functional inventory, never mind trying to assess it qualitatively. It is essential, therefore, to build an overview picture quickly and to narrow down the scope for further investigation using the results of the IS modeling stage to point us in the direction of the functionality likely to be useful in the new solution. As the investigation progresses, you will build up a clearer and more detailed picture of how well the functionality fits the required functionality of the new solution. As this picture clarifies, you will be constantly evaluating the following kinds of decisions.

- Is this functionality a close enough fit to justify the pursuit of this investigation? If not, let's drop it now and spend our efforts more profitably. Otherwise, let's dig deeper and see how close a fit we might have.
- Have I analyzed this component enough to feel reasonably confident that the implementors will be able to adapt it into the new solution? If so, we can stop here and leave it to the implementors. Be careful here, though. You cannot make this decision on purely technical grounds. Of equal weight are the capabilities, maturity, and cultural biases of the implementation team. If team members have a history of NIH (not invented here) behavior, you will need to dot the i's and cross the t's. Better still, make arrangements with the manager of the deployment stage to load the dice in your favor. What you want is for any existing staff with emotional investment in the component to be engaged to wrap it so as to present precisely the desired interfaces to the new solution.
- Can this functionality be incorporated into the new solution if we go back and modify the IS model, and by implication the dependent business processes, to accommodate it? Is the resulting trade-off desirable and acceptable? This kind of trade-off is precisely what the "architectural way" is about, in the sense of making use of available components—the *common-component sense* of "architecture" from Chapter 2. Recall that the essence of the architectural solution-building approach is to craft a solution from existing, available, proven components, resorting to development only when ready-made components cannot be obtained. Using this approach, we expect to cause feedback ripples as we make compromises in component selection to accommodate available components.

8.6.2   Nonfunctional attributes

There is more to assessing an IS component than comparing its functionality—that is, its black-box behavior as observed by a client—with the functional requirements of the new solution. We must also consider other aspects of behavior, which we'll refer to as *nonfunctional attributes.* In this category are such attributes as:

- operational cost—including both the direct expenses of the underlying infrastructure and platform and the ongoing maintenance expense
- security
- performance (response time and throughput)
- scalability
- bug density
- reliability (that is, it keeps working)
- robustness (when it fails, it does so in a sensible way, doesn't cause collateral damage to the IS ecosystem, and gives helpful clues about what went wrong)
- manageability (management interfaces, interfaces to management platforms, and ability to run unattended)
- modularity and extensibility
- maintainability and comprehensibility (implementation language and development system factor into this attribute)
- portability
- backup and restore characteristics
- [interoperability]

"Interoperability" is in brackets because it's preferable to regard it as an attribute of the primary functionality—in other words, the business of using the service that a component provides includes the communication channel that carries the request and response. For example, the local post office provides a service that allows me to buy stamps. Transacting the business using English is part of the defined interface and therefore a functional consideration. However, in some situations, a component may provide functionality through alternative channels—for example, through a GUI, through an API, or through a communications protocol—and it may be more natural to treat the capability to communicate through alternative channels as a nonfunctional attribute for the purposes of the assessment.

The relative importance of the nonfunctional attributes depends on the principles embodied in the IS strategy (which will normally address many of these nonfunctional attributes directly) and on the closeness of fit of the functionality with the desired functionality. The assessment demands a high degree of knowledge and judgment. Suppose the team has identified a component as having suitable functionality for reuse in the new solution. However, the implementation of the component limits its scalability, and it will need to be modified to sit on more solid infrastructure if it is to be a player in the new solution. Do we go ahead and upgrade it? That decision in turn depends on its maintainability and comprehensibility. If the component hasn't been touched in the two years since Joe left, and Joe was a known maverick, then it may be quite risky to attempt the upgrade.

You will need to weigh all of these nonfunctional attributes in making the assessment, using your experience and judgment to evaluate the complex interactions among the various qualities.

8.6.3   Human resource capabilities

You will need to assess the breadth and depth of capability in the IS organization, and its ability to grow and expand its capability, against the demands expected from the solution-building program. Reuse of existing IS assets and orderly transition to full deployment of new IS functionality will need commitment from those with knowledge and experience in the existing IS environment. Assembling and developing components of the new solution may require use of skills and tools that are new to existing staff, and education programs will need to be put in place.

8.6.4   Outsourced services

The team should assess outsourced services in light of the IS strategy and the IS model. It may be possible to identify potential overlap of services currently outsourced with services proposed in the new solution. Conversely, you may be able to expand the role of current outsourcing vendors to obtain nonstrategic services—those of low value to the enterprise—more economically than they could be provided within an internal IS solution.

8.7   Where was the "architecture"?

As in Chapters 6 and 7, we'll conclude by reviewing how the elements of architecture apply to this chapter (see Table 8-1).

TABLE 8-1   Where was the "architecture" in Chapter 8?

Architecture feature	Relationship to this chapter
Solution fitted to client needs	Not applicable to the current IS analysis stage
Empirically validated principles	Not applicable to the current IS analysis stage

TABLE 8-1   Where was the "architecture" in Chapter 8? (*continued*)

Architecture feature	Relationship to this chapter
Design and implementation principles and guidelines	Not really applicable to the current IS analysis stage, although we can see the principle of iterative development (one of the axiomatic principles) in the feedback loop to IS modeling
Components, patterns, and frameworks	This chapter proposed the use of a framework—not a particular framework, but one of your own choosing—to help understand the existing IT environment. Existing IS functionality and IT assets are inventoried and assessed in this stage. This knowledge potentially allows existing assets to serve as prebuilt components in the new solution.
Conceptual integrity and elegance	The current IS analysis stage is one of discovery rather than one of application. We can assess the presence or absence of conceptual integrity and elegance as we conduct this stage. Our findings may suggest subprojects for the solution-building effort to improve these qualities in the existing IT environment.
Formal description and recording	For effective support of the later stages of solution building, the current IS analysis needs to be documented in a user-friendly and accessible way. The notion of the architectural framework helps organize the information collected.

9

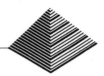

IS Architecture Planning

This chapter describes the IS architecture planning stage. In this stage, we further develop the IS solution design and its supporting technical infrastructure to fulfill the requirements expressed by the IS ideal-object model.

This IS architecture planning stage must develop a model sufficiently detailed to support directly the production of source code. In terms of the OO model set, this model is the *real-object model*. Derived from the ideal-object model, it reflects the impact of real-world constraints and implementation decisions.

An overarching consideration guiding the IS architecture planning stage is the requirement for conceptual integrity, deriving from a clean structure that allows the rapid change and evolution of the IS system built around it.

9.1   IS architecture planning in the context of the total process

9.1.1   Relation to other stages

Figure 9-1 illustrates the relationship of the IS architecture planning stage to other stages of the seven-stage solution-building process. Figure 9-2 expands on the contextual picture by showing the deliverables that flow among the related stages, as well as an overview of the principal activities of the IS architecture planning stage. The deliverables from IS architecture planning are

- the real-object model, which expresses the required application-level functionality
- a set of architectural principles, which
  - guide and constrain the selection of infrastructure technologies
  - provide policies and guidelines to guide the implementation and deployment of the design represented by the real-object model.

Relation to IS modeling   The IS strategy and the IS model, which are developed in the IS modeling stage, are the primary inputs on which the IS architecture planning stage is based.

Relation to current IS analysis   The current IS inventory and the current IS assessment contribute to the formulation of the architectural principles on which the new solution will be based. The real-object model, which is developed in the architecture planning stage, extends the IS model from the IS modeling stage with practical considerations, some or many of which will be derived from consideration of the current IS environment.

Relation to implementation planning   Both the architectural principles and the real-object model, which are developed in the IS architecture planning stage, are primary inputs to the implementation planning stage.

Relation to deployment   The IS real-object model defines the functionality that must be built and therefore is primary input to the deployment phase.

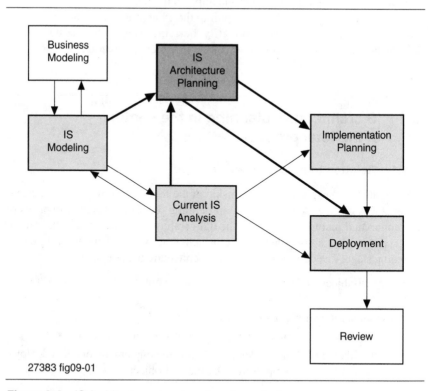

27383 fig09-01

Figure 9-1   IS Architecture planning stage in context.

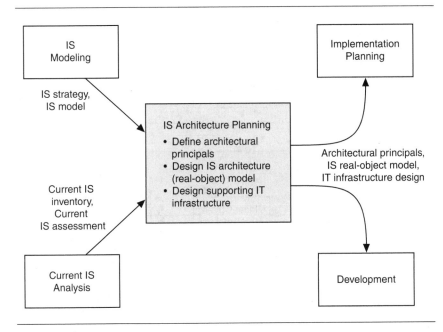

Figure 9-2   Overview of the IS architecture planning stage.

9.1.2   Relation to the OO model set

Figure 9-3 shows the mapping between the IS architecture planning stage and the associated object model in the OO model set, showing that the real-object model of the OO model set is produced in the IS architecture planning stage.

9.1.3   Participants

Information systems professionals on the solution-building planning team have the primary responsibility for completing the IS architecture planning stage. During this stage, the team works with the following people:

- users within the enterprise, to determine the business functions they perform and their information technology needs. The architecture planning team uses this information to design the IS model.
- technical specialists, to understand specific information technologies. The architecture planning team uses the knowledge of the technical specialists to make appropriate technology choices.
- IS managers, to provide continuity with the IS modeling stage and ensure consistency from a management viewpoint. This viewpoint will influence the formulation of architectural principles.

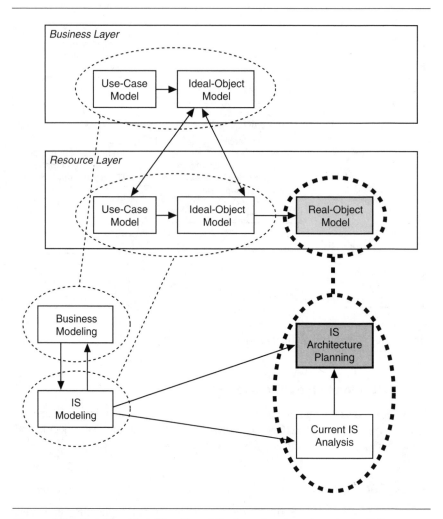

Figure 9-3   Relationship of the IS architecture planning stage to the OO model set.

9.2   Architectural principles

Architectural principles are statements that set ground rules and guidelines governing the building of information systems to serve the enterprise. Based on the business and IS strategy of the enterprise, principles describe the enterprise's philosophy, objectives, and architectural direction. More-specific architectural principles describe technology or business-related constraints and specific technology choices made within those constraints.

Architectural principles govern the translation of the business and IS strategy of the enterprise into language that the IS professionals can use to select and manage information technology. Specifically, architectural principles help an enterprise to:

- evaluate existing technology.
- make technology choices.
- achieve consensus on the technical direction of its information technology.
- design and implement specific information systems.
- ensure consistency among information systems. Principles constrain or encourage conceptual integrity. They provide boundaries within which the solution will be framed, thus constraining the mechanisms that will be used.

Principles can be thought of either as mandatory—in which case we refer to them as "policies"—or as recommended—in which case they become "guidelines." You would lean toward guidelines over policies where the context is complex or unclear and flexibility may be required.

A principle can be classified as a guideline by one enterprise and as a policy by another enterprise. Whether a principle is a policy or a guideline depends on the situation within the enterprise. For example, the principle "All workstations should be upgraded on a three-year cycle" is classified as a policy principle by one enterprise because it wants its IS department to ensure that end-user productivity is not hampered because of working with outdated equipment. But another enterprise classifies the same principle as a guideline because it wants the IS department to upgrade workstations only if the upgrade is of clearly higher budget priority than competing claims on available funds.

9.2.1   How are principles defined?

Definition of principles happens on two levels:

- at the IS strategy level
- at the IS architecture level

Not every facet of IS decision-making is going to go through both levels of definition. Some strategic-level decisions may not need any further refinement.

IS strategy is a set of high-level positions on the overall direction and priorities for IS as it relates to the needs of the business. Decisions made at this level may reach down into IS architecture in areas where senior management regard such decisions as having long-term impact on the IS environment and its alignment with the business.

Principles at the architectural level define a set of policies and guidelines within which the IS solution will be built. They are expressed at a level appropriate for gaining consensus from the interested stakeholders, who at this level include mid-level managers from both the business and IS sides and the key technical leaders.

Each principle enunciation has a corresponding rationale and corresponding implications. The rationale is a short paragraph that expands the principle and explains its need or purpose and what alternatives were discussed. The rationale helps both the business and technical managers understand the basis of the principle. It also reminds everyone why the principle is necessary. An implication describes the impact the principle will have on the enterprise, its IS organization, and its policies. To be useful to the enterprise, the principle must have one or more implications.

At the IS architecture planning stage, principles derive from two primary sources:

- the IS strategy
- principles guiding technology choices or representing actual technology choices

Principles as a refinement of IS strategy   Viewed in the context of the OO model set, principles can be seen as additional information, orthogonal to the models themselves, that gives the additional guidance we need to press forward with the IS solution described in the models. In many cases, principles may be refinements of statements taken from the IS strategy produced in the IS modeling stage. For example, an IS strategy statement may declare that *Solution modeling, design, and development will be done under an overarching component-based development environment.*

This is a high-level statement at an appropriate level of abstraction for establishing the strategic direction. However, we need to refine it into some actionable set of principles before we can meaningfully conform to it. We might refine this statement by constructing the following principles.

- Business modeling and IS modeling will be done using automated tools based on a repository.
- New application functionality will be developed in Java.
- The component run-time infrastructure will be J2EE (Java 2 Platform, Enterprise Edition).

In drawing up principles, there is no one-size-fits-all formula that determines what level of specificity is appropriate to which stage of the solution-building process. Thus, two different enterprises may define the same principle at different levels, at different stages of the solution-building process. For example, here we have shown a principle that defines J2EE to be the choice for component infrastructure. Another enterprise may make this same decision, *but at the IS strategy level.* The higher-level choice would be appropriate where, for example, strong vendor relationships and existing investment dictated the elevation of this technology choice to an enterprise strategic level. Conversely, the choice of Java as the preferred development language for one enterprise may be inappropriately constraining for another enterprise, which may prefer to make the choice of implementation language on a project-by-project basis.

Nonfunctional attributes An important source of architectural principles is the need to be specific about the requirements for the *nonfunctional attributes* of the IS solution. We encountered nonfunctional attributes in Section 8.6.2 in the context of the current IS analysis stage. In formulating architectural principles, we need to be explicit about the requirements we may have for these nonfunctional aspects. By their nature, they cannot reasonably be captured in the IS model.

Principles and technology choices Principles regarding technology choices will represent both guidelines for making technology choices and actual technology choices themselves. Where technology choices are going to have far-reaching effects, it is appropriate to make such choices at the IS architecture planning stage, or even earlier, in the IS strategy. The choice of a particular component-based development and run-time environment is an example of a technology choice that many enterprises would find appropriate to make at this level.

An architectural framework, such as we discussed in Chapter 8, is a useful aid in drawing up principles concerning technology choices. The framework is a structuring device that maps the areas within which principles may need to be formulated. The information carried in, and referenced through, the framework makes for easier understanding of the applicability, relevance, and interrelationships of the principles.

An e-business solution is going to involve many decisions on which technology to choose from competing alternatives. Often, multiple competing technologies need to appear in the total solution, as the enterprise adapts or migrates from current systems. Technology choices are usually complex, involving many trade-offs. By its nature, e-business is a turbulent area, as established businesses jockey for competitive position with each other and new Internet-based upstarts, and competing technology vendors all strive to provide better e-business tools than their own competition.

Making the right technology choices is an important factor in how flexible and agile your e-business solution is going to be. These determinations are a job for the highly skilled. You want your very best people defining your technology infrastructure and indeed your architectural principles in general. The best people are those who know the technology landscape, obviously, but just as importantly, you need people who see the big picture. You want people who see the structure of the forest, not the ones who spend all their energies studying the bark and leaves of individual trees. Using these qualities as the criteria, make sure you staff the architectural-principle definition activity with the people from the thin, right-hand end of the bell curve.

The following are examples of the kinds of principles that might be defined in the IS architecture planning stage:

- Business modeling will be done using SELECT Enterprise.
- IS modeling will be done using Rational Rose.

- All models will be maintained by the Unisys e-@ction Meta Data Engine.
- All modeling and development tools will be compatible with the XML meta data interchange standard (XMI) and the Unisys e-@ction Meta Data Engine.
- New application functionality will be developed in Java.
- The component run-time infrastructure will be Java 2 Enterprise Edition (J2EE).

9.2.2   Guidelines for writing principles

We must recognize that the definition of principles is an iterative process throughout the architecture planning stage. On the one hand, we may find ourselves trying to make a decision in a vacuum, in an area not addressed by any guiding principle. On the other hand, we may find that the best architectural decision conflicts with one or more of our principles.

In the first case, we may choose to spend time and effort understanding the general problem, abstracting to the highest level sensible in order to construct the most general principle that will guide an appropriate decision. In the second case, we may choose to revisit the conflicting principles and revise them to be consistent with our newfound insight.

Our architectural principles are going to help implement the stated IS strategy as well as fill in the necessary information to allow the realization of the real-object model as a working IS business solution. The architectural principles therefore are central to the progress of the solution-building effort, and we must have buy-in from all stakeholders. Defining principles is a consensus-building process. We should not regard our architectural principles as being established until we have validated them with the stakeholders affected by them or having a material interest in them. Interested stakeholders will likely involve at least these people:

- the team that produced the IS Strategy document
- senior and mid-level business management
- IS development managers
- key IS technical leaders
- administrators who will manage the system

Principles of principle writing   Principles must be well-written if they are to serve their intended purpose. There follows a list of useful rules of thumb to assist in the formulation of principles.

- Don't write redundant principles. A principle is redundant if it is covered, implicitly or explicitly, by a more generic principle. For example, a principle that says "Enterprise applications will run on industry-standard middleware" is implicit in the "architectural way" summarized in Chapter 2 and is not specific enough to add further value.

- Write a limited number of principles. Define enough principles so that the vision and intent of the enterprise are clearly articulated, but no more.

- Set a timeframe for this phase to start and stop. Defining principles is a short-term project, measured in weeks rather than months.

- Principles must be easily understood by both technical and business managers.

- A principle should represent a choice or decision that the enterprise has made.

- Principles should be neither too specific—for example, too product-oriented—nor too general. For example, the principle "All development will follow standard industry practices" is too general to be of value. A minimum qualifying criterion for a principle is that it must provide useful guidance in decision making.

- Principles should be forward-looking, with a life expectancy of three years or more.

- Principles can usually be stated in one sentence.

Sample principles   This section gives examples of principles. Each principle has its associated rationale and implication. I want to stress that these examples are just that—examples. I am in no way recommending that these example principles are in any way appropriate to any particular solution development. These examples simply show the kinds of decisions that you may want to enshrine as principles. This section thus has a very different motivation from the statement of principles in Section 5.3, which are indeed intended to apply in every architecture-based IS solution.

- **Principle**—Authentication services will provide a user profile that identifies the users and their access to system resources.
  - **Rationale**—This service allows system access to be customized for each user. Users will not be tied to a physical location and can access the system from anywhere.
  - **Implications**—This principle implies significant constraints on the end-user client software environment. Possible approaches are
    ◊ standardized workstation software environment, with user configuration being downloaded from centralized repository on sign-on
    ◊ dynamic construction of end-user software environment upon sign-on
    ◊ "thin client" workstations, with generic software in each workstation
  - **Comment**—this is a good example of a principle that may appear at different stages for different organizations. For example, to some enterprises, this principle may represent a fundamental business imperative

because of flexibility and security requirements and would thus ideally be reflected in the business model or IS strategy. For other enterprises, the requirement may stem from an IT management requirement to simplify administration of moves, adds, and changes in the IT user population, rather than from high-level business considerations, and thus would not surface until the IS architecture planning stage.

* **Principle**—Data will be centralized, although each business unit will own its own data.

  - **Rationale**—Centralization affords the greatest operational economies of scale. Autonomous business unit data ownership corresponds to the overall management structure of the company.

  - **Implication**—Divisions will have to be trained in database management. The IS department will have to make sure all divisions have access to the appropriate data. Business unit autonomy increases the possibility of redundant data.

* **Principle**—The software development methodology will allow multiple languages to be used for the final implementation.

  - **Rationale**—Use of multiple languages prevents the company from being tied to one specific language.

  - **Implication**—Development environments must provide for implementation in multiple languages.

* **Principle**—File and print servers for general use will be based on Microsoft Windows NT.

  - **Rationale**—Standardizing on NT will simplify operations and support, on both the servers themselves and the client workstations.

  - **Implication**—Existing Novell NetWare and Unix NFS servers will be replaced by Windows NT servers.

  - **Comment**—This is a very product-specific principle, apparently violating one of our rules of thumb for writing principles. Such a principle would appear at this level only if the decision had been made at a relatively high level in the management hierarchy, usually for business and financial reasons rather than technical considerations.

* **Principle**—E-business solutions will be built around those protocols and interfaces that have achieved significant market penetration and therefore promise the greatest capability to interoperate with complementary as well as competitive products.

  - **Rationales**

    ◊ E-business is all about interaction. Without the capability of interoperating with our business partners, we simply do not have the prerequisites for conducting e-business.

    ◊ We must also pay attention to the internally facing interfaces of our IS system—for example, the system management and administration facilities. Conformance to predominant industry standards is important here, because it gives us the widest choice of ancillary tools.

– **Implication**—We need to take inventory of the standards—de facto and formal—deployed in the industry and choose those to which our solution will conform.

– **Comment**—This is a rather obvious requirement, so much so that much of the requirement is being fulfilled by application server platforms and application integration solutions. Applying this principle in practice would likely be a factor in choosing specific application server and application integration products.

9.3   Defining architecture models

The IS architecture model is one of the essential outcomes of the architecture planning stage. In Jacobson's terminology [Jacobson et al. 1994], the IS architecture model corresponds to the real-object model.

The IS model discussed in Chapter 7 is an *ideal-object* model in the sense that it embodies an idealized view of what the business model requires of the information system, unsullied by considerations of—and therefore unaffected by subsequent changes in—development tools or implementation environments and platforms.

In contrast, the purpose of the *real-object model* is to serve as the basis for implementation. It is therefore strongly influenced by development tools and implementation environments. Indeed, the real-object model embodies decisions made about such practical details through application of the principles developed in the first phase of the IS architecture stage.

The form and content of the IS architecture model is going to be strongly influenced by the overall project context, specifically by:

• the scope of the overall project. At what point does it lie on the continuum between full-scale business process reengineering and a tactical narrow-focus incremental improvement? (Refer to Figure 4-2.)

• the existing models and documentation constructed during the development of the existing system.

The larger the scope of the project, and the lower the maturity of the existing models, the more it is appropriate to lean toward replacing existing models with new ones. At the other end of the spectrum, mature existing models and a narrower project scope would argue more for retention of existing models.

The material that follows is written with the assumption that new models will be constructed. In light of considerations of the impact of project context, you may need to make considerable adaptations to arrive at an approach suitable for any given situation.

9.3.1 Forks in the road: solution alternatives

In building a real-object model, you will be continually evaluating alternative designs and alternative technology approaches and techniques. Making these choices among all the competing alternatives is what design is all about. Most of the time, you'll make the choices as you go, because one choice will stand out as being clearly superior in its appropriateness and cost-effectiveness. However, there will be situations where alternatives need to be evaluated in light of more-detailed information, which means you'll have to pursue each alternative far enough to develop the data you'll need to support a decision. For example, should you use a distributed directory, or would a centralized database be more appropriate? Should you use smart cards for customer or employee authentication, or is the cost and inconvenience out of line with the benefit, leading you to stay with user names and passwords? These are examples of decisions for which the real-object model might need to be pursued for both alternatives, to be sure of identifying all the implications that could have a bearing on a properly informed decision.

Having analyzed competing alternatives in sufficient depth, the implementation planning stage is where you ultimately make the difficult choices among competing alternatives, through analysis of their relative costs, benefits, and risks.

As with the forks in the road we saw in IS modeling in Chapter 7, we're almost always better off making these decisions on the basis of what we know at this stage. Carrying forward these decisions to the later stages runs the risk of analysis paralysis and in any event must slow down the project. It may be essential to do quickly something that works, rather than determine the "best" solution and deploy it three months later.[1]

9.3.2 Architecture models for object-oriented development environments

Ideally, both our business model and our IS model are object-oriented. These models flow into software development most naturally when the software development environment is itself object-oriented. A pervasive object orientation helps us avoid the pitfalls so commonly suffered through the translation of business requirements into IT artifacts, which is the "semantic gap" problem we saw in Chapter 3. Use of an object-oriented *development* environment effectively automates much of this troublesome translation by encapsulating and automating

---

[1]By advising a quick solution rather than the "best" solution, I am emphatically *not* proposing a quick-and-nasty solution that ignores architectural principles. I *am* proposing that you choose between competing alternatives based on the level of detail available at this stage. It's implicit that all competing alternatives are equally clean in an architectural sense.

many IT decisions, such as what flavor of middleware and APIs should be employed.

A *real-object model* is necessarily sufficiently detailed that it can directly support the production of executable software. The model will therefore need to invent objects that represent artifacts of implementation and that do not correspond directly to business concepts. The choice of these implementation objects and how they interact is the essence of what concerns us in producing the real-object model. The explicit recognition of a relational database in the IS design is an example of the kind of decision that goes into the real-object model.

In general, the technique for incorporating non–object-oriented aspects is to create object classes that represent them. Thus, paradoxically, we represent non–object-oriented artifacts as objects in our real-world model. Booch [1994, Chapter 10] presents an example of this technique, where he develops a model of a client–server system that explicitly uses a relational database. In a pure object-oriented environment, the existence of the relational database would be hidden from the application developer, who would see the world as a collection of object classes, object instances, and their attributes and methods. By recognizing explicitly that certain object classes will have their attributes held in a relational database, rather than being encapsulated in object instances, we introduce into our real-world model object classes that explicitly refer to artifacts of the relational database, such as the database itself and the tables, records, and relations within it.[2]

Pursuing this example a little further, it is worth pointing out that the decision to recognize explicitly the existence of the relational database will have been documented in earlier stages of the development—perhaps in the IS strategy, perhaps in the formulation of principles, and most usually as a result of the existence of a relational database in the current IS environment.

In keeping with our architectural philosophy, we want to employ components, prebuilt assemblies, and frameworks in building the architecture model, rather than handcrafting the source code line by line. To fill this need, environments for application engineering and development are available from a variety of vendors. The pace of technology evolution is rapid, as is consolidation among vendors. The choice of application development environment is a significant one and warrants consideration in the IS strategy deliberations. In any event, this decision should be resolved before or during the formulation of architectural principles.

This general area—application engineering through prebuilt components—has been growing from complementary starting points. On the one hand, the "fourth-generation" languages (4GLs) that emerged in the 1980s provide highly efficient means for application engineers to build applications through high-level constructs. These high-level constructs are effectively prebuilt components that

---

[2]At the risk of wandering beyond the scope of this book, I must mention that the problem of interfacing object-oriented systems with relational databases is a well-known discontinuity that many developments will face. For an architectural approach to this problem, see the white paper *Integrating Object and Relational Technologies,* by Rational Software Corporation, at *http://www.rational.com/sitewide/ support/whitepapers/dynamic.jtmpl?doc_key=296*

generate equivalent tracts of third-generation language (3GL) source code. In addition, the development environment provides standard infrastructure software to interface the generated application software components to its surrounding run-time environment, such as databases, networks, interprocess communications, transaction environments, and so on.

On the other hand, the application server environments that emerged in the late 1990s grew "upward" from origins in integrating middleware, fueled by the needs of e-business. To allow application engineers to take maximum advantage of the integrating middleware environments, it was natural for application server vendors to extend their product lines up into the application environment space, thus competing in the same space as the 4GLs.

What does all this mean for the architecture model in the context of architectural object-oriented solution building? In practical terms, it means that some of the decisions that a designer would need to make in building a real-object model become subsumed by the application engineering environment. The boundary between the ideal-object model and the real-object model becomes blurred. This boundary is determined by the design tools and application engineering environment you select. In the limit, all the decisions that take you from the ideal-object model to the real-object model may be conveniently handled within the application engineering environment.

9.3.3 Architecture models for non–object-oriented development environments

Object-oriented development technology has not yet (as of the year 2000) attained the degree of acceptance that would allow us to be confident of being able to work in pure object-oriented methods throughout the IS solution life cycle. At the point where we need to begin designing models that can directly guide the implementation, in practice we are often going to have to make some concessions to non–object-oriented concepts. Object-oriented developments are the norm in e-business developments, because the platform we'd like to choose is the application server platform, which by its nature is a component-based (and therefore object-oriented) environment. However, in projects fitting the Incremental Improvement Paradigm, we will probably need to accommodate non–object-oriented development systems.

We will begin our discussion of non–object-oriented environments with a reprise of some observations from Section 3.5.2:

> *the difference between an object-oriented environment and a non–object-oriented environment lies more in the* mindset of its users *than in the* inherent capabilities of the tools *or the characteristics of the delivered designs and systems*

One corollary is that it is quite possible for developers with the "wrong" (non–object-oriented) mindset to completely subvert the object orientation of their tools and produce horrible designs with all the built-in problems that object orientation is intended to solve.

The more positive corollary is that it is quite feasible and practical to apply an object-oriented mindset in working with development tools that are themselves non–object-oriented. And indeed, that is the mindset we need. What, then, are the essential differences between object-oriented and non–object-oriented development environments?

An object-oriented development environment

- provides a framework that encourages designers to think in object-oriented terms, to design systems with conceptual integrity and clear separation of function from internal implementation.
- provides substantial assistance to the developer in automating the production of executable software from the object-oriented model. Interface logic, and the underlying middleware, are generated by the object-oriented environment—oops! I really mean the *component-based development environment*[3]—without consuming precious developer brain cycles.

What do we do when our tools and existing environment are non–object-oriented? We have to create a conceptually object-oriented environment out of what we have. Rather than having the benefits of an object-oriented design environment provided to us automatically, we have to use the available tools with a disciplined mindset to compensate for the inherently non–object-oriented nature of the tools. We have to apply consciously the clear separation of function (that is, external interface) from internal implementation. We will need to think harder about *information hiding*[4] in designing a flexible system that is robust in the face of change.

In the run-time environment, we'll need to choose our own integration middleware rather than have such choices made inherently in the development environment. Here, we'll need to pay attention to *conceptual integrity,* making sure we use the same mechanisms for similar purposes wherever they arise.

9.4   Defining supporting IT infrastructure

In Chapter 8, we saw how an architectural framework assists in the solution-building process. We used the architectural framework in structuring our analysis of the existing IS environment. In the same way, we use the architectural framework as the central reference model to help us define the technical infrastructure to support our applications. For ease of reference, the same example architectural framework diagram shown in Figure 8-3 appears in Figure 9-4.

---

[3]The "oops!" is a reference to the explanation of the distinction between "components" and "objects" in Section 3.4.

[4]The information-hiding principle is almost a corollary of the principle of separation of interface and implementation and is discussed in that context in Section 2.4.2.

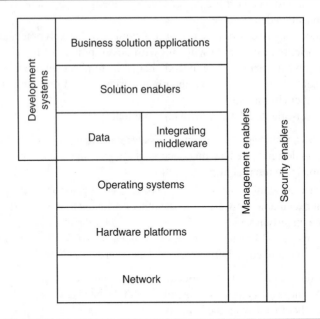

Figure 9–4 Example architectural framework.

Defining the supporting infrastructure is going to involve an exercise similar to the one we went through in constructing the current IS inventory. This time, of course, we're defining our future desired infrastructure rather than the current installed infrastructure. Once again, we use the framework as a checklist and organizing device.

In each area of the framework, we make technology choices according to:

- the architectural principles we defined in the first part of the IS architecture planning stage
- the requirements of reused, or packaged, application-level components

Conflicts will sometimes occur. For example, a packaged solution that we chose, based on its fit with our business processes, may turn out to be incompatible with our preferred infrastructure direction. In these cases, we have to examine the trade-offs and make the best compromise. Do we reconsider the application package? Do we try to find a way to have the two infrastructure environments interoperate? Or can we wrap the incompatible application so that it operates within our preferred infrastructure environment? Each case needs to be decided on its own merits.

In practice, of course, we usually know enough about packaged solutions that we implicitly take into account their infrastructure requirements as part of the selection process at the IS modeling stage. Where the technical infrastructure direction is unclear, however, we may well find ourselves dealing with these kinds of issues late in the solution-building process.

Using the architectural framework as a basis for technology selection makes for an orderly entry into the implementation planning stage. We have both the current IS environment and the desired IS environment expressed according to the same structure. It is therefore easy to see where the differences are and to assess what is going to be involved in the transition.

9.4.1 Technology evaluation criteria and considerations

Table 9-1 lists some considerations that the team can apply to help in making technology decisions and weighing trade-offs.

TABLE 9-1   Technology evaluation criteria and considerations

Criteria	Considerations
Level of consensus	Is the technology based on an accepted standard and available across applicable hardware and software platforms? What other standards compete in the same space? What is the outlook for competing standards? (Recall from Chapter 2 that leading-edge technology that will give you the more significant competitive advantage is going to be—by its nature—proprietary, or based on standards that enjoy vigorous competition. Choices are not easy in this space, but you're going to have to make them anyway.)
Product availability	Is there a wide variety of products available from various viable vendors across different platforms? Are proprietary products readily available?
Completeness	To what degree does the technology cover the key features needed to support the application components of the IS model?
Maturity	If the technology is based on a reference model, is the reference model well understood? Are appropriate concepts of the technology in widespread use?
Stability	What degree of flux is expected in the future? Are there incompatibilities between current and future releases of the technology?
Problems and limitations	Are there restrictions on the use or capabilities of the standard (for example, are intellectual property rights an issue?) Are there known problems too numerous or difficult to overcome?

9.4.2   Filling technology gaps

The results of the preceding evaluation will indicate that the technology is

- **Currently defined and available.** The team can safely make substantial investments and long-term plans with this technology. However, as we saw in Chapter 2, stable technology is likely to apply to lower-value strata of the IS solution.
- **Emerging and turbulent.** High-value IS solutions are, by their nature, at the leading edge of innovation. The state of supporting technology is likely to be turbulent, featuring several competing and broadly incompatible models. It is here that you must make your most critical judgments. Backing a loser is likely to be expensive if its ecosystem later disappears in the competitive maelstrom, forcing a conversion to the eventual victor.

Choosing technology undergoing the emerging and turbulent phase will likely require you to provide some custom bridging of your own, especially where interfacing to existing assets (often referred to as "legacy systems") is concerned. The bad side of this situation is that the decision making is complex and the development expensive. The positive side is that this is where the greatest potential exists for realizing significant competitive advantage. If this stuff were easy, anyone could do it. Your IT excellence and capability to execute are the keys to getting ahead of your competition.

9.4.3   Identifying hardware and software products

The final act of IT infrastructure definition is the process of identifying the hardware and software products that the application components of the IS model need in order to be successfully deployed. Guided by the principles of the IS strategy, as further refined in the principle-definition phase of IS architecture planning, the team evaluates available products against the technological criteria crystallized in the previous phases of technology infrastructure definition. At the product-selection stage, it may be appropriate to revisit the architectural principles if the team finds itself without an adequate framework for decision making. The team should ideally capture the logic used in resolving this kind of decision and consider carefully whether there is value in abstracting that logic to an appropriate level, and thus define a new principle.

9.5   IT infrastructure for e-business

This is not a book that gets very far into technology details. Obviously, any attempt to describe, in any amount of detail, the information technologies that could be attached to the example architectural framework would run to many volumes of description and many lists of references. In general, the scope of this book extends to the depth of giving an example framework, and no further.

However, e-business displays some particular characteristics that distinguish it from the information systems of the disconnected past. These characteristics place different demands on the underlying technology—or rather, the set of demands is the same, but the relative emphasis is shifted. In this section, we'll look at the environmental influences on e-business and the ways in which the technology has adapted in responding to those influences.

9.5.1   Environmental influences on e-business technology

In the world of living things, organisms adapt to their environments or perish. IT infrastructure has performed a similar organism-like transformation to respond to its shifting environment. Some characteristics of e-business are so hugely exaggerated in comparison with plain old IS-as-we-knew-it that they radically alter the nature of the beast. Just as bears trapped in the polar north evolved with thick white fur coats, e-business technology has evolved its own set of responses to its challenging new environment.

Interoperation is everything in the e-business environment. The very essence of e-business is communication and interaction. If you can't interoperate, you can't communicate or interact, and so you can't do e-business. This situation is very different from the way IT products, and products in general, normally evolve. As we discussed in Chapter 2, the introduction of a technology category normally involves many competing and noninteroperable standards, as the early entrants seek to build and promote their "best of breed" product suite in the new category. Eventually, the technology category becomes more valuable with interoperation capability, a small number of standards take hold, and product differentiation battles move to other fields. In the e-business arena, the situation is upside down. Because interoperation is the *sine qua non* of e-business, e-business technology vendors were constrained to provide interoperability from the very beginning. Standards to provide the required interenterprise interoperability are being developed and promoted by such industry consortia as Oasis (*http://www.oasis-open.org/*) and RosettaNet (*http://www. rosettanet.org/*).

Speed of development and deployment is essential. E-business has arrived with startling suddenness. Brand-new upstarts are challenging established businesses in just about every sector of the economy. You really don't have a choice about e-business. You have to do it. You have to do it now. And you have to do it fast.

A large customer base for e-business infrastructure vendors is a natural consequence of the first two characteristics. Recognizing the e-business imperative, a large number of enterprises are involved in, or are preparing to be involved in, e-business enabling themselves. Responding to the need to act quickly, enterprises are building e-business solutions on "standard"[5] frameworks, the basis of which is the *application server,* a technology class that we'll discuss shortly. The "standard" nature of the frameworks attracts customers and vendors alike, causing a positive-feedback loop. A larger customer base encourages the development of more products; a more complete line of interoperable products creates more potential customers.

Traffic loads are at best difficult to predict and at worst impossible. When you open for business to a national or even international consumer audience, you usually can't predict with any certainty what volume of sales you're going to attract. Aggravating the uncertainty is the phenomenon of supply-created demand, which we saw in Chapter 6, where the availability of a new product or service creates a demand impossible to project from previously measured customer behavior and preferences.

In the e-commerce world, it has been observed that you have a good chance of losing the sale to a competitor if your Web site keeps your customer waiting more than seven seconds (there's that number seven again). You probably don't want to invest vast sums on a huge server farm—if you build it, they may not come. On the other hand, if they come, and you haven't built it, they won't stay and most likely won't come back. The reality is that when it comes to e-commerce, scalability and availability are not optional. It pays to overbuild for traffic you don't expect. Order-of-magnitude growth is normal in e-commerce,

The 7-second knockout.

[5]The quotes around "standard" refer to the *de facto* status of these framework architectures, which are controlled by individual vendors rather than standards bodies or even multivendor consortia. At the time of writing, competing product suites based on the same architecture have generally not yet achieved transparent interoperability within the *intra*enterprise environment.

and unpredictable demand spikes of two orders of magnitude are not uncommon. Overprovisioning and built-in scalability—providing for rapid expansion of capacity—are less expensive than starting afresh.

Customer expectations in conducting e-business will continue to rise and will continue to stimulate the development of technology to satisfy those expectations. Here in this technology chapter, we're not talking about the business functionality facing the customer. Rather, we're concerned with the nonfunctional qualities of the e-business experience, particularly system availability and security. Customers expect your system to be available for business 24 hours a day, 365 days a year. They have no patience for scheduled downtime, taking the system offline for backups, system crashes, backhoe cuts on the communications lines, power failures, or anything else that interrupts service. Customers also expect security. They don't want personal information flowing between your server and their browsers in the clear, for any interloper and Echelon[6] to snoop on.

9.5.2   E-business technology: its responses to environmental demands

To set the context for this discussion, let's return to the example architectural framework shown in Figure 9-4. Again, I stress that this framework is an *example* and that I'm in no way promoting it as the definitive framework that you should adopt. This framework, albeit a nondefinitive one, is helpful in our discussion for the same reasons that a framework is helpful in actual architectural solution building—it helps us structure our thoughts and serves as a comprehensive roadmap of the technology landscape. Although the example framework may not be structured and categorized exactly how you'd like it, it does provide a container for technology categories across the entire e-business and general IS spectrums.

We'll discuss each technology category in turn, as it relates to e-business. Along the way, we'll meet the *application servers* and *enterprise application integration solutions* that are establishing themselves at the epicenter of the e-business explosion.

Business solution applications   Business requirements and supporting application functionality are the subjects of Chapters 6 and 7. With regard to this particular layer of the framework, the effect of the e-business environment drivers is being most felt in the need for interoperation. An enterprise's business applications—be they packaged solutions or various vintages of custom-crafted software—need to work harmoniously together as a precondition for participating in e-business relationships. The need for applications to work "harmoniously together" is also being fueled by the need to integrate custom software with packaged ERP software, which a large number of enterprises have adopted, prompted

---

[6]What's "Echelon"? See Hager [1996] (if you can find it anywhere), or search the Web for "Echelon," "spy," "surveillance," etc. You get the idea.

in part by the need to solve the Y2K problem. Finally, ongoing activity in mergers and acquisitions places many organizations in the situation of having to deal with overlapping and inconsistent application environments.

The holistic technology response to these stimuli has been the emergence of comprehensive solutions for application integration. First known as enterprise application integration (EAI) solutions, these products now take on the challenge of interenterprise integration—which is of course what e-business is all about—and in this context have become known as Internet application integration (IAI). We'll look at application integration solutions shortly, under Integrating middleware.

Solution enablers   The solution enablers layer includes horizontal business components and information interchange facilities. The workflow framework that we've seen several times qualifies as a horizontal business component. General-ized to e-business, a workflow framework would enable interenterprise workflow, and thereby enable interenterprise process integration, allowing such phenomena as virtual companies. Supply-chain integration is another example of an e-business-specific target for horizontal business components.

Information interchange facilities are a central feature of enterprise applica-tion integration (EAI) technologies, which we'll discuss in a subsequent section.

Data   The data category includes databases, data warehouses, directories, and metadata repositories. Of particular interest in the context of e-business are direc-tories and metadata.

A *directory* can be thought of as a set of facilities layered above a set of data-bases. The value added by the directory layer is to provide a scalable, distributed interface to a possibly heterogeneous and distributed collection of underlying databases. The characteristics of a directory make it particularly well suited to finding IT system resources—particularly business services in a generalized e-business environment—and system users in a distributed environment.

Metadata repositories store and manage metadata, which is "data about data." Metadata is key in building adapters for integrating applications by letting them intercommunicate without having to modify the applications themselves, thus adhering to the architectural principle of reuse. We'll discuss these adapters shortly, under Integrating middleware.

Integrating middleware   Integrating middleware is the heart of e-business tech-nology infrastructure. As we saw in Chapter 6, e-business has been a key stimulus for enterprises to integrate their business applications, both within the enterprise and with business partners beyond the enterprise boundary.

Integrating middleware provides a coherent platform—a consistent set of patterns, methods, and templates—on which our enterprise application environ-ment can be supported. It thus conforms to one of our key definitions of "architec-ture." In the absence of such a framework, integrating applications would involve a multitude of ad hoc bilateral interfaces forged one at a time. And indeed, before the arrival of mature integration products, such nonarchitectural approaches were the usual way that pioneer enterprises approached the problem.

As I write this section (in early 2000), integrating middleware is in a state of rapid development and flux. Many vendors are represented in this space—a common indicator of a rapidly growing market—and much consolidation among these vendors is inevitable, and indeed is already in progress. In the present state of evolution, integrating middleware technologies fall roughly into two camps, which are generally referred to as *application servers* and *enterprise application integration solutions*. We'll look at the characteristics of each and then compare them.

Application servers   The term "application server" has been adopted in the industry to refer to a particular set of integrating middleware and supporting functionality. The heart of the application server is the component framework. This segment of the technology spectrum has been reduced essentially to two ecosystems: the Microsoft ecosystem and the Sun ecosystem (or should that be solar system?). The terms used in describing the constituent parts of these ecosystems change continually, and by the time you read this there may well be new terms in the mix. I'll cover the more significant terms that are current at the time of writing.

The Microsoft ecosystem is named DNA (which originally went by the full name "Distributed interNet Applications architecture"). Microsoft is using DNA as an umbrella term to describe a large part of its product line—even including the whole of Windows 2000—but such a broad catch-all isn't very helpful to us in understanding integrating middleware. Focusing down to this integrating middleware piece, the component model at the heart of DNA is COM (Component Object Model), which is sometimes referred to explicitly by its later variants DCOM (distributed COM) and COM+ (DCOM with transaction support). Transaction support is provided by MTS (Microsoft Transaction Service). Store-and-forward messaging (as opposed to synchronously executed remote procedure calls) is provided by MSMQ (Microsoft Message Queue). DNA is available only for Microsoft Windows environments and supports various programming languages.

The Sun ecosystem is currently named J2EE (Java 2 Platform, Enterprise Edition). The component model at the heart of J2EE comprises EJB (Enterprise Java Beans) and a companion Servlet[7] API. Other significant technologies are JNDI (Java Naming and Directory Interface), JTI (Java Transaction API), and CORBA (Common Object Request Broker Architecture), a standard developed by the OMG (Object Management Group), an industry consortium. J2EE implementations are available from a variety of vendors and run on a variety of operating system platforms. At its core, J2EE supports only components written in Java,

---

[7]A "servlet" is a Java component that modifies and extends the behavior of a Web server, analogously to the way an "applet" extends the behavior of a Web browser.

although interconnectivity with non-Java components is provided through CORBA interoperability.

Application servers provide a platform for integrating applications in a *tightly coupled* way. Interacting components are tightly dependent on precise data interchange formats, and operations are performed synchronously, so that transaction semantics and internal state can be maintained with integrity. Tight coupling is best applied within the scope of a single architectural authority, such as within the confines of a business domain within an enterprise. Tightly coupled sets of applications spanning architectural domains are brittle, because changes in one domain can break dependent applications in other domains.

Each of the application server environments provides development tools for the creation of application components and the integration of legacy applications. Legacy integration involves "wrapping" the legacy software with an adapter layer that effectively turns the legacy software into a component, thus providing a service in the application server environment. Because of the tight coupling of the application server environment, the wrapped application is fully able to participate in transactions in which cooperating applications need mutually to synchronize their state.

As well as wrapping legacy applications, J2EE application server environments usually provide connectivity with COM components, thus providing a bridge between the two environments. In a sense, J2EE interoperation with COM components is a special case of interoperation with legacy components, in that it is a way to bring non-native components into the environment.

As we can see, the component model is the nucleus of the application server model. Surrounding this nucleus, it is logical for application server environments to provide functionality that supports e-business in other necessary ways, and application server vendors are indeed building into their products such functionality, which includes the following:

- **Scalability and reliability features.**   Application servers provide scalability through the ability to replicate system components to cope with increased load—which in an e-commerce environment is at best difficult to predict. This same ability to run on replicated components provides reliability and performance management through load balancing, thus avoiding stressing any given system component, which leads to slow response or system failure. Failure of a system component can be handled by switching out the failed component and moving its load to a replicated component.

- **Manageability features.**   These features allow all aspects of the application server to be configured, monitored, and controlled.

- **Development environments.**   Development environments support development teams with visual tools in creating application components, wrapping legacy components, and building Web interfaces.

Enterprise application integration solutions   Where integration is needed across architectural domains—and in e-business, interenterprise integration is what we're aiming for—*loosely coupled* integration is more appropriate than a tightly coupled arrangement.

Enterprise application integration solutions provide a loosely coupled integration in which application components are integrated with a lower degree of mutual dependence on precise details of behavior. Rather than synchronous interactions between components, a component invokes an operation in another component by sending a message. The operation is thus invoked asynchronously—the message may be stored and queued along the way. Furthermore, the target component of the message may be busy, or may not even be running, yet the operation may still be able to complete satisfactorily when the target component resumes. There are situations, of course, in which functionality being integrated inherently calls for tight coupling, yet organizational reality dictates loose coupling. Additional application logic will be necessary in such situations to handle maintenance of state, perform error checking, and maintain integrity.

Application integration solutions provide standardized features for applications to exchange data. These features are built on *metadata* facilities that we saw earlier in the data layer of the framework. XML is becoming dominant as a vehicle for defining standardized information interchange. An application integration framework supports standard XML schemas and provides tools that allow developers to define the required mappings onto the data formats expected by the applications being integrated. Thus, an application being integrated into a cooperating environment does not need to negotiate a bilateral relationship with every other application of interest—it merely translates its external interactions into the standard XML format. This technique can be viewed as an "architectural" one, using a small set of standard patterns rather than a multitude of ad hoc ones.

Another aspect of loose coupling that an application integration solution provides is the message broker. In a tightly coupled integration, a component needs to know the name of the service it wants to call. In a loosely coupled integration with a message broker, an application makes its request by sending a message, in proper standard format, to the message broker. Based on the message content, the message broker forwards the message to the application that can deal with the message. The mechanism may be based on a content-based *publish–subscribe*[8] model, where applications that can deal with particular message types "subscribe" that interest to the message broker. The sending of a message to the broker amounts to the publishing of an event, which the broker passes on to those applications that have subscribed to deal with it.

Up to this point, I have glibly described a loosely coupled integrated application environment interacting through the passing of messages. This tidy scheme would work fine if there were only one messaging software model in the world, but of course there isn't. Message-oriented middleware is still in the noncommodity part of the technology spectrum, so there are competing standards and proprietary models at large. However, technology for performing conversions between

---

[8]See *http://www.research.ibm.com/gryphon/home.html* for a quick overview of publish–subscribe.

message models is available, and enterprise application vendors supply this capability with their solutions.

Application servers and application integration solutions compared
We've seen that application servers represent tightly coupled environments, and that application integration solutions represent loosely coupled environments. In the future, we can expect greater overlap of these categories. Indeed, the trend has already begun. With the support of JMS (Java Messaging Service) in J2EE application servers and the presence of MSMQ (Microsoft Message Queue) in DNA, application servers become well equipped to provide loosely coupled integration. Application server vendors are also developing XML-based features for the creation of data interchange adapters, a key feature of integration solutions.

At the same time, application integration solutions are themselves leveraging more of the underlying technology of application servers. It seems likely that there will be a significant degree of coalescence between these categories. Microsoft already has both models under its DNA umbrella, and IBM has made acquisitions in filling out its product line. We can expect ongoing vendor consolidation and fusing of their offerings.

Development systems   Development tools for e-business, in addition to the familiar facilities required in developing any IS solution, require tools for creating information interchange adapters. These kinds of tools were discussed earlier. They are provided in application server suites and application integration solutions and may be thought of as more appropriately belonging to the solution enablers layer of our example framework.

Management enablers   Application servers generally include management facilities, which allow console monitoring and control over system resources, events, clients, and business components. The management facility may also be capable of being integrated into a more global management environment—through SNMP, for example.

Management capability is a particularly critical consideration. Application, system, and network management are often not given the serious attention they warrant, except as an afterthought. The reality is that e-business systems, with their need for scalability, failover, and 100 percent uptime, place very stringent demands on the systems management environment. E-business deployments often find that that cost of *managing* the system hardware and software assets exceeds the cost of the assets themselves.

Security enablers   Each of the core development systems associated with the application server models provides a rich set of security features to address the security services: authentication, access control, confidentiality (through encryption), and integrity (detection of tampering). Ideally, however, application developers do not need to concern themselves with security. Security is one of the functions provided transparently by the framework. Web servers provide SSL, a security layer that can be inserted underneath HTTP by appropriate configuration and without impact on Web page content or Web-enabled applications.

Within the application server, interactions among components take place over standardized communication mechanisms (such as CORBA IIOP in tightly coupled environments and messaging middleware in loosely coupled environments), and security functionality can be applied to these standard interaction transports. There are, however, issues of security compatibility when bridging between different messaging environments, and early interenterprise integrations have avoided employing a secure messaging envelope.

An approach that has gained currency in loosely coupled interenterprise integrations is to run sensitive communications over an "extranet" or "virtual private network" (VPN), which amounts to a private club of cooperating enterprises using the Internet for their private communications, but with the messages being encrypted and integrity-protected so that only members of the club can read them. This kind of solution works well as long as the club has only a few members. However, as more and more enterprises join the e-business party, everyone will need potentially to do e-business with everyone else—which brings us back to the global Internet we started with.

In a sense, using a VPN is a bit like trying to keep the bad guys off your street when there are an ever-increasing number of people who have legitimate reasons to be on your street. Who's going to distinguish the bad guys from the good guys, and who are you going to rely on to keep the bad guys off the street? Ultimately, you'll have to give up on the street-policing idea and police the door to your house yourself. *You* decide who gets in your door, whichever route the visitor took to get there. The way you make that decision is by looking at the credentials of the would-be communicant, which are provided in the secure envelope of the message. The point is that the validation of credentials needs ultimately to be performed at the application level. However, there is a certain comfort attached to living in a gated community, and VANs (value-added networks) are somewhat analogous in the network world. We'll come back to VANs later when we discuss networks.

Operating systems   Operating systems evolve slowly. Requirements of e-business have been influencing operating system development for some time, and will continue to do so. Perhaps the greatest contribution of the operating system—considered narrowly on its own merits—to your e-business environment is how well it stays up. E-business is 24*365. Can your operating system cope with that requirement, or can it at least cooperate with the replication and scalability features of your application server to give that effective capability?

Hardware platforms   E-business requirements for hardware mirror those for operating systems. Ideally, you need hardware that can be upgraded, or have components replaced, without being taken offline. You need all the features of non-stop operation, such as redundant power supplies and clustering with failover capability.

Backhoe fade.

Network   Your network, being your enterprise's lifeline to the Internet, is akin to your e-business oxygen supply. Lose it, and you suffocate. You don't want to be a potential victim of the proverbial backhoe. Geographically distinct cable routes to your ISP will give you the redundancy to survive a single backhoe attack—perhaps.

There are many horror stories on record of enterprises that, on digging deeply enough (so to speak), discovered that their "geographically diverse" cable routing shared a common cable group and traveled in the same conduit or traversed the same bridge over a river together with the other cables in the group.[9] How much money would you lose if that bridge were knocked out? Could you even stay in business?

And how about your ISP? Your geographically diverse connections *do* terminate in physically distinct ISP facilities, don't they? And are you sure that your ISP itself is backhoe-proof?

Network redundancy is perhaps the most difficult kind of redundancy to acquire in the entire chain, because so much of it is outside your control. It's worth your serious attention.

In addition to the physical requirements on the network, we also need to consider the logical characteristics. For B2C e-commerce, our connectivity to our consumers is necessarily through the Internet. However, for back-office B2B

---

[9]See *http://catless.ncl.ac.uk/Risks/20.85.html#subj1* for a typical example.

interactions, a VAN may be more appropriate. The value added by the VAN is that it's run by an identified enterprise that's responsible and accountable for providing guaranteed quality of service in terms of availability, throughput, transit delay, and security. The VAN provider is therefore going to keep thorough audits and be careful who it lets onto its network. VAN providers have interconnection arrangements with each other, so that an enterprise needs to deal with only one provider to participate in VAN connectivity, regardless of the VAN providers used by business partners.

9.6   Where was the "architecture"?

As in Chapters 6, 7, and 8, we'll conclude by reviewing how the elements of architecture apply to this chapter (see Table 9-2).

TABLE 9-2   Where was the "architecture" in Chapter 9?

Architecture feature	Relationship to this chapter
Solution fitted to client needs	In the IS architecture planning stage, we're drilling down and refining the solution designed in earlier stages. The IS model designed in the IS modeling stage fulfills the client needs, and the IS architecture planning stage determines in greater detail how the IS model will be realized in a working IS solution.
Empirically validated principles	The IS architecture planning stage reaffirms empirically validated principles as guiding principles for solution building. The principles themselves guide the design of the IS solution, expressed through the building of the real-object model.

Architecture feature	Relationship to this chapter
Design and implementation principles and guidelines	The IS architecture planning stage defines a more specific set of principles, refining those defined in the IS strategy. The asset selection and technology selection activities defined in the IS architecture planning stage are conducted according to these implementation principles.
Components, patterns, and frameworks	We use an architectural framework to help support our decision making in defining the technology infrastructure layers. Furthermore, we look for comprehensive frameworks—such as application servers and enterprise application integration solutions—that bring a coherent set of patterns to our technology infrastructure design.

(continued)

TABLE 9-2   Where was the "architecture" in Chapter 9? (*continued*)

	A clearly nonarchitectural alternative to application servers and EAI solutions would be ad hoc bilateral interfaces between applications.
Conceptual integrity and elegance	In the context of IS architecture planning, there's not much new to say about conceptual integrity and elegance that we haven't already seen in this space in earlier chapters. It's a matter of adhering to well-chosen principles and using patterns and frameworks in a consistent way.
Formal description and recording	The real-object model is documented through the use of an object-oriented modeling tool, where the scale (e.g., reengineering) or nature (e.g., e-business) of the project justifies using such a tool. Otherwise, an incremental improvement project will use less formal tooling, such as natural-language descriptions of the changes to be made in the existing environment.

9.7   Where to find more information

Application servers, enterprise application integration, and Internet application integration. These areas are in a state of rapid development. Any specific references I could give would be out of date by the time you read this book. You can of course do some searching around the Web, but expect to have to sift through a lot of material before you find true enlightenment. To trade money for time, I recommend getting into the research prepared by the Giga Information Group (*http://www.gigaweb.com*), which produces excellent research reports in this area.

10

Implementation Planning

This chapter describes the implementation planning stage, in which the team develops a transition strategy that describes how the current IS environment will be migrated to the target IS environment. In this stage, the team

- evaluates and prioritizes implementation options identified in earlier stages.
- establishes a transition strategy.

10.1 Implementation planning in the context of the total process

10.1.1 Relation to other stages

Figure 10-1 illustrates the relationship of the implementation planning stage to other stages of the seven-stage solution-building process. Figure 10-2 expands on the contextual picture by showing the deliverables that flow among the related stages, as well as an overview of the principal activities of the implementation planning stage. The deliverable from the implementation planning stage is the transition strategy.

IS architecture planning   The primary input to the implementation planning stage is the IS real-object model—actually a set of related models—which was created in the IS architecture planning stage. The IS real-object model identifies available components to be reused and defines the functionality that needs to be built. In addition to the real-object model, the IS architecture planning stage produces the architectural principles, which may influence choices made in implementation planning.

Current IS analysis   The implementation planning team uses the current IS inventory and assessment to determine in detail how the current IS assets will be deployed in supporting the new solution, in line with the architectural principles and IS real-object model.

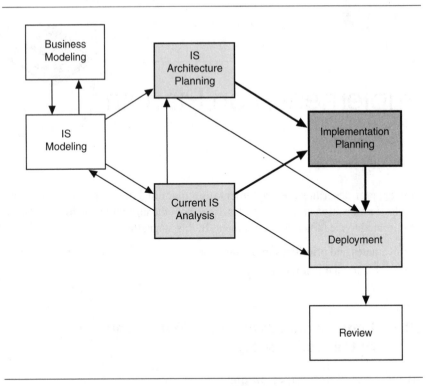

Figure 10-1   Implementation stage in context.

Deployment   The transition strategy is the primary deliverable from the implementation planning stage. It identifies the implementation options, their relative priorities, and the business process and organizational implications of deploying each option.

10.1.2   Participants

The information systems managers and professionals on the implementation planning team have the primary responsibility for completing this stage. During this stage, the implementation planning team works with

- business managers and end users within the enterprise, to understand the impact of the various implementation options on the business processes and organization and their relative priorities.
- technical specialists, to understand the specific information technologies needed to deploy the different implementation options.

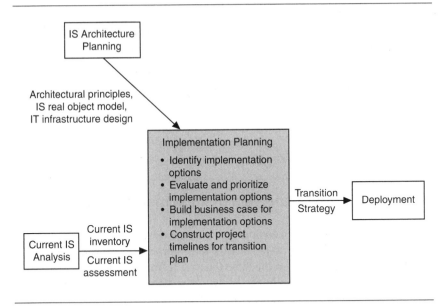

Figure 10-2   Overview of implementation planning stage.

10.2   Identifying implementation options

The first activity in the implementation planning stage is identification of implementation options. This activity should flow naturally from earlier stages and involves capturing and organizing earlier work more than creating new material.

The business modeling phase identified a set of business initiatives to pursue. The IS modeling phase identified ways to support, enable, and enhance those business initiatives. Sometimes, different alternatives emerge from the IS modeling stage and from the IS architecture planning stage, where we build the real-object model. These alternative solutions may need to be evaluated in the implementation planning stage if resolution could not be reached earlier. The purpose of the implementation planning stage is to consider all the options from earlier stages.

For the options emerging from the business modeling stage, we need to evaluate their relative priorities, interdependencies, and conflicts. Through this evaluation, the implementation stage

1. resolves the conflicts.

2. evaluates the relative priorities.

3. considers organizational impacts.

4. considers resource requirements of the various options and the availability of resources.

5. considers costs, benefits, and risks.

Where alternative solution designs for the same business initiative are being evaluated, as opposed to alternative business initiatives, then clearly only items 4 and 5 need to be examined. The result of the analysis is the production of a transition plan from which the deployment stage will be conducted.

10.3 Preliminary analysis of implementation options

After identifying the implementation options, the team evaluates them to determine which are of the highest priority for the enterprise. However, more implementation options may be on the table than the team has time and resources to evaluate. The process can get bogged down if the team tries to evaluate too many options. The objective of implementation planning is to create a plan that describes which implementation options the enterprise will deploy during its planning timeframe. The length of the timeframe naturally varies with the nature of the implementation options. E-business solutions are the most time-critical, with timeframes measured in weeks or months rather than years.

To keep the process moving, the team can complete a preliminary analysis of the implementation options and identify a manageable subset of the options for a more thorough evaluation. Options not carried forward in this round will be evaluated during a future review of the IS environment.

10.4 Analyzing the implementation options

For the transition strategy, the team identifies those options offering the least risk to the enterprise while providing the greatest benefits. Clearly, these low-risk, high-benefit options are the implementation priorities for the enterprise. This section describes the use of a cost–benefit and risk analysis to evaluate implementation options.

Note that it is entirely inappropriate to perform any kind of detailed cost–benefit analysis for a reengineering program. By its very definition, reengineering promises *dramatic* results. If you have any fears at all that success in your reengineering program will bring less than dramatic results, then what you're doing is probably not reengineering, and you should reevaluate the program. Risk analysis, however, is certainly appropriate. It will give you a handle on your probability of success and will point out areas where corrective action is needed.

10.4.1   Cost–benefit analysis

For each implementation option, the team gathers data on the costs and benefits associated with each option and completes a cost–benefit analysis. A cost–benefit analysis focuses on identifying those options that will either reduce costs[1] or enhance revenue for the business. This type of analysis provides the team and the business managers with a reasonable estimate of the costs and benefits associated with each implementation option and allows them to compare implementation options.

Analyzing costs   The team analyzes the costs associated with each implementation option. The cost analysis estimates the money, time, and resources the enterprise needs to invest to develop, deploy, and maintain the implementation option. Table 10-1 lists examples of the types of costs the team may identify. To complete the cost analysis, the team compares the costs of the implementation option against the costs associated with the existing business process, if any, and identifies those options that provide a cost savings to the enterprise.

Perhaps surprisingly, "architecture" in the sense of reusing patterns can have a powerful positive effect on the analysis of the costs of the identified implementation options. This is not a book about project management, which is another discussion altogether. However, certain aspects of the architectural approach have substantial benefits for project managers: models and the disciplined approach to implementation planning make things more understandable and quantifiable. Metrics captured from earlier projects and reuse of standard patterns and frameworks

TABLE 10-1   Types of Costs

Cost	Description
Development	Costs associated with developing and deploying the implementation option, including costs of personnel, training, equipment, materials and supplies, overhead, and any external consultants or subcontractors.
Operating	Costs associated with operating and maintaining the implementation option over its entire life cycle, including costs of user training, user documentation, communications, leases and rentals, hardware, administration and management, maintenance, enhancements, and so on.

---

[1]Reducing costs has an old-fashioned ring to it in the e-business era, when creating strategic advantage and innovative enhancement of customer value is the exciting stuff we'd rather think about. But think about the huge cost savings the Web allows you to realize—for example, by moving functions to customer self-service that previously needed an expensive human intermediary. Examples are legion: tracking a package on Federal Express or UPS, checking the status of an airline flight, trading stocks, and placing a catalog order.

enable the building of validated work-breakdown structures—including task lists, resource needs, and elapsed-time requirements. Projects can thus be planned and managed with a higher confidence level and a higher degree of repeatability. Continuing to keep records of the costs incurred and resources used by projects built around reused patterns and frameworks allows continuous refinement of project metrics. The result is a potential for accurate estimation of the cost of future projects built around those same reusable patterns.

Realistically, however, it must be said that realizing this kind of project repeatability is not likely to be a viable option for the enterprise's own IS function. Rather, the building of an estimation database is a more practical proposition for a consultancy performing many engagements across many client enterprises. However, automated software tools, with supporting knowledge bases of project data, are available for automation of the construction of project plans. Be aware, though, that their effective use requires skilled and experienced handlers. These are tools to leverage the scarce skills of capable professionals and increase (significantly) their productivity; they are not tools for *replacing* scarce skills.

Analyzing benefits Table 10-2 lists the types of benefits an implementation option can provide. Economic benefits are direct and can be estimated easily. Technical and operational benefits are often indirect and cannot be quantified easily. Nevertheless, technical and operational benefits provide a desirable outcome for the enterprise and are as important as economic benefits.

The team, as it completes the cost analysis, also analyzes the benefits of the implementation option and identifies those options that provide a specific economic, technical, or operational benefit for the enterprise.

10.4.2 Analyzing risks

Each implementation option carries a certain risk. Risk is the possibility that the implementation option will violate established criteria (for example, cost, required resources, and time) or not attain established goals (for example, functionality and

TABLE 10-2 Types of Benefits

Benefit	Description
Economic	Enhances the revenue of the enterprise, or tangibly reduces costs
Technical	Uses information technology to provide competitive advantage, or uses information more effectively, and provides the enterprise with more flexibility or more functionality
Operational	Improves the efficiency, personal productivity, or workflow of the enterprise

performance). Risk occurs in proportion to the scope of the implementation option—the larger the scope, the greater the risk. But scope is not always the only risk; an implementation option can encounter several different types of risks. Table 10-3 lists some different types of risks.

For the implementation planning team, the challenge is to identify the type of risk in each implementation option. Once risks have been identified, the team can actively manage and structure them to reduce their impact—or send the project back up the management chain for thorough rethinking, if risks appear too serious.

To revisit the architectural principle of pattern reuse once again, notice that there is a connection between pattern reuse and project risk. We saw in Section 10.4.1 how reusing familiar patterns allows more accurate estimation of elapsed time and resource needs. Thus, pattern reuse lowers project risk—obviously. Perhaps less obvious is the corollary that, faced with competing alternative solution designs, the one with the better-documented history of reuse—and therefore with

TABLE 10-3   Types of Risks

Risk	Characteristic symptoms
Financial	The near-term costs exceed the near-term benefits, and the enterprise cannot afford to deploy the implementation option.
Technical	The implementation option uses leading-edge technology available only from small start-up companies that may suffer execution problems.
Project	Because of the technical complexity of the implementation option, or the skills and expertise of the IS department, the enterprise cannot successfully deploy the option.
Functional	The implementation option supports a redesigned business process that breaks new ground—after deployment, we fear that it may not meet the needs of users.
Political	The implementation option does not have organizational support consistent with its ambition. For example, a reengineering program needs unwavering support from the very top of the enterprise if it is to succeed. A more constrained implementation option still needs support from affected key business managers, IS managers, and users.
Organizational	The implementation option implies far-reaching organizational impacts, with radical effects on job descriptions.
	End users do not have the skills, training, or knowledge to operate a technology that the implementation option uses. Unexpectedly high surge in demand from newly deployed e-commerce initiatives may place untenable demands on the enterprise's physical and logistical infrastructure.

the more accurate available project statistics—carries the lower project risk, a factor that should help determine the final choice.

10.4.3 Analyzing organizational impact

The preceding section mentioned organizational impact briefly, in terms of the risk it can present to an implementation option. In reality, however, that risk is merely the tip of the iceberg. The whole issue of organizational impact and its management is a substantial professional discipline in its own right.

From the business process reengineering era of the early 1990s and through the e-business era of the late 1990s and beyond, we have been radically redesigning business processes. This radical redesign brought with it not merely a different set of tasks for workers to perform, but also required a fundamentally different approach to work: "culture shock" would not be too dramatic a label. Managing this kind of culture change in the workplace has given new momentum to the specialty of organizational change consultants—people with knowledge in information systems but with backgrounds in the humanities and psychology.

Any substantial discussion of organizational change management is beyond the scope of this book. However, proper attention to organizational change management is essential if any radical change in business processes is going to be successful. Organizational change specialists should ideally be involved in the entire solution-building process, beginning with the business modeling stage.

For our purposes in this chapter, we need to consider organizational impact to the extent that we need to understand the broad implications of the implementation options on the organization. We need to decide whether we'll need the help of organizational change consultants to make a successful transition to the new business processes.

10.5 Establishing a transition strategy

The implementation planning team, after it has analyzed the costs, benefits, and risks associated with each implementation option, defines the implementation priorities and establishes a transition strategy for the enterprise. The transition strategy describes those implementation options that are priorities for the enterprise, which the project planners and developers will deploy in the next stage.

Any transition implies risk. By carefully selecting the implementation priorities, the team can create a transition strategy that provides an acceptable level of risk while still retaining the benefits of the IS architecture.

This section provides guidelines to help the team establish a transition strategy. We discuss the following topics.

- using a risk–benefit matrix
- selecting short- and long-term priorities
- diversifying risk
- determining a transition sequence
- building a business case and determining a transition strategy

10.5.1   Using a risk–benefit matrix

To help identify low-risk, high-benefit implementation options, the team can complete a risk–benefit matrix. By graphing each implementation option on the matrix, it is easy to see how the options compare with each other in terms of their risks and benefits. The team uses a risk–benefit matrix to identify low-risk, high-benefit implementation priorities for the transition strategy. The benefits considered in this exercise should be net benefits (that is, benefits minus cost).

Figure 10-3 shows an example of a risk–benefit matrix. Clearly, options A and B are the most appealing, with options F, G, and C worth considering. Options D and E, with low benefit and high risk, are of the lowest priority.

10.5.2   Selecting short- and long-term priorities

To keep morale high and retain stakeholder commitment, business managers and end users must see benefits quickly. Consequently, for the transition strategy, the implementation planning team should select implementation options that the IS department can deploy over time with some short-term benefits. By deploying implementation priorities that provide benefits in the short term, the team can quickly establish a series of successes that increase the confidence of end users and business managers in the solution-building process.

This approach does not, however, mean that the team should ignore medium- and long-term implementation priorities in the transition strategy. Not all implementation priorities can be completed in the short term. The transition strategy should include a mix of both short- and long-term implementation priorities.

The success of the solution-building process depends on the ability of the team to deliver a continuous stream of benefits to the enterprise. Whether short- or long-term, the business objectives of the enterprise are what determine the relative priorities of the implementation options. Figure 10-4 illustrates the concept of selecting short- and long-term implementation priorities.

10.5.3   Diversifying risk

In the transition strategy, the team should try to diversify risk. You have the following options.

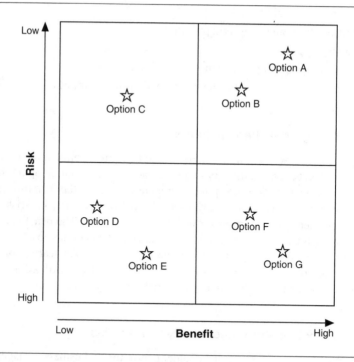

Figure 10-3 Risk–benefit matrix example.

- **Diversifying risk across the entire transition strategy.** In addition to considering the risk of the individual implementation priorities, you should consider the risk of the entire transition strategy. The transition strategy should include a mix of low- and high-risk implementation options (provided, of course, that the expected net benefit is high), because, in general, both low- and high-risk options are needed to provide the benefits that the enterprise needs to fulfill its business goals and objectives. A balance between low- and high-risk options still provides the enterprise with an acceptable level of risk.
- **Diversifying the type of risk.** As we already saw, there are several different types of risk. The team should try to diversify the types of risk in the transition strategy. The implementation options in the transition strategy should not all involve a technical risk, for example, but a mix of technical, project, and political risks.

10.5.4 Determining a transition sequence

For the transition strategy, the team determines which implementation priorities can be deployed in parallel and which need to be deployed sequentially. Typically, the transition strategy will include a mix of both parallel and sequential

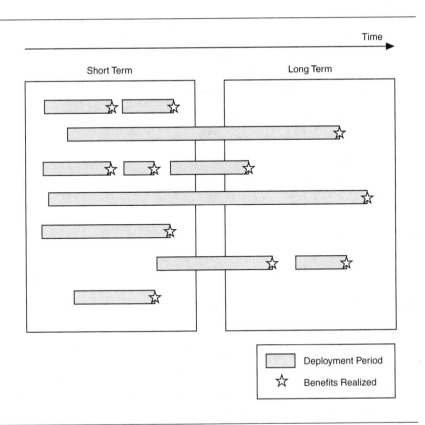

Figure 10-4   Selecting short- and long-term implementation priorities.

deployment. The decision to pursue parallel or sequential deployment depends on the interdependencies among the implementation priorities, the aggressiveness of the enterprise in deploying its solution, and the time and resources available. Although a well-managed parallel deployment produces results faster, a sequential deployment is usually easier to manage and therefore carries less risk. Figure 10-5 illustrates the concept of parallel and sequential deployment.

To evaluate the implementation options properly, the team should build a milestone map that shows the approximate milestones associated with each implementation option. The project milestones are determined by:

- the expected effort and elapsed time for each implementation, using previous similar projects as guidelines[2]

---

[2]The accuracy of the estimates made at this stage can significantly affect the success of the project. It is here that mature knowledge bases from earlier projects are invaluable. Such knowledge bases allow planners to estimate with much greater objectivity and precision than would a "wet finger in the wind" estimate based on subjective assessment.

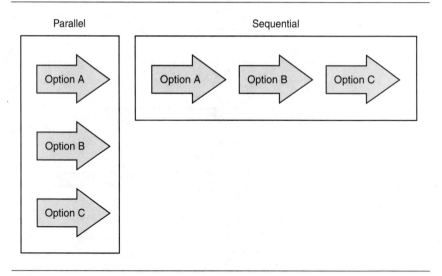

Figure 10-5   Parallel versus sequential deployment.

- interdependencies between implementation options
- constraints on available staffing and other necessary resources

Figure 10-6 gives an example of a milestone map and illustrates how such a map shows the relative timing and interdependencies of the implementation options.

10.5.5   Building a business case and determining a transition strategy

Once planners have analyzed the costs, benefits, and risks of the implementation options, they can consolidate this information into a business case. The business case summarizes the following information about the implementation options:

- business need or objective
- priority
- costs, benefits, and risks
- timing or sequence

A business case helps users and business managers understand how the team prioritized the implementation options. The business case also helps secure the commitment of users and business managers to the transition strategy.

The timing and sequencing derived from the milestone map are very important to the business case. The time at which the enterprise can bring a new capa-

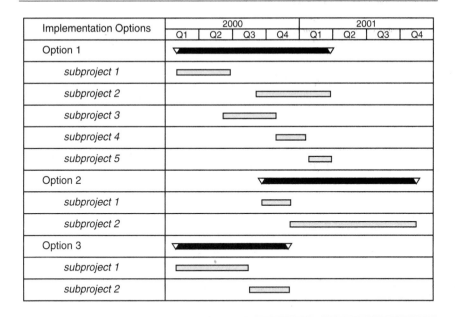

Implementation Options	2000				2001			
	Q1	Q2	Q3	Q4	Q1	Q2	Q3	Q4
Option 1								
subproject 1								
subproject 2								
subproject 3								
subproject 4								
subproject 5								
Option 2								
subproject 1								
subproject 2								
Option 3								
subproject 1								
subproject 2								

Figure 10-6   A milestone map.

bility online very much affects the revenue, cost savings, and competitive advantage that can be realized. As a result of the insight gained through the milestone map and its effect on the cost–benefit analysis, it may be necessary for the team to rework the milestone map so that high-impact implementation options are moved forward in the transition sequence.

The results of these evaluations and decisions are drawn together in the transition plan. The transition plan includes:

- implementation priorities and the business case for their deployment
- specification of assets to be acquired or reused, as opposed to being developed:
  - outsourced services
  - packaged software
  - reused functionality of existing IS assets
- a project plan, which comprises a refinement of the milestone map, taking into account:
  - interdependencies of implementation options
  - resource availabilities and limitations
  - any revision of implementation option priorities indicated in the course of analyzing the business case

To help communicate the transition strategy and business case to end users and business managers, the team should present the strategy with appropriate levels of detail and emphases for the particular audience. Presentation of the strategy is the culmination of the planning process, with the desired result that the deployment phase will be given the go-ahead.

There should be no surprises in this presentation, because successful projects necessarily keep all interested stakeholders properly informed and involved throughout the course of the project. Rather, the presentation of the transition strategy is a formal review of everything that has been decided, with all issues resolved. It is a checkpoint in the management of the overall project, where decision makers can review project status, initiate changes where appropriate, and reaffirm their commitment to proceed.

10.6   Where was the "architecture"?

By this point in the solution-building process, most of the "architectural" principles have served their purposes in earlier stages, and we're now in the mode of using good project management practices to get the solution built and deployed. However, architectural principles still have some benefit for us, even at this late stage in the process (see Table 10-4).

TABLE 10-4   Where was the "architecture" in Chapter 10?

Architecture feature	Relationship to this chapter
Solution fitted to client needs	We prioritize implementation options based on the value (cost–benefit) and risk to the client. Participation of affected stakeholders in the decision-making process helps ensure the best match of solution to business need.
Empirically validated principles	Not applicable in this chapter
Design and implementation principles and guidelines	These principles were defined in the IS architecture planning stage and used in that same stage to guide the asset and technology selection process. Any principles governing the implementation planning stage will of course be observed in the conduct of this stage.
Components, patterns, and frameworks	Project planning is assisted and made more accurate by applying known work-breakdown structures and associated resource needs from previously conducted projects based on similar patterns.
Conceptual integrity and elegance	Although we want to have conceptual integrity and elegance permeate everything we do, I can't summon up any specific advice in the context of this chapter.

TABLE 10-4   Where was the "architecture" in Chapter 10? (*continued*)

Architecture feature	Relationship to this chapter
Formal description and recording	The transition plan and business case are presented to end users and business managers as the culmination of the participative solution-building process. The formal description and recording—one of the key vehicles for stakeholder participation and communication—helps ensure the building of an appropriate solution. The project plan is recorded and maintained in a specialized project planning tool. (Although this practice is obviously integral with any sensible project management approach, it fits our definition of architecture, so by golly we're going to claim it.)

10.7   Where to find more information

For an example of a software tool that supports solution building with, among other features, *work-breakdown structures* and *task estimates,* see Client/Server Connection, Ltd. at *http://www.cscl.com/.* See the Bibliography and References section for material on managing *organizational change.*

11

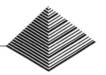

Deployment

Deployment is a phased process in which individual projects are planned and implemented according to the framework identified in the IS architecture and the transition strategy. The deployment stage encompasses all the steps normally considered part of the project development life cycle. Individual projects follow their own development schedules on the basis of the resources available and the priorities assigned to them in the transition strategy.

11.1 Deployment in the context of the total process

11.1.1 Relation to other stages

Figure 11-1 illustrates the relationship of the deployment stage to other stages of the seven-stage solution-building process. Figure 11-2 expands on the contextual picture by showing the deliverables that flow among the related stages, as well as an overview of the principal activities of the deployment stage.

Relation to IS architecture planning stage During the deployment stage, project developers build solutions that implement the real-object model, based on the IT infrastructure designed in the IS architecture planning stage and observing the architectural principles formulated in that stage.

Relation to implementation planning stage During the deployment stage, project developers plan and construct projects according to the transition strategy developed in the implementation planning stage.

Relation to current IS analysis stage Developers refer to the current IS inventory and current IS assessment in drawing up the deployment plan and during the course of solution implementation.

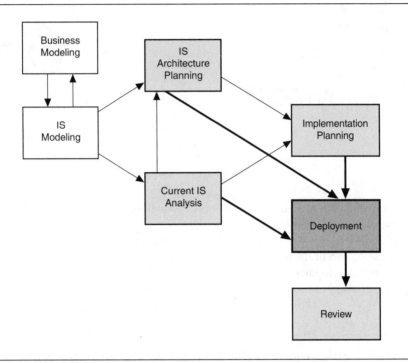

Figure 11-1   Deployment stage in context.

Relation to review stage   Because individual projects proceed according to their own schedules, the process cycles back and forth between the deployment stage and the review stage as individual projects are completed.

11.1.2   Participants

The deployment stage involves IS personnel and users working together to define, implement, and test the individual projects called for in the transition strategy.

- **IS managers and IS professionals**. Guided by the architectural principles formulated in earlier stages, IS personnel:
  - develop the information systems that fulfill the real-object models developed in the IS architecture planning stage
  - build the required technical infrastructure
- **Users and business managers**. End users and their managers work with IS professionals to validate requirements and verify the performance and suitability of the information systems being deployed. In an e-business deployment, some users of our system are going to be external to the enterprise. E-business is, after all, the integration of our business processes with

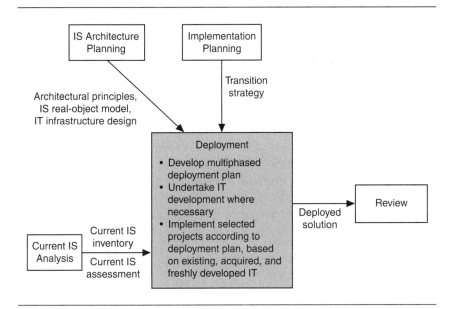

Figure 11-2   Overview of deployment stage.

those of our business partners and the extending of direct self-service to our end consumers. Ideally, these external users need to be involved in pilot deployments of the system so as to participate in performance validation and system suitability along with internal end users.

11.2   Deployment activities

In the deployment stage, the work completed in earlier stages begins to produce results visible to the rest of the enterprise. Deployment consists of all the activities needed to create the IS solution described by the IS architecture. These activities are of several different types.

- **Building the infrastructure**. These activities involve building—acquiring and installing—the technical infrastructure according to the IT infrastructure design developed during the IS architecture planning stage.
- **Purchasing or developing new applications**. These activities involve acquiring or creating the new applications identified as necessary to fulfill the IS real-object model. In developing our own application logic, we will of course be paying proper attention to architectural principles. We will therefore try to leverage the *reuse* and *conceptual integrity* principles by employing recognized programming patterns. Pattern reuse is covered in the general

reuse discussion in Chapter 16. Of course, everything we do in the deployment stage is guided by the architectural principles formulated in earlier stages, but it's worth reiterating here that application development should be conducted incrementally and iteratively.

- **Upgrading existing applications**. These activities consist of reverse engineering, reengineering, or otherwise modifying an existing application to enhance its functionality or make it easier to maintain. Note, however, that plunging into an application such as this violates one of our axiomatic principles and should not be undertaken lightly. We prefer to retain the application intact, using the wrapping technique.

- **Integrating existing applications**. The IS model and transition strategy identify functions of existing applications that will play roles in the new solution. These applications need to be integrated into the new framework through the application integration strategy identified in the Integrating middleware subsection of Section 9.5.2.

- **Educating users**. These activities relate to the orientation, training, and documentation needed to help users become productive with new or modified systems.

- **Conducting simulations**. Simulations are particularly important for e-commerce solutions. In many situations, it's almost impossible to predict the level of traffic a Web site will attract, whether on initial launch or through such events as a publicized launch of a new initiative. By running simulations, driven by tools that generate loads on the system representative of a chosen population of Web browsers, we can test how our systems behave under expected and higher-than-expected traffic loads. This kind of simulation reduces the risk inherent in live deployment.

- **Conducting pilot deployments**. For internally focused systems, pilot deployments in the context of the real business environment are necessary to work out the kinks in the new IS solution and to determine how it melds with the people and processes it is designed to support. E-business is fundamentally different from internally focused IS solutions in that e-business solutions are necessarily exposed directly to users external to the enterprise, including users who are end consumers as well as users from our business partners' offices. Coordination of acceptance and usability testing in this environment presents a correspondingly greater challenge than did yesterday's purely internal systems. More careful coordination of live rollout is needed. It is much more difficult to overcome the bad initial impressions of customers and partners than to work toward peace and harmony with your internal users. Consumers especially are very likely to go elsewhere if their experience is a bad one. The most aesthetically pleasing Web site in the world will still drive your potential customers away if they have to wait too long for its pages to download. An awful lot of companies find creative ways to get their Web sites to irritate customers. Try to make sure, through usability testing with representative customers, that your Web site isn't one of them.

11.3   Project management

Project management is a substantial subject in its own right, and any significant discussion on this subject is outside the scope of this book. The material in this section is limited to descriptions of how the deployment stage relates to the earlier stages of the solution-building life cycle.

11.3.1   Management tasks

Regardless of the particular activities involved in a project, the basic steps for conducting it are much the same.

- Development managers use the transition strategy to determine priorities and interdependencies among projects. Does project B have a higher priority than project C? Does project A have to be finished before project C can begin?
- Development managers assign people to work on a project. They must identify the tasks needed to complete the effort—that is, determine the work-breakdown structure (WBS)—and gauge the scope of the effort and how soon it needs to be finished when allocating resources. Some projects may be able to proceed simultaneously. Others must wait until other projects are done, because of either resource limitations or project interdependencies. The project WBS is an area where reuse again comes into play. As we saw in Chapter 10, there exist tools that provide substantial automation in the generation of task lists. By harvesting empirical data on completed projects, exhaustive task checklists are developed, which are then tailored to particular situations by matching the IS model with standard models in the database. By applying sizing parameters against the model, the tool associates resource requirements with the tasks of the WBS. Clearly, a tool of this kind, supported by a comprehensive knowledge base, can take a lot of risk out of a project plan, compared with an ad hoc all-in-people's-heads approach.
- Development managers clearly define the role of the project within the overall IS architecture. Every project is intended to implement some portion of the real-object model and its associated use cases. Architecture planners must make sure project developers have a thorough understanding of relevant portions of the architecture models and principles as well as of the business objectives on which their projects are based.
- Project developers produce a plan for their project covering
  - a project-specific schedule.
  - detailed requirements, including descriptions of assets to be used, developed, or acquired.
  - tools and methodologies.
- Development managers and project developers agree on a process for documenting project status. Development managers need periodic updates in

order to monitor the progress of individual projects and to assess potential impacts on other deployment activities.

A large enterprise can have many deployment projects going on simultaneously, possibly in many different places. Centralized management of all those projects may be neither practical nor desirable. The projects must be coordinated, however, to ensure that they remain in step with the transition strategy and relevant portions of the IS architecture.

11.3.2   Feedback loops

The projects conducted during the deployment stage are likely to generate large quantities of detailed plans, specifications, and other recorded materials. These documents are an important part of the solution process, but they are not part of the IS architecture itself.

What's important is that new insight gained from the deployment stage needs to be fed back into the earlier stages where the new knowledge is relevant. We can expect deployment-stage insights sometimes to ripple back all the way to business modeling, when newfound awareness of technical capability leads to breakthrough innovation in business processes. This kind of feedback effectively means that the models of the OO model set are, in principle, in a constant state of continuous improvement. Ensuring the timely—and controlled—updating of the models is but one of the many tasks of managing the total solution-building effort.

Managing feedback loops is important because, in a healthy IS environment running under architectural principles, the entire process is continuous. We don't go through the solution-building process from beginning to end and then stop and take a breather. We iterate back and forth between all stages of the process, and when we're done with one project from the master plan, other projects have taken their places in the queue. The whole process is iterative, continuous, and organic, and in its steady state all stages are in progress simultaneously. Managing the feedback loops is an integral part of managing the total steady-state solution-building process.

11.4   Where was the "architecture"?

We're almost at the end of the solution-building process, and "architecture" is still rendering yeoman service. Table 11-1 shows how architecture applies in the deployment stage.

TABLE 11-1 Where was the "architecture" in Chapter 11?

Architecture feature	Relationship to this chapter
Solution fitted to client needs	The incremental, iterative approach to development—one of the axiomatic principles—is a key factor in ensuring that the ultimate solution fits the client's needs. The incremental, iterative approach to development applies particularly to the deployment stage, but also applies to the entire solution-building process across all stages as they relate to one another.
Empirically validated principles	The empirically validated principles (see Section 2.4.2) apply to the software development activity of the deployment stage in microcosm, just as they applied to earlier design stages at a more global level.
Design and implementation principles and guidelines	Implementation principles are whatever the team decides they need to be, and they may therefore come into play during this deployment stage. In particular, the axiomatic principles of *iterative development* and *object-oriented development* will come into play here.
Components, patterns, and frameworks	Components, patterns, and frameworks apply in microcosm to the software-development task in the deployment stage. Reuse of established patterns comes into play in matching the deployment with those in tool-based knowledge bases, which generate project plans and work-breakdown structures based on accumulated experience. Even the use of established e-business simulation tools is an example of reuse of an available component. Writing our own simulation environment from scratch would be the "nonarchitectural" equivalent.
Conceptual integrity and elegance	Conceptual integrity and elegance are qualities that we want to permeate the solution at all levels, all the way down to the source code. In the deployment stage, these qualities come from the competent developers that we assign to the project.
Formal description and recording	In the deployment stage, we're really into the project management discipline, rather than the architectural discipline. However, for effective life-cycle management, we need development and deployment tools that integrate well with earlier-stage development tools, and we need to provide project managers with sufficient insight into what's really happening in the development environment.

12

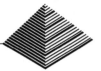

Review

Developing and deploying an IS solution is an evolutionary process. Both the business environment in which an enterprise operates and the information technologies on which it relies are perpetually changing.

Running an information system is an ongoing activity that must keep pace with changing business demands. An architectural approach helps enterprises manage change, but only if the architectural underpinnings remain flexible and responsive. Regular reviews make this possible.

The purposes of the review stage are

- to assess how well the deployed system actually meets the needs of the business processes and activities it is designed to support.
- to confirm that systems being deployed comply with the IS architecture and to evaluate their impact on other deployment plans. (In this chapter, the phrase "IS architecture" means the collection of the deliverables produced throughout the planning stages of the solution-building process—notably the IS models, the technical infrastructure models, and the principles and guidelines.)
- to assess whether changes in the enterprise's operating environment, business strategy, or technology options require revision to the IS architecture or any of the analyses on which it is based.

12.1 The review stage in the context of the total process

A formal review takes place after each completed deployment project. The results of the review need to be fed back into the appropriate earlier stages. Reviews generally identify things that can be improved and highlight areas that were not perfectly understood during earlier stages. The insight gained through the completion of the project allows IS functionality—and perhaps the business processes relying on them—to be redesigned.

Figure 12-1 shows the flow of information from the review stage to other stages. The completed project has led to a change in the current IS inventory. More important is that insight gained through the completion of the project may suggest improvements in all prior stages.

12.1.1   Participants

Many different people participate in various stages of the solution-building process. All these participants should have an opportunity to review the parts of the process with which they are concerned.

- **IS managers and IS professionals**. As the people responsible for implementing most aspects of the IS architecture, IS representatives are concerned that project schedules and budgets are met. They also must assess on an ongoing basis whether the systems being developed are consistent with the IS model and serve the needs of their users in their performance of the business processes.

- **Business managers**. Managers are concerned with how information systems support their business processes and how the resulting processes affect their budgets. They need to assess whether the new system and business processes meet their expectations. They also need to make sure that the insight and experience gained from the project are captured and fed back into the next round of business and IS modeling.

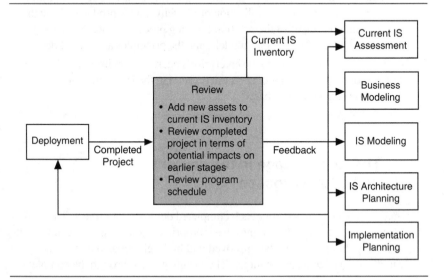

Figure 12-1   Review stage.

- **Executive management**. The enterprise's leaders must be satisfied that the information systems being implemented promote the enterprise's mission and strategy and justify the resources being invested in them. They are also responsible for communicating changes in business mission or objectives that may place new demands on the enterprise's information systems. The review stage presents an opportunity for upper management to see how their enterprise is working at a more detailed level of business process than they normally deal with. The greater understanding of the business processes by both upper and middle management contributes to the attainment of tighter alignment of business mission with business processes and their supporting IS systems. *Alignment* is, after all, the first fundamental driver of the architectural discipline that we saw in Chapter 2.

- **Users**. Members of this group, which encompasses people from all levels of the enterprise, must judge whether the information systems and services being deployed perform properly in helping them do their jobs. We want users to feel that our systems are a joy to use, not an irritation. We will usually not attain the "joy to use" label the first time around, and here, perhaps, is the tightest feedback loop in our solution-building process. We need to capture the user suggestions and irritation reports and feed them back into the deployment stage so that we continually improve the user-friendliness level. Of course, we'll need to prioritize and spend more effort on the base-load applications that support the core processes of the business, rather than those that are used only infrequently. End users are one of the best sources of ideas for improvements in IS systems and business processes. These ideas do not, however, flow automatically. If users send in suggestions and irritation reports, only to be ignored or given vacuous responses, then be assured that the flow of suggestions will quickly dry up. Don't make the mistake of spending hundreds of thousands of dollars on outside consultants to revamp your business while ignoring your own people.

- **Customers and business partners**. E-business, by definition, involves external consumers and business partners. We need to involve these people in an e-business review stage for the same reasons that we involve our internal end users in an internal IS review stage. Involving consumers in usability tests and collecting meaningful feedback presents its own set of challenges. On the other hand, business partners in B2B arrangements generally have as much at stake in the outcome of an e-business initiative as you do, so bringing them into the review loop amounts to a logical extension of the cooperation that brought the project this far.

12.1.2   Relation to other stages

Deployment stage   Deployment consists of individual projects that are planned and implemented according to an overall architectural design. Each of these projects has its own unique set of requirements, its own development schedule, and possibly a particular set of developers and users working together to ensure its success. The development life cycle for each individual project typically includes a testing, pilot, or evaluation phase in which developers, users, and business managers determine whether a system performs properly and meets all design requirements. Strictly speaking, this phase of an individual project is part of the deployment stage, not the review stage.

The review stage should ideally be undertaken after the system has been in live deployment long enough for its impact to be realistically appreciated.

Current IS assessment   As soon as the system is deployed, it becomes part of the IS asset base and should therefore be reflected in the current IS inventory.

Other stages   All other stages in the solution-building process may be affected by feedback from the review stage.

12.2   Reviewing projects

The review stage is different from the iterative review activity that occurs within each stage, and between associated stages, of the solution-building process. The review stage, applying as it does to the deployed solution in its entirety, involves a higher-level assessment of whether the project as deployed complies with relevant architectural specifications and meets the business objectives for which it was intended. At this level, team members assess the potential impact of the project on other projects in various stages of their life cycles and on the IS architecture itself.

12.2.1   Activities in the review stage

During the review stage, various members of the team perform the following activities:

- review the results of a completed project or phase of deployment. It may not be possible to evaluate the economic and other impacts of a project until the completed systems have been in operation for some time. Initially, however, planners should be able to judge whether the project follows architectural principles and implements relevant aspects of the architecture models.
- add any newly purchased or developed assets to the current IS inventory. Each completed project results in new assets that become part of the enterprise's IS environment. By updating the current IS inventory, planners maintain an evolving baseline on which new projects are constructed.
- reassess the business strategy, business model, IS strategy, IS architecture, and transition strategy in view of experience gained with the completed project

and any changes in conditions since those plans were devised. Planners must judge whether earlier conditions and assumptions still apply and determine whether changes in pending projects are required.

- if necessary, return to earlier stages and revise the business strategy, business model, IS strategy, IS architecture, or transition strategy. The IS architecture will be useful only as long as it is kept accurate and up to date.

- keep a written record of decisions made during this stage and the rationale for those decisions. This record serves as a history of deployment and can be the basis for progress reports to management.

- return to the deployment stage and continue with the next project or phase in the transition strategy.

12.3   Maintaining the IS architecture

No matter how carefully it is constructed, the IS architecture loses its value over time if it is not properly maintained. Many circumstances both internal and external to the enterprise can require changes in the IS architecture.

12.3.1   Ongoing maintenance

Even when everything works as planned, the enterprise can expect to make regular changes to the current IS architecture models.

The IS model evolves as applications are enhanced, new applications are developed, new systems are purchased, and old systems are retired. The current IS inventory should be kept up to date to ensure that planners and developers always have an accurate picture of the enterprise's resources. This information is also vital to any financial assessment of the enterprise's investment in its information technologies. An inventory update should be a routine part of every deployed project.

12.3.2   Ongoing maintenance: reacting to change

Changes in the enterprise's internal or external environments provide another reason for revising the IS architecture. For example, an unanticipated change in the regulatory environment could create a new set of requirements for the enterprise's information systems. New information about its competitive position may prompt the enterprise's leaders to adopt a new business strategy.

Any condition that seriously alters the analyses on which the IS architecture is based should be examined. Planners must determine whether they need to return to earlier stages of architecture planning to revise the results.

12.3.3   Scheduled maintenance

Besides reacting to changes in the enterprise's environment, planners can take a proactive role by scheduling periodic reviews with executive management. At regular intervals—such as once a year, depending on the enterprise—executives should be given the opportunity to review the high-level business objectives of the IS architecture. This occasion can also serve to review progress in deploying the architecture.

Regular reviews periodically extend the planning horizon to ensure that the IS architecture remains aligned with the enterprise's business needs.

12.3.4   Benefits of proper maintenance

Proper maintenance is more than just a matter of good work habits. It is essential to achieving important objectives of the IS architecture.

- **Managing change**. An up-to-date IS architecture is the foundation that allows the enterprise to respond quickly to a changing environment or to a new business opportunity. It also provides a framework for making deliberate decisions about emerging information technologies in order to minimize disruption to existing systems.

- **Integrating systems**. Unless refinements and revisions that result from every project are incorporated into the architecture models, all later projects will be based on inaccurate information. The discrepancies will grow until the enterprise's information systems no longer constitute an integrated whole.

- **Streamlining costs**. Keeping the IS architecture current allows new systems to be developed more quickly by freeing developers from much of the up-front analysis and planning. Systems based on current, well-defined data and process models are also less costly to maintain.

PART III

LET'S GET PRACTICAL

I've said several times that this book doesn't claim to be a how-to guide—for one thing, it's not thick enough. This book is more of an architecture for an approach to solution building, which I know amounts to a recursive description. (Perhaps if you reread Chapter 2 you'll be able to see what I mean.) Okay, if I'm not claiming this book as a how-to guide, what am I doing with a Part headed "Let's Get Practical?"

Part II, with its more-detailed treatment of the seven-stage solution-building process, could be viewed as an outline sketch of a how-to guide. Part III looks at some topics that, by their nature, span several of the stages. And yes, they're topics relevant to an application of the principles of earlier sections in practice, so this part moves us just a little further down the how-to path.

13

Enlisting Outside Help:
the Role of Consultants

The body of this book has talked about the participants in the solution-building process largely in the abstract, as far as their company allegiances are concerned. There is perhaps an expectation that most or all of the participants are associated with the enterprise whose business processes are being enhanced. It is certainly true that company insiders best know the business and its IS environment. Moreover, they have a personal stake in the company's future.

However, there is much to be gained by enlisting outside help in the solution-building effort. Outside help, in the form of consulting companies, provides an objective view, fresh ideas, and a potentially large knowledge base to support its consulting engagements.

13.1   Consultants for cross-enterprise leverage

Company "insiders" know the business and its IS environment, but there is another, equally important viewpoint that the insiders are usually missing—the experience and knowledge that come from building solutions for other enterprises. Whether or not these enterprises are in similar lines of business, the experience and knowledge a consulting organization gains from this wide exposure can bring enormous leverage.

Outside consultants are invaluable in the business modeling stage. They have seen many other businesses like yours, and they are not limited by having been immersed in your status quo. They can provide the objectivity to see past obscure constraints that you may be living with unwittingly and needlessly. They can apply their knowledge of what other organizations in your situation have done, have thought about doing, or have failed in trying to do.

"Architecture" in the sense of reused components, subassemblies, patterns, and frameworks becomes a more practical pursuit when the store of those reusable artifacts is well stocked. For a consultant, each engagement potentially adds new artifacts to the reuse store. A consultant with a wide range of experience is much more likely to be able to abstract reusable patterns from one industry to another—from repair dispatching to delinquent account collection, for instance—than either of those industries is likely to do for itself.

Also remember that reusable artifacts can be found and manufactured at every level of abstraction in a solution, from low-level basic technology all the way up through domain-independent business-solution enablers and into domain-specific business processes and supporting information systems. Obviously, choosing a consultant with a proven track record in your enterprise's line of business will give you a better opportunity to profit from reapplication of domain-specific artifacts.

As well as the potential to apply reused patterns at each level of the solution, the reuse of patterns has benefits throughout each stage of the solution-building process. Patterns apply to business processes just as they do to information systems. "Nobody knows your business better than you" may be true, but most of what you know is tacit knowledge: it can't be written down in a manual that someone else could pick up cold and use to run your business. Translating your business into the processes that run it and seeing the patterns in the business that can be applied in effective IS systems—this is where you'll tend to need help from a neutral third party. The third party has seen lots of other businesses and thus is in a better position to recognize what's common about your business to others and what unique value your business has.

The reuse of familiar patterns carries with it the confidence that, since we've done all this before, doing it again will not produce any unpleasant surprises. Each time we apply a pattern, we add to our knowledge base of everything associated with it, including the work-breakdown structure and the all-important cost and schedule data. Using a consultant with a track record and a well-populated knowledge base takes a lot of risk and uncertainty out of your solution-building effort.

Of course, using consultants has an obvious downside, too. Any consultant who comes in and helps you develop a world-beating solution can obviously go right next door and do the same for your arch enemy. And since he's so good at reusing things that work, he'll take your good ideas with him. Ah, the dilemma! Use a consultant and he'll steal your ideas and give them to your competitors. Don't use a consultant, and you'll never get the solution built, or it will take too long, cost too much, and still not be very good. What to do?

Fortunately, you can have the best of both worlds. Practically speaking, you'll gain much from the consultant, because of the breadth and depth of his knowledge base. He will already have developed some of the systems you need, and you can integrate these systems relatively quickly and cheaply into your enterprise. These kinds of systems are, of course, going to be at the low-differentiation end of the spectrum, where you're fulfilling low-value business needs or responding to business imperatives. At the high-differentiation end of the spectrum is where you may feel the need to be concerned about your good ideas—or even the good ideas the consultant had with your help—walking down the street to the competition.

Various legal remedies are available here. Nondisclosure agreements have been used effectively in these situations. In the United States, business processes can themselves be patented, which gives you much stronger protection. Whichever way you feel inclined to handle the issue of intellectual property in regard to your business innovations, you need to discuss it openly at the outset of the consulting engagement. You certainly don't want to get into a fight after someone has had a major breakthrough of an idea.

13.2   Consultants for technology expertise

In all but the very largest client organizations, it is usually true that consultants are more knowledgeable about current and emerging technologies than internal staff. Not only is their research time amortized against a broader base of application, but their involvement with many client organizations gives them greater opportunity for hands-on real-world application of newer technologies.

13.3   Consultants as project managers

Earlier remarks notwithstanding, experience in the field shows that IS personnel in client organizations are usually quite capable and knowledgeable on technology issues. Where internally run projects usually encounter trouble is in the project management. This is another area where consultants can help.

We can trace back to architecture one of the principal reasons why consultants are so much more effective in project management. Because consultants perform many engagements for a variety of clients—reusing components, patterns, and frameworks—their ever-expanding knowledge base provides them with the resources they need to be able to construct accurate work-breakdown structures and associated resource and elapsed-time needs.

13.4   The bottom line on consultants

You will find that there is great benefit in engaging a well-chosen and capable consultant. The best strategy is to nurture and actively sustain a relationship with a consultant whom you have used successfully. Your needs and his needs are mutually supportive. He wants to see you succeed—because this means that *he* has succeeded. He wants to find ways you can improve your competitive position and business processes—because he makes money helping you get there. The benefit of a long-term relationship is that the consultant becomes intimately familiar with your business and is therefore positioned to be able to apply new ideas and new technology to *your* business as he becomes aware of innovations in his interactions with other companies and IT vendors.

14

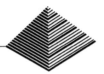

Methodologies: Patterns for Solution Building

At the beginning of this book, I said that it wasn't a "how-to" guide but rather an introduction and an overview. Yet I went on to give some detailed information about the seven stages of solution building and what needs to happen in each stage. If, however, you actually tried to use this book as a how-to guide, you'd quickly realize how much information you were missing and how much you'd have to make up for yourself.

What you'd need to do to flesh this book out to the point where it became a how-to guide would be to develop a *methodology* around it. In this context, a methodology, according to its dictionary definition, is a body of methods and principles. What we need is a step-by-step guide that can be followed *by capable people,* who understand business and IS concepts, in order to build IS solutions that create business value.

I want to stress here that I'm talking about a "methodology" in its generic, dictionary-definition sense.[1] The term "methodology" has connotations in our industry of a ready-made set of methods and principles, packaged and delivered under a product name such as "The XYZ Method." I am not suggesting here that you go out and buy such a packaged methodology, although that's certainly one of your options. What I am suggesting is that you need to formalize the detailed steps you will take in building your information solution.

---

[1]"A body of practices, procedures, and rules used by those who work in a discipline or engage in an inquiry; a set of working methods" (*American Heritage Dictionary*).

14.1 What's in a methodology?

The essential contents of the methodology are as follows:

- A list of activities, their descriptions, and their deliverables
    - a list of tasks within each activity
        - ◊ a list of steps within each task
- At appropriate points in the methodology:
    - templates (patterns by another name) for deliverables
    - a list of applicable techniques, and references to technique papers
    - a list of applicable tools, and references to information on them
    - a list of applicable information resources:
        - ◊ on use and application of tools
        - ◊ on widely applicable technology infrastructure
        - ◊ on further information to amplify technique papers
    - a list of references to examples from previously completed projects

Although not part of the methodology itself, a supporting knowledge base greatly enhances the effectiveness of the methodology. The knowledge base, or repository, is built up through application of the methodology in practice. In it, all deliverables are captured and serve both as knowledge support and as a reusable artifacts repository for future solution-building efforts.

Using a methodology in solution building amounts to reusing a set of patterns. It's essentially meta-architecture—using architectural principles in the very process of applying architectural principles to solution building.

14.2 Developing or acquiring a methodology

Developing a methodology requires a seasoned and capable team with practical experience in IS solution building and an understanding of the architectural principles discussed in this book. Of course, there's a bootstrap problem here—if the team has practical experience in IS solution building, then what methodology were they using when they gained that experience?

In practice, methodologies evolve like everything else, from try-it-and-see experimentation and from earlier methodologies. New insights gradually gain currency. The "architectural way" that I've tried to describe in this book is by no means built into the modus operandi of every active IS solution builder. If it were, then we would have better agreement on what "architecture" really means in the context of information systems. We'd also be much better at reusing our IS artifacts—components, subassemblies, patterns, and frameworks—and we'd be better at producing new artifacts, themselves amenable to reuse in different business domains.

When we assess all the components of a comprehensive methodology, it's clear that it contains a great deal of knowledge and experience, and that it represents significant value. Methodologies are the intellectual capital of the companies—usually consulting organizations—that create them. As a client organization, you could expect to benefit from the methodology by retaining the owning company as your IS consultant or perhaps by buying the rights to the methodology.

In summary, developing your own methodology will take time and commitment and will involve a maturation period while the methodology is honed by practical experience. Purchasing a methodology or engaging a consultant (who you first verify as already having a mature methodology) will give you immediate access to the benefits of the methodology and effectively amounts to reuse of existing knowledge.

14.3   Using a methodology in practice

A methodology can be a very powerful leveraging force in the building of IS solutions.

- The orderly step-by-step approach frees practitioners' brains from the mechanics of the process to concentrate on the essence of the solution itself and its surrounding business environment.
- The methodology amounts to a framework for teaching and mentoring new and less experienced IS professionals in the gentle art of architectural solution building.
- An orderly framework, with validated templates and collected references to resources and examples, empowers less skilled and less experienced IS professionals to contribute to the project.
- A methodology provides a framework for capturing the experience and knowledge of each solution-building exercise for reuse in future efforts.

A methodology also has pitfalls for the unwary. Sometimes these pitfalls can exert black-hole-like force in dragging practitioners into them. Be on your guard always! The following sections describe the pitfalls that are easiest to fall into.

14.3.1   Pitfall 1: "This stuff is easy!"

The orderly step-by-step method tends to make any IS solution-building effort look like a paint-by-numbers exercise. All we have to do is follow the steps and a wonderful solution will pop out at the other end, on time and within budget.

I know—said like that, it looks pretty ridiculous, but hard experience indicates that this phenomenon is a real problem. As I said a couple of times before, good people will produce good solutions regardless of the methodology they're using, and poor-performing people will somehow contrive to produce poor solutions in spite of having the world's best tools at their disposal. You can't staff every project exclusively with superstars, but make sure your nonsuperstars are capable journeymen rather than abject losers, and arrange things so that the superstars keep an eye on the journeymen.

It is difficult for a methodology to ensure proper adherence to all the architectural principles. For example, we can keep saying "reuse existing components" all we like, but it's very easy for designers with a not-invented-here mentality to convince themselves their situation is unique so that they can justify going off to design and build neat stuff from scratch. It comes back to staffing with good people and recognizing that following the methodology is an aid, not an automatic formula for success. At all times, we have to apply good judgment and sound principles, embodied in a proper mindset.

14.3.2 Pitfall 2: You can't fly a Boeing 747 just by reading the manual

You can't produce good IS solutions just by reading through the methodology manual and then getting straight down to business in a solution-building effort. It

Flying by the book.

doesn't matter how good you are, you need some quality right-seat time, mentored by people who can already fly. Although knowing the principles of flight (architectural principles) will help, you'll still crash the plane unless you're first given a controlled introduction to the art of flight.

14.3.3 Pitfall 3: Methodology bloat

It's terrifically tempting to want to dot all the i's and cross all the t's—but don't do it. You'll soon have a bloated methodology that will drag your projects into the mire. The temptation to become overdetailed gets worse as time goes on, because mistakes are inevitably made in the course of building solutions. What's tempting is to try to head off future mistakes by putting a "fix" into the methodology. Fixing the methodology is all very well if that's truly where the failing occurred, but ask yourself honestly if the person or team that made the mistake was acting reasonably or was displaying immaturity or inexperience below what's expected of IS professionals performing that role. Often we get back to the business of needing capable people or proper mentoring, rather than inflicting unnecessarily burdensome and bureaucratic requirements on our methodology.

15

Practical Considerations in Conducting Solution Building

As we've already seen, the principles covered in this book need a lot of fleshing out before we have an adequate basis for a viable "how-to" guide. This section covers some additional considerations pertaining to practical solution building that may be difficult to capture adequately in the formulation of a methodology.

15.1   Feedback loops and whirlpools

The solution-building model described in the main body of this book often showed feedback arrows to earlier stages of the process. In practice, there are many more of these feedback loops than are practical to illustrate. Activities from different stages are often inevitably mutually interdependent, leading to a situation that's more like a whirlpool than a feedback loop.

You may wonder why, if the stages ever get so interdependent that a whirlpool of parallel activity results, we even try to separate the stages. The answer comes back to one of the reasons for doing "architecture" at all, which we discussed in Chapter 2: we need to divide and conquer, for the sake of intellectual manageability. And it's probably not a coincidence that our solution-building process breaks down into seven stages, the magic number of concepts that a human brain can deal with simultaneously.

Even though the activities making up a stage may be interdependent with other stages, the deliverables from each stage are themselves well defined. These deliverables should be used as the basis for formal feedback loops with interested stakeholders, and through them to earlier stages of the solution-building process.

The fact is that whirlpool-style feedback is easier to apply, because the need for it is obvious in real time. It's the lower-frequency feedback that may get missed, because it requires conscious effort on someone's part to make sure that it happens. But happen it must. For example, if your IS modeling stage has produced a maelstrom of activity that is threatening to take your business processes through a major revolution, way beyond the competition, you had better tell executive management all about it before forging ahead any further.

15.2   Duration of solution building

It is difficult to say precisely how long it should take to produce or evolve an IS environment. Business drivers vary greatly in size and in complexity. The length of the process also depends on the resources allocated to it and on the percentage of their time that team members are able to devote to the effort. For planning purposes, it is useful to note that the process described in this book can be divided roughly into two parts.

- The first four stages end with the creation of the IS architecture. Most of the intense involvement of the senior people on the solution-building team occurs during these stages. Experience shows that, if these stages are not completed quickly, the rush of events can often overtake the planning activity.

- The last three stages encompass the individual projects necessary to plan, design, and deploy the various systems and services identified in the IS architecture. This part of the process corresponds to the kind of ongoing project development activities the enterprise is probably accustomed to. Once the overall requirements and priorities have been set, each individual project will have its own timetable and its own project team.

Determining the proper scope and level of detail at each stage helps ensure that the architectural solution-building process will produce tangible results as quickly as possible. You will find that the technique of time boxing, which we first met in Chapter 6, is a pragmatic, albeit brute-force, tool for keeping the project on track.

15.3   Architectural solution building
and ongoing projects

In a typical enterprise, IS personnel probably have a long list of activities underway for enhancements, modifications, and new systems. It is not realistic to expect work on high-priority IS projects to wait until architecture planning is complete, nor should the importance of ongoing projects serve as a rationale for delaying the start of architecture planning.

15.3.1   Allocating resources

In deciding to undertake architectural solution building, you must also make a decision about where the necessary resources will be found. Regardless of the long-term benefits of architectural solution building, in the short run it may require the redirection of resources from lower-priority projects.

Provided that the strategic risk is not great, you may choose to suspend low-priority projects until after completion of the IS architecture or significant portions of it. In the case of essential maintenance or strategic new system development, you may need to continue those efforts in conjunction with architectural solution building.

15.3.2   Integrating multiple projects

For projects that must be planned and implemented in parallel, developers have three broad options.

- Ignore architecture by integrating the projects after their completion. This option places no additional burden on individual projects, but it creates the risk that the completed projects will not be consistent with each other or with overall business goals. Planners and developers will have to decide whether any additional effort is required to bring the individual projects into alignment.
- Incorporate unifying features into each project before it is completed. Depending on what stage of its life cycle each project is in, developers may be able to accommodate such unifying features. For example, if a new application is still in the design stage, developers could incorporate a Web-browser-based user interface selected for use across all applications.
- Be prepared to return to earlier stages of the project life cycle to bring the projects into line with each other. This option risks delaying one or more important projects. The risk is partially offset by the possibility that the project as originally conceived is not in the best long-term interests of the enterprise. If planners identify significant new operational or strategic goals, reevaluating ongoing projects to ensure that they are consistent with those goals costs less in the long run.

Awareness of these issues is important to both business planners and project developers. They need to evaluate projects on a case-by-case basis to minimize risks and impacts on project schedules.

16

Issues Concerning Reuse

One of the major themes of this book has been reuse. In every stage of solution building, we've tried to reuse the results of earlier efforts—both ours and other people's. Reusability is a lofty aim that we, the IS industry in general, have not hitherto been very good at attaining. Reuse initiatives have had some success in limited areas where the right supporting conditions were in place, and there are useful lessons we can draw from those experiences [Schmidt 1999].

In this chapter, I have leaned toward the use of the more general term "artifact," rather than "component," because the usual connotations of "component" are overly restrictive in a more general discussion of reuse.

16.1   Benefits of reuse

Reuse has many benefits, some obvious, some less obvious. Among the obvious benefits, we can list

- speed of development, and therefore reduced time to market
- reduced development cost (a quarter of the cost of developing from scratch [Jacobson et al. 1997])
- predebugged software, raising product quality and reliability
- higher population of users, leading to flushing out of more bugs

Among the less obvious benefits are

- worked examples serve as learning materials
- reuse leads to familiarity with common patterns
- reuse of common patterns promotes intellectual manageability

- reuse of common patterns leads to growth of ecosystems of conformant components
- reuse of common patterns facilitates application of prebuilt methodologies to the design and development process and therefore promotes process repeatability and predictability
- common patterns facilitate automated production of project support materials
  - functional documentation
  - design documentation
  - work-breakdown structure
    - ◊ automated documentation of tasks
    - ◊ task resource and elapsed-time requirements

Reuse also has drawbacks. We'll discuss the problems of launching a reuse initiative later, but as far as ongoing operations are concerned, we have to note that developing with the intent to create reusable components carries additional overhead. Not only must developers complete the abstraction of reusable artifacts and deposit them into the repository, they must also maintain, throughout the development process, a mindset toward producing reusable artifacts. Experience shows that design for reusability costs 50 to 200 percent more than equivalent pure custom design for a single application [Jacobson et al. 1997]

16.2   Reuse domains

The reuse principle applies at all levels of the solution-building process. We find that different types of issues arise at the various levels, and so for discussion purposes we'll break down the reuse landscape into three domains: source code, middleware, and business logic.

16.2.1   Source code

Inspired by the so-called "Gang of Four" book [Gamma et al. 1994] and reinforced by Buschmann et al. [1996], a movement to promote patterns at the source code level has grown up. These two books, and others cited by Schmidt [1999], document a number of reusable patterns that can be applied in the production of source code, with the resulting advantages of comprehensibility through standardization, fewer bugs, and all the other bonuses we expect from reuse.

To promote pattern development and use, a "patterns" movement has formed several online communities to discuss, develop, and share patterns. These communities and their pattern repositories are rather informal, and I will not risk giving references that may turn out to be transient. However, a few searches on the

Web should allow you to find the active areas. The Portland Pattern Repository, which houses the paper by Best [1995], is one worthwhile starting point. (Paradoxically, this site is itself was built without benefit of any discernible underlying recognizable pattern for a Web site, which makes for awkward navigation.)

Patterns for source code are available essentially for free. You can find them in books, in repositories on the Web, or through Internet mailing lists. People are happy to develop and share patterns collaboratively, without payment.

16.2.2   Middleware

Middleware is the software infrastructure that holds our business logic together. We're taking advantage of reuse whenever we select a standard middleware environment for our IS solutions. Of course, the term "middleware" covers a broad spectrum of capability, and some middleware solutions will leave a lot of "plumbing"-type considerations for the application programmers to worry about.

Because we have reuse as one of our basic tenets (or axiomatic principles), we should choose a middleware environment that removes as much domain-independent consideration as possible from our application programmers' concern.

In addition to our reuse tenet, we also have an object-orientation tenet. In concert, these tenets mean that we should select an object-oriented middleware, or a component framework, to give object-oriented middleware its in-vogue characterization. We discussed component frameworks and allied middleware concepts, in the Integrated middleware subsection of Section 9.5.2.

16.2.3   Business logic

Reuse at the business logic level has the highest potential payoff. In business terms, we can characterize middleware reuse as making the right strategic call for the IS environment and characterize reuse at the coding level as efficiency of execution. However, reuse at the business logic level is where the real leverage is created.

At the business level, we're talking about reusing bigger chunks of things. We need reuse not only for efficiency of development but also because often we simply don't have the time to develop from scratch.

The remainder of this chapter discusses issues of reuse that apply particularly to reuse in the business logic domain.

16.3   Impediments to reuse

Several types of impediments have historically combined to limit the effectiveness of practical reuse. These impediments are both technical and nontechnical in nature. Technical problems include

- insufficient depth of developer skill
- insufficient breadth of developer knowledge
- inadequate technology and insufficient resources to support effective reuse
- the not-invented-here developer mindset

Insufficient depth of developer skill has the result that developers are unable to draw effective abstractions from their designs. Designing for reuse requires the designer to abstract generally applicable behavior from behavior pertinent only to the particular problem at hand. Less experienced and less skilled developers are often unable to draw these kinds of abstractions.

Insufficient breadth of developer knowledge is a problem when the developer has insufficient domain-related knowledge, and is therefore ignorant of fundamental design patterns well established in the business domain in which she's working. She is therefore unable to recognize appropriate reusable assets. Worse, she is likely to invent design patterns inconsistent with the accepted model, leading to a loss of conceptual integrity.

Inadequate technology and insufficient resources to support effective reuse is both a technical and an organizational problem. To be able to reuse artifacts effectively, designers have to be able to search effectively through component repositories to know what's available. Providing the technical infrastructure to support the depositing, cataloguing, and retrieval of artifacts is one problem. Overcoming the organizational difficulty of making the facilities available across organizational units is another. The organizational challenge applies whether we're talking about reuse within an end-user enterprise or by a consulting organization.

Not-invented-here is a well-known dysfunction that may be suffered by engineers of all stripes and is perhaps better classified as a psychological problem rather than a technical one. This syndrome results in the engineer's rationalizing the need to create a solution from scratch, rather than use or adapt an available component.

Nontechnical impediments to reuse include

- start-up overhead
- an ongoing funding model
- employee reward systems

Start-up overhead will be incurred in any reuse initiative. It takes resources—both human and IS—to establish a reuse repository and the tools and organization to make use of it. It takes time, skill, and commitment to populate the repository with reusable artifacts. During the start-up phase, while the pump is being primed and the repository is sparsely populated, few artifacts will see reuse, resulting in a net negative in the ledger. Experience has shown that it takes two or three product cycles, usually about three years, before net benefits begin to be realized. Another observed rule of thumb is that a component needs to be

Not Invented Here.

reused three to five times to amortize the cost of building and maintaining it [Jacobson et al. 1997].

An ongoing funding model is needed to sustain the reuse initiative. How are its costs covered? Do the organizational structure and accounting practices allow for costs to be distributed in a palatable and sustainable way? Companies have found it difficult to answer these questions, to the detriment of their reuse initiatives.

Employee reward systems need to be consistent with the reuse initiative. You can't expect developers to go looking for artifacts to reuse if they're being rewarded, officially or not, by the number of lines of code they produce or by how many hours they spend in the office. You have to put teeth into the "work smarter, not harder" doctrine.

16.4   Essential enablers of reuse

Essential enablers of reuse include, reasonably enough, effective countermeasures against the impediments listed in the preceding section. While some of these countermeasures are implied by the nature of the impediment, others need further explanation, specifically:

- a supportive organization and culture
- skilled developers

A supportive organization and culture are needed to combat the negative effects of the start-up overhead. The organization needs to accept the overhead of reuse, devise effective systems to fund the reuse utility, and stay the course with determination and commitment through the apparent drought of the start-up period. The start-up period must produce a well-documented framework and component repository, well maintained and with conspicuous management support—not just lip service—to give developers the confidence that the repository will support their needs. Developers and their managers need to be rewarded based on their reuse from, and contributions to, the repository.

Skilled developers, or the lack of them, will make or break a reuse initiative. Producing reusable components and frameworks is difficult, even for the capable. It takes a supportive climate, constant mentoring, and continuous learning to develop the skill and awareness needed to produce reusable designs. The supportive climate includes the acceptance of longer development elapsed times than would be incurred in producing strictly custom designs. In short, you need to hire capable developers, empower them, create a mentoring and supportive environment, and reward them appropriately.

16.5   Environmental drivers of reuse

In practice, successful reuse initiatives have needed the right environmental conditions to exist. Necessity is the mother of invention, and it seems that necessity is a key driver of reuse, even when the organizational and technical conditions are aligned for its support. Specifically, for reuse to be successful we find we need

- a competitive market
- a complex application domain

A competitive market demands that solutions be developed quickly to hit the critical time-to-market constraints. A less competitive market gives more room and nurture for all the reuse impediments to thrive.

A complex application domain dissuades developers from reinventing the wheel simply because it's so hard, in an intellectual sense, to do. Developers willingly seek out reusable components in highly complex domains, driven as much by a search for enlightenment as by a desire to reuse.

16.6 Sources of reusable artifacts

Reuse is our goal, but it's only practical to the extent that there are things available in the reuse store. And having things in the reuse store is only half the problem—how do we know what's in the store, where they are, and what they do?

16.6.1 Reusable artifacts from ongoing development

In practice, it has been found that successful production of reusable components and frameworks has arisen from solving real problems rather than from trying to work top-down in the abstract. Although we need to keep reusability and abstraction in mind as we're developing, paradoxically we need a domain-specific environment from which to abstract and generalize reusable behavior. We find that the discipline and ongoing feedback of tying reusable abstractions to real, working developments is a requirement for producing truly useful components.

16.6.2 Reusable artifacts from current IS assets

Existing applications represent a wide range of rich functionality. The problem in figuring out how to adapt existing applications or reuse them in new solutions is in discovering exactly what they do, where their interfaces are, and how those interfaces can be used in fitting them into new solutions.

Taking inventory of current IS assets is what the current IS analysis stage of the solution-building process is about. To prepare properly to take full advantage of current IS assets, you'll need some tooling help. Software products exist that help catalogue the functionality of existing business software, storing the catalogue in a repository. At the time you're looking for functionality to satisfy the IS model, the repository allows the location of suitable components that have been discovered.

Whatever tooling you have, experience shows that taking stock of current IS assets is time-consuming. It needs to be started early in the solution-building process, and it needs to be confined to those assets that reasonably can be expected to play roles in future developments.

16.6.3 Reusable artifacts from packaged software

We've discussed this topic several times throughout the course of this book, but it's worth another look in the context of reuse.

One of our axiomatic principles said that we have a bias toward keeping applications intact on their existing platforms. In reuse terms, this principle says that we reuse existing installed software, and indeed that is our first choice. However, if for some reason our existing software is inadequate in some way, perhaps we should consider packaged software against the alternative of fixing the inadequacy of the existing software.

This line of thinking was exactly the reason behind many installations of packaged software—specifically the ERP (enterprise resource planning) category—in the period leading up to the end of 1999, when the Y2K bug was known to exist in many older software systems. Many companies had home-grown IS solutions that had evolved over the years and that were imperfectly understood and hard to maintain. In terms of our five-era model from Chapter 7, those solutions may have been leading-edge solutions and yielded competitive advantage at the time they were built. But in today's world, when all those functions have been built into standard packages, there is no advantage in maintaining custom software. Companies realized they could save maintenance costs as well as fix their pressing problems by going with standard commercial software packages. Adopting the standard package often caused impacts on business practices, but this effect was accepted as a necessary cost of getting the benefit of the standard solution. In some cases, the modified business processes were simpler than their predecessors and a welcome relief from processes that had become convoluted through uncontrolled growth and ad hoc modification.

Packaged software can do only so much. It is rather obvious that packaged software cannot itself give your business a competitive edge. If your business can buy the software, plug it in, and automatically jump out in front of the competition, then clearly your competitor can go out and do the same thing. Packaged software can usefully help your business only at the low-differentiation end of the spectrum.

Using packaged software to run your business has similarities to the way you use electricity. You can't run your business without the functionality it provides, but using it doesn't give you any competitive advantage. And you surely cannot generate your own any more cheaply or reliably than you can buy it from the power company.

16.6.4 Reusable artifacts from the specialty store

We've established by now that your competitive advantage is going to come from the domain-specific end of your IS solution, the highest link in the food chain. The challenge, then, is how to find the high-value domain-specific artifacts from which to assemble your solution.

Initially, the most promising source of reusable artifacts is likely to be your consultant. Your consultant will have developed a methodology as an aid to conducting the engagement, and supporting that methodology is a knowledge base built from and including completed projects. If your consultant is as good at the reuse game as you'd like him to be, that knowledge base is going to be the source of your reusable artifacts. If your consultant is a specialist in your industry segment, it's likely he will have built standard frameworks around your standard business processes. These frameworks are "standard" for your consultant, not for the industry at large, and they represent intellectual capital of the consultant. You're paying as much for the reuse of this intellectual capital as you are for the consultant's time.

Standard frameworks are good news and bad news of the kind we've discussed before—good news because you get your solution built quickly but bad news because your competitor gets the same thing. However, given that the consultant has built the framework, it's clear that you're likely to fall behind the competition if you don't use it. Your discriminating value will come from the components you plug into the framework, not from the framework itself. Remember, no one can build a general information solution that provides your unique distinguishing business value. If they can, and do, then you don't have any distinguishing business value and you'd better invent some fast.

If you're successful in realizing your reuse philosophy, you will begin to populate your own enterprise repository with reusable artifacts. Realize, though, that a reuse initiative will need considerable commitment to establish and sustain—it will not just happen as a bottom-up effort from a few disconnected projects. First of all, infrastructure needs to be put in place to support the reuse initiative, in the form of a repository and its management and administration. More importantly, effective education and evangelism will be necessary to get your IS and business process staff on board. Furthermore, you need a certain critical mass before the reuse repository can begin to sustain itself. In the nascent stages, while the repository is being developed and populated, solution builders searching for reusable artifacts are going to be coming up empty-handed. Unless a relatively large cross section of the enterprise is committed to the reuse initiative, the population of the repository may grow too slowly for it ever to attain credibility.

No one can build a general information solution that provides your unique distinguishing business value.

Certainly there's room for debate here. After all, your unique business value could be your low prices or your exceptionally friendly and helpful customer service agents, which have nothing to do with information systems.

Huh, really? How did your prices *get* to be so low? Wasn't it because your information systems wrung the inefficiencies out of your supply chain, and your IS-collected sales data kept your finger on the pulse of what the market wanted, and . . . (you can fill in other examples). And how come your customer service staff are so much more friendly and helpful than your competitors'? Could it be perhaps because they're so well supported by information systems that give them exactly the information they need and support them in their daily tasks with a user-friendliness that keeps their stress levels down? In all likelihood, in any enterprise bigger than a mom-and-pop operation, we're going to find that each distinguishing attribute of the business has a capable information system not far behind it.

16.6.5   Reusable artifacts from the specialty broker

Here I'm being futuristic. What I'm proposing is that reusable artifacts be bought and sold like any hardware component. It's not a new idea, by any means. Companies have been set up to perform exactly this business function. As far as I know, none has yet been successful. But the eventual reality seems inevitable. When all the required conditions exert enough force, then surely the market will emerge.

In this business component market, you might develop a component that gives you a useful jump on your competition. Let's color in the story with an example. Say you're a retail bank, and you figure out how to make your Web site deliver an on-screen statement to your customer, which allows her to painlessly and automatically reconcile her Quicken accounts with a single mouse click. You might want to patent this business innovation to keep your competitors from doing the same thing. But at the same time, you might want to sell the capability to banks in different markets that don't compete with you. So you let a component broker resell the capability for you, subject, of course, to your restrictions on who's allowed to buy it.

In a healthy market, the artifact catalogues of these business object brokers would become very large and comprehensive. IS solution building would involve much research through these catalogues. The nature of solution building would shift from reuse as the happy exception to reuse as the expected norm. Software engineers would do their jobs in the same way that engineers in the physical world—and, dare I say, architects—have become accustomed to doing theirs.

EPILOGUE:

TAKE-HOME THOUGHTS

This epilogue is a grab-bag of ideas that I feel are important to retain as the "footprint" on your brain that remains after reading this book. I purposely didn't cross refer to the expanded material in the body of the book: that would have involved far too much effort on my part. Writing this book has been a long, hard slog, and I'm ready for a rest. No, seriously—if you feel the need to reamplify these points (as I hope you will), then your scan back through the book will lead you serendipitously across other nuggets you might not otherwise have rediscovered. So, open up your own grab-bag and start loading it up with these thoughts.

Architecture   Architecture is:

- design of elegant form to fulfill desired function, aligning IS support with business objectives.
- reuse of standard, catalogued, or existing components, patterns, and frameworks.
- maintainence of appropriate forms of "blueprints" for effective communication among stakeholders.
- disciplined design and construction according to prespecified guiding principles
- a pervasive mindset of maintaining intellectual manageability through simplification, conceptual integrity, and the specific techniques listed above.

IS requirements   IS people: don't expect business people to be able to tell you what their "requirements" are before you've helped them express precisely what it is that they want the *business* to do—by building the business model.

E-business   E-business technology will not be a business differentiator—it's table stakes, the cost of playing the game and staying in business. E-business is mandatory.

E-business is infrastructure, not business strategy.

Availability, scalability, and security are not optional. Overcapacity is cheaper than rebuilding.

Your e-business environment can be built—based on sound architectural principles—around application server (AS) and enterprise application integration (EAI) products. Choose loose coupling (EAI) between different organizational and management domains. Choose tight coupling (AS) where you're confident that the closeness of the domains is sufficient to reduce risk to an acceptable level relative to the efficiencies gained through tight coupling.

E-business, with the possible exception for customer-facing e-commerce, takes you inexorably toward reengineering. Recognize the political and organizational implications of where your project is headed.

Reengineering   Reengineering involves entire end-to-end business processes, spanning the enterprise. Unwavering top-down executive commitment is a must. Reengineering is never a grass-roots phenomenon.

The major business breakthroughs come from looking at new technology and figuring out how to apply it for business advantage. Keep abreast of emerging technology and constantly look for ways to apply it.

Business-driven thinking is complementary to technology-driven thinking—you need business-driven thinking to figure out what business advantage *is*.

Project scope   Organizational commitment needs to be aligned with project scope. If organizational commitment for reengineering cannot be marshaled, use the expedient "bolt-on" approach for e-business initiatives, or fix obvious areas of pain through an incremental improvement effort.

Costs, benefits, and risks   Reengineering brings *dramatic* benefits. If you don't have a deep visceral conviction that your results will be dramatic, then what you are doing is probably not reengineering. If reengineering is truly what you're doing, don't waste time on detailed cost–benefit analysis. You can't predict the demand for supply-driven new products in any event.

Recognize that leading-edge technology is by nature proprietary. Embrace it for competitive advantage.

Tread carefully in the turbulent zone, where interoperability is becoming more valuable than differentiation for most players. Recognize when your choices lie in this zone, and make your choices with extra care.

Beware of persisting with proprietary nonstandard technology after the value it offers has been commoditized. If maintenance costs are nontrivial, think about discarding it in favor of standard packages or outsourcing—even if human procedures need to change as a result.

Don't apply high-cost solutions to low-differentiation strata of your business.

Create custom solutions at the high end of the business value spectrum, where you need to differentiate yourself from the competition and offer unique value.

Intellectual Manageability   Object orientation. Apply object-oriented techniques, and use object-oriented modeling and component-based development tools. Working within an object-oriented environment makes it so much easier to adhere to sound architectural principles and maintain intellectual manageability.

Principles. Carefully formulate your guiding principles, adhere to them where they make sense, and review them where they don't. If an important design decision is not covered by your principles, you probably need to formulate a new principle.

Elegance. Look for elegance always. Choose the simple and elegant solution over the clever and complex. Choose solutions with a clear, straightforward, and elegantly simple relationship to the problem.[1]

Conceptual integrity. Maintain conceptual integrity—always. Use similar mechanisms, patterns, and idioms to achieve similar behavior wherever it occurs.

Methodology. Formalize your approach to solution building in a step-by-step methodology that guides the capable journeyman.

Architectural frameworks. Consider underpinning your methodology with architectural frameworks that explain the relationships among technology categories and provide checklists of areas to be designed.

Iterate, iterate, iterate . . . and develop incrementally   A complex system that works is invariably found to have evolved from a simple system that worked. Develop incrementally. The big bang may have worked for the universe, but it doesn't work for software. Apply feedback and whirlpools throughout the solution-building life cycle.

Reuse   Reuse components, patterns, subassemblies, and frameworks for efficient and cost-effective development as well as for intellectual manageability.

Hire consultants who are familiar with your business domain so as to reuse the solutions they've developed. But be sure your agreement protects your own breakthrough business ideas.

If you *have* to design from scratch, design so that you have reusable pieces to apply in the future. Constantly look for domain-independent patterns and concepts, and keep the domain-specific aspects of your solution separated from domain-independent aspects that may be reusable in other domains.

---

[1]"Everything should be made as simple as possible, but not simpler." —Albert Einstein. "Any intelligent fool can make things bigger, more complex, and more violent. It takes a touch of genius, and a lot of courage, to move in the opposite direction." —Albert Einstein.

Reuse is hard. You'll have to be persistent and determined to put in place the technical and organizational foundations necessary to make it work. Keep at it, and don't give up.

Application servers, enterprise application solutions, and packaged (ERP) solutions are viable large-scale reuse foundations for e-business infrastructure.

The right resources for the job   Carefully consider building, nurturing, and sustaining a good relationship with a consulting organization. The knowledge resources, business intelligence, project management capability, and technology skill the consultant brings will amply offset any leakage of your own breakthrough ideas to your competitors.

The right approach, the right tools, and the right methodology will all be subverted by people operating with the wrong mindset.

Even good people need mentoring. You can't learn to fly a Boeing 747 just by reading the manual.

Stamp out all vestiges of the not-invented-here mentality.

People   Find and retain capable people. Yes, I know—"well, duh!" But the list above contains some warnings about some of the problems that even apparently "good" people may be susceptible to.

Successful IS deployments achieve a balance among people, processes, and systems.

Pay proper attention to organizational change—the people side of reengineering.

Bibliography and References

Alexander, C. *The Timeless Way of Building*. Oxford University Press, 1979. Although Alexander is a bricks-and-mortar architect, the audience for this book seems to be dominated by software designers. As I write these words, six out of six reader reviews on Amazon.com are by software people. Alexander explains how a relatively few patterns—themselves arranged in patterns of patterns—can be employed to create buildings, towns, and so on, with that indefinable quality (his *quality without a name*) that balances the place in perfect harmony with the events intended to happen there. The writing is so eloquent, and the ideas are so carefully developed and presented, that the book is pure joy to read. This was the book that spurred the rise of the patterns movement [Gamma et al. 1994] in software.

Alexander, C., Ishikawa, S., and Silverstein, M. *A Pattern Language*. Oxford University Press, 1977. Although it predates *The Timeless Way of Building,* Alexander regards this work as the second in reading sequence. It develops the set of patterns in a more systematic and comprehensive way, while the 1979 work dwells more on the qualitative and creative aspects of applying patterns to the job at hand.

Bahar, M. *Object Technology Made Simple*. Simple Software Publishing, 1996. An informative, entertaining, and easy-to-understand guide, this book is for busy IS executives and IT vendors who want a basic understanding of object technology. It is also useful for object developers and experts who'd like to be able to explain object technology to their bosses, their end users, and their families.

Bass, L., Clements, P., and Kazman, R. *Software Architecture in Practice*. Addison-Wesley, 1998.

Best, L. "What Is Architectural Software Development?" *http://www.c2.com/ppr/ams.html,* AMS, Inc., 1995. This short paper makes the case that the term "architecture," used in various unclear senses in the context of software development, properly refers to construction using available and catalogued components.

Boar, B. *Constructing Blueprints for Enterprise IT Architectures*. John Wiley & Sons, 1998. This book builds on Zachman's paper [1987], and thus takes a different approach to architectural solution building from the one I describe in this present volume.

BOC. *Adonis. http://www.boc-us.com/.*

Booch, Grady. *Object-Oriented Analysis and Design with Applications, 2nd ed.* Redwood City, CA: Benjamin/Cummings, 1994. This book aims to show practicing software engineers how to use object-oriented technology to solve real problems and to show analysts a path from requirements to implementation using object-oriented analysis and design. Examples are given throughout. The book predates the development of UML, and the notation used is consequently out of date.

Booch, G., Jacobson, I., and Rumbaugh, J. *The Unified Modeling Language User Guide* (*The Addison-Wesley Object Technology Series*). Addison-Wesley, 1999. Presents the UML and explains its use in a concept-per-chapter format. The book is well written and assumes no prior knowledge of object-oriented techniques. However, readers with no prior knowledge of UML are likely to find Fowler's work [Fowler 1997] more approachable.

Booch, G., Jacobson, I., and Rumbaugh, J. *Complete UML Training Course.* Addison-Wesley, 2000. The three amigos' collaboration on a UML training course, complete with CD-ROM. This is a substantial work with a substantial price to match.

Brooks, F. *The Mythical Man-Month, Anniversary Edition: Essays on Software Engineering.* Addison-Wesley, 1995. Perhaps the most influential and important book ever written on the human, psychological, and management factors that bedevil software development. The 1995 edition updates the original (1975) with Brooks' recent observations. Brooks' lessons are timeless. We're still making the same mistakes today that we made 25 years ago. Only the technology and its tools change; the human psychology remains the same.

Buschmann, F., Meunier, R., Rohnert, H., Sommerlad, P., and Stal, M. *Pattern Oriented Software Architecture: A System of Patterns.* Wiley, 1996. A useful catalogue of patterns—in the sense of Gamma et al. [1994]—that can be combined into software designs analogous to Alexander's bricks-and-mortar patterns in the physical world [Alexander et al. 1977, Alexander 1979]. The book gives advice on implementing the patterns and discusses pros and cons of the individual patterns.

Champy, J. *Reengineering Management: The Mandate for New Leadership.* Harper-Business, 1996. As its title suggests, the focus of this book is the effects of organizational change brought about by reengineering, particularly as it affects those in middle-management roles.

Cook, M. *Building Enterprise Information Architecture.* Prentice Hall, 1996. This book is essentially a manager's-eye view of building information systems. Cook avoids technical details and explains the broad characteristics of the evolutionary stages that brought us into today's IT landscape. Managers can gain useful insight into the process of aligning information systems with the business processes they must serve. IS professionals can also benefit from this business-centric viewpoint.

Dijkstra, E. "The Structure of the THE Multiprogramming System." *Communications of the ACM,* May 1968.

Fowler, M. and Scott, K. *UML Distilled, Second Edition: A Brief Guide to the Standard Object Modeling Language.* Addison-Wesley, 2000. Primarily intended to give a practical appreciation of the Unified Modeling Language, this excellent and concise book also gives a very good and very pragmatic introduction to the object-oriented solution-building process. The book is written in an entertaining style, stays within its intended scope, and gives well-focused annotated references for further reading.

Gall, J. *Systemantics: The Underground Text of Systems Lore—How Systems Really Work and How They Fail.* General Systemantics Press, 1986.

Gamma, E., Helm, R., Johnson, R., and Vlissides, J. *Design Patterns.* Addison Wesley, 1995. This is the famous "Gang of Four" book, which gave rise to the patterns movement in software and opened the cross-pollination channel between Christopher Alexander's bricks-and-mortar architecture and the software world. The book shows how pattern languages and pattern catalogues can be applied in object-oriented software design. A pattern is a description of a common software problem that can be solved by a relatively standard set of connected objects. The book describes some standard design patterns and how they may be implemented as a set of collaborating objects.

Gause, D. and Weinberg, G. *Exploring Requirements: Quality Before Design.* Dorset House, 1989. A thorough exploration of the process of specifying product requirements. This book is not confined to the world of information systems but rather deals with products in a general sense. In relation to this book, the Gause and Weinberg volume applies at the juncture of business modeling and IS modeling, where IS functionality (IS use cases) are being formulated in support of the business processes.

Hager, N. *Secret Power.* Nelson, New Zealand: Craig Potton, 1996.

Hammer, M. *Beyond Reengineering.* HarperCollins, 1996. The third book in Hammer's reengineering series, this volume looks at the consequences of reengineering—how reengineered "process centered" enterprises shape themselves. This is a holistic treatment that expands on the theme of harmonious balance among people–processes–systems.

Hammer, M. and Champy, J. *Reengineering the Corporation: A Manifesto for Business Revolution.* HarperCollins, 1993. The original work on reengineering, which introduced the concept to the world. This book is about business reengineering and the kinds of creative thinking that make it happen, illustrated by case studies.

Hammer, M. and Stanton, S. *The Reengineering Revolution: A Handbook.* Harper-Business, 1995. A sequel to Hammer and Champy's 1993 work. This volume focuses on the practical aspects—including organizational change management—of making reengineering work, with war stories on what works in practice and what doesn't. The book is required reading for those who would attempt large-scale redesign of business processes as the first stage in an IS solution-building endeavor. The authors provide a thorough discussion of the organizational, political, and other nontechnical hurdles that stand in the way of reengineering and offer practical advice for overcoming those hurdles.

Handy, C. *The Age of Unreason.* Harvard Business School Press, 1990, 1998. It is really quite eerie to read what Handy predicted so long ago and is now happening around us. Handy foresaw the technology-facilitated changes that are now reworking our economy and society. If we can all become a little more unreasonable, perhaps today's "e-business" will expand to embrace "e-society."

Herzum, P. and Sims, O. *Business Component Factory: A Comprehensive Overview of Component-Based Development for the Enterprise.* John Wiley & Sons, 1999. This is an important book that advances the state of the art in the practical application of object-oriented techniques through a component-based software life cycle. "Object-based" systems worked for programming "in the small," but ran into heavy weather in the scaling up to industrial-strength systems. Herzum and Sims present the principles and methods they have developed for overcoming those scaling problems, and show how large-scale systems can be realized through component-based software development and deployment.

IBM. "Ten success factors for e-business." *http://www-4.ibm.com/software/info/soul/st/tenfactors.pdf* 2000. This short paper reinforces some of the e-business-related ideas developed in this book.

IDS Scheer. "Aris." *http://www.ids-scheer.com/.*

Intelligent EAI. http://www.intelligenteai.com/. A periodical and Web site devoted to coverage of enterprise application integration solutions and technology.

Jacobson, I., Ericsson, M., and Jacobson, A. *The Object Advantage: Business Process Reengineering with Object Technology.* New York: Addison-Wesley, 1994. This book shows how to apply object technology—particularly object modeling—to the business process reengineering life cycle, through to system implementation. Jacobson's framework of models is one of the foundations on which I have built this book. Jacobson pursues the technique of object modeling in greater depth.

Jacobson, I., Griss, M., and Jonsson, P. *Software Reuse: Architecture Process and Organization for Business Success.* Addison-Wesley, 1997. This book builds on the work of Jacobson et al. [1994] on object-oriented business process reengineering and object-oriented software engineering. It is a thorough treatment of those disciplines from an overarching viewpoint of the institutionalization of reuse. The book also covers the organizational considerations that affect reuse initiatives, although this discussion is much less detailed than the engineering discussion.

Larman, C. *Applying UML and Patterns.* Prentice Hall, 1997. A very practical and very readable treatment of object-oriented modeling using UML. This book focuses exclusively on modeling information systems as opposed to business processes.

Marshall, C. *Enterprise Modeling with UML: Designing Successful Software Through Business Analysis.* Addison-Wesley, 2000. Marshall applies UML to business processes themselves, as opposed to the information systems that support them—an approach that is innovative in its own right. His treatment gives guidance on reuse at the business process level.

Moynihan, J. "Propositions for Building an Effective Process." *Journal of Information Systems Management,* Vol. 5, No. 2, Spring 1988: pp. 61–64.

OMG. "OMG's Reading Room." *http://cgi.omg.org/library/reading.html.* OMG 1999. A useful, although far from comprehensive, bibliography of titles related to object-oriented technology.

The Open Group. *The Open Group Architectural Framework.* The Open Group 1998. *http://wwopengroup.org.togaf/.*

Parkinson, C. Northcote. *The Law of Delay.* John Murray, 1970. Parkinson is the British civil servant who gave us Parkinson's Law (work expands to fill the time allotted to it), and a half dozen lesser-known laws, including the Law of Delay, which states that "delay is the deadliest form of denial."

Parnas, D. "On the Criteria to Be Used in Decomposing Systems into Modules." *Communications of the ACM,* December 1972.

Rational Software Corporation. "Rational Rose." *http://www.rational.com/.*

Rational Software Corporation. "UML Resource Center." *http://www.rational.com/uml/index.jtmpl.* A comprehensive listing of resources of all kinds—books, papers, and presentations—on UML.

Rosenbluth, H. and Peters, D. *The Customer Comes Second and Other Secrets of Exceptional Service.* William Morrow & Co., 1993.

Schmidt, D. "Why Software Reuse Has Failed and How to Make It Work for You." *C++ Report,* January 1999. Also available at *http://siesta.cs.wustl.edu/~schmidt/reuse-lessons.html.* Schmidt gives a good account of the reasons that effective reuse has been a problem in practice, and suggests some remedies.

Schneider, G. et al. *Applying Use Cases: A Practical Guide.* Addison-Wesley, 1998. A highly regarded text that illustrates use cases by example. The use cases relate to an *information system* (as opposed to a business process), and the material thus corresponds to IS modeling as I have applied it in this book.

Sethi, V. and King, W. *Organizational Transformation Through Business Process Reengineering.* Prentice-Hall, 1998. An eclectic collection of papers on reengineering topics, mainly from the business, management, and organizational viewpoints. Papers are organized into eight subtopics, with each subtopic being illustrated by a case study.

Skarke, G. and Holland, D. *The Change Management Toolkit.* WinHope Press, 1999. A step-by-step how-to-do-it guide to implementing the organizational changes resulting from business process engineering.

Slonim, J. *Building an Open System.* New York: Van Nostrand Reinhold Company, Inc., 1987.

Spewak, S. *Enterprise Architecture Planning.* Wiley, 1992. Now dated in this fast-moving world, the chief value of this book for today's practitioner lies in its analysis of organizational and political impediments faced by large-scope IS development efforts. Focusing more on discovering existing business processes than on inventing new ones, the book goes into some detail on developing an enterprise-wide information system through the support of a "blueprinting framework." While the goals of the blueprinting framework are instructive, the practical details have been overtaken by today's modeling tools. As far as I am aware, no present-day tool is based on the blueprinting framework philosophy.

Treese, G. and Stewart, L. *Designing Systems for Internet Commerce.* Addison-Wesley, 1998. A comprehensive compilation of descriptions and explanation of e-business drivers and relevant technologies. There is enough detail in the descriptions to convey a useful understanding of how to apply particular technologies.

UUA. "Business Survival Strategies for the 21st Century." Unisys Users Association, *http://www.uuae.org/,* 1996. The result of a collaboration between Unisys customers and the Unisys Corporation, this 60-page report defines the "requirements of user organizations wishing to put in place flexible, adaptable IT infrastructures capable of supporting business needs in times of rapid and never-ending change."

Zachman, J. "A Framework for Information Systems Architecture." *IBM Systems Journal,* Vol. 26, No. 3, 1987: pp. 276–292. The "Zachman framework," as it has become known, is a systematic formalization of enterprise information architectural design as practiced in the structured design and functional decomposition approaches, which predate the object modeling approach. The emphasis of the framework is the effective communication with the various stakeholders throughout all stages of solution building.

Index